Highly Favored
of the Lord

Volume III

Michael Stroud

DEDICATION

To Janet, the mother of our children.
May The Lord bless you for your service and sacrifice.

CONTENTS

	Acknowledgements	i
	Introduction	3
25	Opposition in all things	13
26	The Celestial World Part 1	41
27	The Celestial World Part II	67
28	The Powers of Heaven	90
29	Power in the Priesthood	112
30	Temple Thoughts	135
31	Progression in Eternity	153
32	Why Temples	173
33	The Law of Justice	196
34	Temples: The Purpose of Gathering	216
35	The Remnant of Jacob	237
36	Glory	266
	About the Author	287

ACKNOWLEDGMENTS

Thank you to Shelle McDermott, author of the "NoFearPreps.com" site for her help in encouraging, organizing, and bringing this all to fruition. Nothing would have happened without her.

Editors
Phillis Ann Postak
Elizabeth Postak

Transcribers
Carol Crisp
Pat Crisp
Robert Briscoe

https://www.podomatic.com/podcasts/mstroud

Introduction
Exchanging Bullets for Bubbles:
Toward a higher and more exalted sphere
By Wayne Shute

Bubble

I hope you catch the significance of what is said here and try to move along the path that leads to eternal life with a greater vision of Heavenly Father's love for us and His desire to protect us from all calamities in the last days.

While Mike and Margaret Stroud were serving their mission in the Philippines, we stayed in close touch. I was pleased to read their reports and look at the pictures with captions which described their activities. One day, along with a very sobering letter, they sent pictures that a tourist woman took while staying in a hotel in Cebu. In the picture taken from her hotel balcony and taken both in the night and during the day, you can clearly make out a bubble of light which covered over "one of the city's buildings." She saw the bubble of light surrounding a distant building and was very curious and determined to find out what the building was. Taking a taxi over to the building, she discovered that the building was the recently dedicated LDS Cebu Temple.

She went inside the nearby Mission Office and showed the pictures to Sister Ernstrom who was serving at the time as the Mission Secretary. Sister Ernstrom explained the temple complex to her and asked the tourist woman if she could have copies of the pictures. She was agreeable to that, and it wasn't long before President Schmutz, Cebu Mission President, gave all the senior mission couples copies of the pictures. Needless to say, the woman was astonished and very impressed with the fact that a Mormon Temple would have such a protective bubble shield over and around it.

Sometime prior to this experience, Mike and Margie had been contemplating the pending geopolitical problems developing in the world, and re-thinking their "What will we do when these awful calamities that are plaguing the world get worse as predicted by prophets?" They had decided sometime earlier, that there will always be those with "bigger guns" and more armed personnel than the prepared family in Zion could possibly match. One day Margie said, "Mike, all we need to do is raise our right arm to the square, and use the power of the priesthood to defend and protect our family and possessions." Margie's strong assertion started a focused study aimed at discovering what kind of people have the power to call down the powers of heaven, and who can successfully maneuver and survive the tribulation period we have now entered in these the last days. Their belief in calling on the powers of heaven drove them to an in-depth scripture study in an effort to make sense of this unusual phenomenon as the pictures by this tourist woman showed.

Their study also led to a discovery of periods of time in history where God has established Zion societies. There are only two recorded historical accounts where Zion societies were *fully developed*: Enoch, and Melchizedek. And there is enough recorded information as to what is entailed in these societies. So, what's the bottom line? To quote Mike:

> It all boils down to this: If we want to survive and thrive in the coming period of upheaval and turmoil, we will need to trust completely in the Lord Jesus Christ, and His power to protect and preserve.

They came to realize that Heavenly Father shields buildings that He wants to protect from the calamities of the world and that through priesthood power and with the exercise of our faith, we can expect Heavenly Father to protect us also.

Mike and Margie's background

Let me now back up a bit and show you the significance of the bubble phenomenon it has had in the lives of Mike and Margie Stroud. As with all of us, Mike is greatly defined by the things he has suffered—his first wife was killed in a car accident and died in his arms; his second wife died of cancer; Margie came into the picture about ten years ago as a wonderful companion and helpmeet. In addition to tragedy, Mike knows a great deal of suffering with regards to his children. We know a little about that but not to the degree Mike does. In most ways, this pain is bitter and causes us great sorrow.

Yet, as we all must do, he carried on with faith in our Savior. He has made every effort to build the Kingdom of God by being a faithful missionary—he served his first mission in Germany; he and Margie served a mission to Mongolia, a second mission to the Philippines and a third to Morristown, New Jersey. In all other ways, he has been faithful in fulfilling his callings in the Church.

Although Mike has spent most of his career as a top seminary teacher, he really is a cowboy and outdoorsman at heart. During most of his lifetime, he has been around farm animals, especially horses. Because of his love for *all things cowboy*, he had collected guns and built up a veritable armory in his house— cowboys tend to collect guns. His gun collection ranged from antique guns to modern firearms. Many of the guns were rare and worth a lot of money. Also, he had weapons for protection and a huge arsenal of ammunition.

Margie is not at all behind Mike—she has lived a very interesting and successful life. She has a background on a farm and has qualified herself as a mechanic and is well acquainted with animals and all kinds of work that are associated with this lifestyle. Over many years, she has taught elementary education and is a superb teacher. She has filled all kinds of assignments in the Church and is a student of the scriptures. She is perfectly yoked with Mike in their love of the Gospel and their faith in Jesus Christ.

A Powerful Example to all of us in becoming Self-reliant

When they came together, they were determined to follow the

prophets and build a self-reliant environment in their home in Eagar, Arizona. They threw their full hearts into building a self-sustaining home and built a place that is completely independent of outside support. They have followed the admonitions of prophets and apostles to be prepared. You know what their counsel has been. Accordingly, they have, in my opinion, the best food storage, emergency storage system probably in the Church. You have to see it to understand what I mean. They have prepared themselves beyond measure. They define for us what it means to be fully prepared for the turmoil, even the horror of the last days. In our view, we will face indescribable hardship; to do so, we must be fully prepared. As the scripture notes, "if you are prepared, you need not fear."

> Behold, this I have given unto you as a parable, and it is even as I am. I say unto you, be one; and if ye are not one ye are not mine.
> And again, I say unto you that the enemy in the secret chambers seeketh your lives. Ye hear of wars in far countries, and you say that there will soon be great wars in far countries, but ye now not the hearts of men in your own land.
> I tell you these things because of your prayers; wherefore, treasure up wisdom in your bosoms, lest the wickedness of men reveal these things unto you by their wickedness, in a manner which shall speak in your ears with a voice louder than that which shall shake the earth; but if ye are prepared ye shall not fear (D&C 38:27-30).

Naturally, they have been concerned about protecting what they have worked so hard to build. They, like all of us, have a great desire to protect our property, our homes and the lives of all of us. The modern weapons they have stored have been to protect their family and their possessions.

A few years ago, Mike spoke to our family about food storage and emergency preparation. He gave a lot of interesting information about the coming trials and test in these the last days. He talked about how we all will face many trials whether they be economic, political, or spiritual. In many cases, our lives will be threatened, and there will be vandals, thugs, even murderers who may threaten our lives and our property. He didn't hold back in painting a clear picture of what to expect in the coming years.

He spent some time during that talk about the need for weapons to protect our lives and the lives of our loved-ones.

The Relevance of the Bubble for us

While visiting with us recently, they shared the scriptures that have turned their lives around and given them a new perspective on what we can expect if we seek protection from our Father in Heaven and His Son, Jesus Christ. They have a completely different focus now and have reversed themselves 180 degrees. I'll say more about this later, but for now, let's walk through some of the scriptures which have changed their lives so dramatically.

From the Book of Revelation 13:10, we read the following:

He that leadeth into captivity shall go into captivity; he that killeth with the sword must be killed with the sword. Here is the patience and the faith of the Saints.

In explaining this scripture, Mike offers the following:

The patience of the Saints in this verse refers to a previous verse (7) which talks about Satan making war upon the Saints and OVERCOMING THEM. I believe that at some time in the future, we as Americans, and as Latter-day Saints will be led into captivity by foreign invading powers, and that we like Alma will need to learn to submit to these powers. We will be delivered miraculously, by the Power of God, but will need to put our trust in him, and WAIT (the patience of the Saints) for His deliverance. The two stories of Ammon/Limhi, and Alma and his people, teach us a powerful principle of trying to escape captivity by the force of our own arm, or by trusting on the Arm of the Lord. (Read Mosiah 21 -22, and Mosiah 23-24)

Mike and Margie were pretty sobered when they read these and other scriptures. Those who have weapons may be tempted to kill the thugs or marauders who may be beating and pounding on the door. But if you answer in kind, with guns yourself, someone will get hurt or killed. And it may be you or your loved ones! No, we have greater weapons at our disposal than guns!

In addition to that scripture above, they were mightily impressed with another from Doctrine and Covenants 105:14. Here's what that verse says:

> For behold, I do not require at their hands to fight the battles of Zion; for, as I said in a former commandment, even so will I fulfill—I will fight your battles.

Mike enlarged on this scripture as follows:

> See also D&C 45:66-75, Moses 7:13-14, JST Genesis 14:25-40. Pay close attention to these scriptures! Notice that the people of God in these references do not take weapons. God fights their battles and uses men and women endowed with priesthood power to command elements and call down the powers of heaven in their behalf.

When these scriptures were reviewed with us recently, we talked about how in the *Book of Mormon*, much time and energy was spent by the Nephites in making preparations for war. They had weapons and fielded the best-equipped armies they could muster. I said to Mike, "Those folks had weapons of war to protect their homes, families, etc. Shouldn't we also?" Here, Mike taught us a great lesson. He said, "You have to remember, we are talking about the concept of Zion. You won't find the concept of Zion had much meaning to the Nephite generations. When Zion is mentioned in the *Book of Mormon*, it is through Isaiah and his vision of our times, or it is a vision that Nephi had concerning our times in which we covenant to build up Zion. We must remember that in Nephite times, they fought wars to protect their families and land, etc. but they were not fighting to build up a Zion society. You never read about them building up Zion. They were not a Zion people—in effect, they were fighting to save their country. In order to protect their country, they needed weapons of war. When the time comes that we must fight to protect our country and our Constitution, we will no doubt need weapons of war."

A Zion People

But when we're talking about building Zion that is a different matter. There will be *a_small remnant* (Joel 2:32) from within this people (Latter-day Saints) who will become Zion men and women. The rights and privileges of these Saints (Sanctified Ones) are described in the following verses of scripture: D&C 67:10-14, D&C 76:50 -70, D&C 84: 18-25, D&C 88:63-68, D&C 93:1-2, D&C 107:18-19. These people are best described In *JST Genesis 14:25-40*. Enoch and Melchizedek were patterns of the type of people we will need to be in order to survive what's coming. Notice also what Abraham is seeking for in Abraham 1:2-4. Read closely also **D&C 50:26-30**. This is a very powerful scripture about a bestowal of power from Christ himself. Again, this pertains to this life.

But, as we review these scriptures, they are referring to us as a Zion people. We are talking about building and protecting Zion. So, when building Zion—and we do that by being faithful to our Heavenly Father—it is clear that the Lord God Almighty will protect us. He will "fight [y]our battles" and protect His people. So, faithful people of the Lord don't need guns to protect what they have—God Himself will extend His mighty arm and protect His people.

All of this can be said in a different way. Said, Mike:

> *When we are fighting for the cause of Zion, we don't need weapons of war. But we can't get this confused with the Second Amendment of the Constitution which purpose is to protect the Constitution of the United States. That has nothing to do with establishing Zion. It's OK to have arms to protect the country, but we don't need weapons of war to establish and protect Zion.*

When we make an effort to have a food storage program for the blessing of our families, that food storage program becomes part of our faith in building the Kingdom of God. To repeat, it is part of building the Kingdom of God on the earth and strengthening Zion. The Food Storage program of the Church is first and foremost about obedience. Everything we do within the program of temporal preparedness can vanish in the coming day.

Our obedience to this command qualifies us to become Zion individuals and to perform miracles when the need arises. Those who have not been obedient in following the prophets will not be able to become the men and women who can command "the very trees, the mountains, or the waves of the sea," and have them obey. (Jacob 4:6)

Here are two other scriptures of great significance for us:

And their arm shall be my arm, and I will be their shield and their buckler; and I will gird up their loins and they shall fight manfully for me and their enemies shall be under their feet; and I will let fall the sword in their behalf, and by the fire of mine indignation will I preserve them (D&C 35:14).

And I the Lord, would fight their battles, and their children's battles, and their children's children's, until they had avenged themselves on all their enemies, to the third and fourth generation (D&C 98:37).

Faith to move mountains

What we're talking about here is a completely different look at the power of the priesthood and the power of faith in the Lord Jesus Christ. When we do have the faith to call down the powers of heaven to protect us, then God will lay bare His mighty arm and protect us. He will put a bubble over our houses and lands in so much that no one will dare to try to hurt us or if they do want to hurt us they will become the victims of God's wrath. It is not beyond reason that people who want to hurt us or steal our food storage won't be able to see us or our possessions. There is no reason to doubt but what Heavenly Father could make our places invisible to those who would hurt us or want to take by force the things we have.

Some of us may say, "I don't have that kind of faith, so I'm going to rely on my guns to protect me." Well, there are consequences to that kind of thinking. As I've said above, you or someone you love may be the ones who will suffer (D&C 45:68).

What I've decided to do is try to show my love for a kind and merciful God. I will show this love by expressing daily my gratitude for His tender mercies; by acknowledging His power and inviting His protection. And when I do this, I can expect bubbles of protection to be above and around the ones I love and cherish.

Mike and Margie add the following to this discussion:

If God our Father is the same yesterday, today, and forever...and if he is unchanging, then it stands to reason that every miracle, sign, power, endowment, and gift received by others mentioned in the scripture, is available to us today. If not so, God is a respecter of persons and ceases to be God. This is the beauty of the Gospel of Jesus Christ: Not only is it TRUE, but it WORKS! Everything we read about God's dealings with his children in history is available to us today. We can face the future with faith and confidence that through the Lord's power, we can become invisible to our enemies, we can traverse time and space, we can stand in the presence of the Father and the Son, and do ALL THINGS according to HIS WORD! And all of this, WHILE IN THIS LIFE!

Once we came to this realization and had it powerfully confirmed through the Holy Spirit, it all made sense, and we felt the "Call to Zion." To demonstrate to the Lord that we were willing to not only "see and hear," but to "do," (D&C 84: 54-49) we made plans to offer a sacrifice to Him as a token of our faith and trust. The first thing we did when we returned home from the Philippines, was to sell all of our battle weapons and thousands of rounds of military ammunition. This was ironic because at the time we did this, millions were buying these weapons and ammunition, and thought we were crazy for selling. From that time to this, this principle continues to grow stronger and stronger as we Ask, Seek, and Knock to be bestowed with the

privileges and promises found in the scriptures,
and in the temple.
The Spirit of the Lord is hovering over, and
persuading a remnant of this people to come up to
this level, and claim these blessings. This isn't
something we become on our own; it is the person
He makes us_through the cleansing, purifying,
and sanctifying power of the Atonement of Jesus
Christ. (Alma 13:12) It is our desire to become a
part of this remnant (Joel 2:32).

My Personal goal and I hope the goal of all Shute Family members

All of this has a great meaning for me, and I think for our entire family. For me, I have set a personal goal to become worthy to become one of the remnant of people who are full of faith and become, therefore, worthy to be a part of Zion. This will come through my exercise of faith and strict obedience to Heavenly Father's commandments—all of them. I must, as we are informed in the *Lectures on Faith,* "pursue a course of life that is pleasing to God" and no sacrifice is too great in order to have this sure knowledge.

As for our entire family, the same goal should apply. Most of you, according to my observation, are heading in the right direction, but there is still a long way to go for some of us, less of a journey for others. I urge us all to take a spiritual inventory and begin now to have a greater vision of what is required of us to become a Zion people.

Part of that spiritual journey will be to be faithful temple attenders for it is in the temple that, if we are observant, we will see the greater vision of what is possible for us.

Chapter Twenty-Five
Podcast 025 Opposition in All Things

Today in church, we had a lesson in priesthood on 2 Nephi 2:11; Opposition in All Things. In that conversation, there were a lot of subjects that came up. One of the subjects had to do with the purpose of having a physical body in this life. Another was whether there is opposition in the world to come and in the spirit world. Lots of different discussions came up.

I'd like to turn to *Doctrine and Covenants* 121 and take a look at something. Margie and I have found out that patterns are the key to opening up great mysteries and doctrines. We read verses like 39 all the time, and we limit it to this earth's experience. What if these principles that we have in verse 39, apply in eternity, everywhere, and are not just limited to mortal life? For example, verse 39 says:

> *We have learned by sad experience that it is the nature and disposition of almost all men, as soon as they get a little authority, as they suppose, they will immediately begin to exercise unrighteous dominion.*

We see that everywhere. What if it existed before we came here, it will exist in every realm after we leave here, and it exists in eternity as a principle of opposition? It's just always there.

Now, with that in mind, I want to read to you a couple of

statements by the Prophet Joseph Smith. This is out of a book called *The Words of Joseph Smith,* and the authors are Ehat and Cook. Joseph said this:

> *It is a natural thing with those **spirits** that have the most power, to bare down on those of lesser power.*

Now, notice that he's talking about *spirits* here. And so, here we have this principle found in section 121 that's operative when we go into the spirit realm. The traditional understanding of Latter-day Saints, when we think about pre-mortal existence is that it was a place of extreme happiness and joy. We lived in the presence of our Father in Heaven, and there was no contention or difficulty, except for the rebellion of Lucifer. So, for however long we were there, it was just peace and bliss, except for one point that we call *The War in Heaven.* The nature of that rebellion was a little nebulous in our minds, and generally, we think of it as being fairly short in duration. It was there, it only lasted for a short period of time, and then it was over. Other than that, the eons, countless thousands of years, maybe billions of earth years have been lives filled with peace and contentment as we prepared to come into this probationary state. That's generally the way we think about the premortal life.

Here's what I want to chat about tonight and here's your pattern: Joseph Smith has made some statements that indicate that life there was not all that different from life here. So, if you want to know what it was like there then look at what it's like here. There were great difficulties in our premortal existence, according to what Joseph said:

> *difficulties which were so severe that only knowledge and the obtaining of corporeal [physical] bodies could enable us to overcome them.*

I want to point out that the two things Heavenly Father said were necessary for us in that premortal life as spirits, to cope with the difficulties that were so severe, were knowledge and a physical body. Now, one of the things that comes up is "What's the purpose of earth life?" and the missionaries always teach that the main purpose was to come here and get a physical body. And that's true! But to what end? For what purpose? Why was it important that we come into a telestial world and obtain a physical body? Let me reason with you just a little bit. Now, think about this statement by Joseph again:

> It is a natural thing with those **spirits** that have the most power, to bare down on those of lesser power.

So, in the premortal life, some beings had more power than others, and they used that power unrighteously, just like section 121:39 says:

> as soon as they get a little authority, as they suppose, they will immediately begin to exercise unrighteous dominion.
>
> [40] Hence many are called, but few are chosen.

This unrighteous dominion in the premortal life was the cause of the fall of a third-part that was cast out into the telestial world to provide opposition. Now, that sounds a lot like mortal life, the strife that we have, and the power struggles that we see in this world.

My premise for us tonight is that what took place there is not exactly the rosy picture that we have in mind. I'm going to give you some quotes that will show you that it's a lot different there than we usually think. Let me give you another statement. Now, this statement was quoted by Boyd K. Packer during the last 10 or 12 years of his life in several general conference addresses. It also comes from the book *The Words of Joseph Smith* page 60. This is a blanket statement regarding power that the Prophet Joseph Smith gave. He said:

> All beings who have bodies have power over those who have not.

You've all heard that quote. So, as we reason together, let's take these quotes and put together an interesting little idea. Now, all Latter-day Saints have no problem and accept that. It's for this reason that evil spirits don't have any power over us unless we allow them or permit them. Just the fact that we have a physical body gives us power over them. So, if we who have bodies end up subject to those who don't, it's because we permit them by the improper use of our agency. If you couple these statements with the previous one, then you can deduce that there were tabernacled beings, who dwelt in our premortal state, who exercised unrighteous dominion over us who were spirits. Now, that's not what we usually think. When we usually think of the premortal life, and we think of people who have bodies, we usually think of our Heavenly Father. In fact, we teach in the missionary discussions that we looked on Him, we saw that there was something different about Him, we realized that He had a body and we didn't, and we longed to be like Him, so it became necessary for us to have a body. What Joseph Smith is teaching here is that it is necessary for us to have a body so that we could compete against embodied, tabernacled evil that existed in our premortal state and exercised unrighteous dominion over us. In other words, in the first quote by Joseph Smith, what did he say? It says that they *"bare down on"* us. It is natural that those spirits who have the most power bare down on those of lesser power.

Now, you're going to see here that Joseph taught that there were evil beings in the premortal life that had physical bodies. Here's another quote from the book *The Words of Joseph Smith*:

> God is good, and all His acts are for the benefit of inferior intelligences. God saw that those intelligences [who were inferior] *had NOT power to defend themselves against those that had a tabernacle,*

Now, in place of tabernacle put what? Body:

> *therefore the Lord calls them* [the inferior intelligences, spirits] *together in counsel and agrees to form for them tabernacles.* [bodies]

God saw that these intelligences, which He calls inferior, weaker ones, had not power to defend themselves against those that had tabernacles, or bodies. So, we learn that in our premortal estate, God called a counsel together to present a plan so those that do not have tabernacles could be provided with corporal bodies. Joseph explained that:

> *the express purpose for granting tangible bodies*

*to the children of God was **so they could defend themselves against the oppressions of an unrighteous group that already had tabernacles.***

Isn't that interesting?

Student 1: You're telling us in the premortal life there were spirits that had mortal bodies?

Mike: There were tabernacled beings. There were persons who had physical bodies in the premortal world who were unrighteous and wicked.

Let me give you another quote. Again, from *The Words of Joseph Smith* page 62:

> *Before the foundation of the Earth, in the Grand Counsel, the spirits of all men were **subject to oppression and the express purpose of God in giving it a tabernacle*** [these spirits who were being oppressed] ***was to arm it against the power of Darkness.***

Student 2: These two gentlemen who compiled the book, where are they getting these words of Joseph from?

Mike: All of these words come from the journal entries of scribes who were present, five or six scribes, who were present when Joseph Smith gave these discourses. These discourses were all given in Nauvoo. The greatest of all was given just two months before his death. That's called the King Follett Discourse. And then his final address in Nauvoo was given just a week or so before his death. But he had scribes. Some of his scribes were Wilford Woodruff, John Taylor, and William Clayton and there were usually around four or five of them. There were 21,000 people that were at the King Follett Discourse, outdoors around the uncompleted temple in April of 1844. When Joseph gave these addresses to the Saints, there were no loudspeakers or microphones. In fact, Joseph starts out the King Follett Discourse basically saying, "I hope the Lord will bless the weather and give me the lungs to do this." And as he spoke, these five scribes, some of them in very early shorthand, were all writing down what he's said the best they could in longhand. Then afterward, they compared notes and compiled it so that they agreed as much as possible with each other. Some would pick up one nuance; another one would pick up another nuance. Brother Ehat and Brother Cook went back, and pulled out all these original journals and wrote down all of them. You can get all of that in the book called *The Words of Joseph Smith*. You can find it online. The book, when it was first published, sold out quickly and they didn't print any secondary editions, so for years and years, it was out of print. I remember when I was trying to find a copy while visiting Nauvoo. We went into a bookstore and saw a copy of it there, and they wanted $400 for it. I couldn't afford that. So, it was a rare book at that time. You can now get it online in PDF version, and it's all there, *The Words of Joseph Smith*. That's excellent stuff! We're finding a lot of things, and it's coming into its own now, especially with the advent of the *Joseph Smith Papers Project*. So, it's now being quoted, and of course, Brother Packer quoted that portion of it over and over and over.

I want to read just a little summary here of what we've talked about.

> *Clearly, the oppressive tabernacle beings* [these are people in the premortal life with bodies who are evil] *mentioned in the earlier quotes and the tabernacled powers of darkness Joseph mentioned in this passage are one and the same. They are the ones who oppressed us in our pre-mortal state, and it is because of their oppression that God desired to extend to us the privilege of mortality. In other words, there were some wicked, evil, tabernacled beings who resided in our pre-mortal existence who bore down upon and oppressed those who did not have bodies. God saw that this was not fair and so said in effect, "I will organize an earth and allow man to take upon them tabernacles of flesh **for the express purpose of placing them on equal footing with these wicked tabernacled beings who are oppressing My spirit children.***

Comment?

Student 2: That makes it sound secondary to obtain a body, a proper body so that we could become like our Heavenly Father and experience what He experienced.

Mike: If this is the pattern, then this is the way it has been and Heavenly Father at some time obtained a physical body for the same purpose. It's just an area that we don't talk about. Here's a thought: Lucifer was a "Son of the Morning" and that implies a very high status of light and truth. His very name, Lucifer, indicates where he was and who he was before his fall. Lucifer means "Light Bearer" or "One who carries light." Lucifer is a good name, only it's been associated with a bad boy, but it's a good name. And so, the question comes up, what caused his fall?

Go over to Section 76 for just a minute and let me show you something. I'm going to surmise something with you tonight. Part of this is going to be doctrine and part of it is Stroud chapter 26 verse 3. I always tell you when I do that so that you'll know, okay? Let's go over to 76:25. Section 76 is really interesting because after the first 24 verses, which talk about Joseph and Sidney Rigdon seeing Christ *"on the right hand of God,"* they have this great vision, this manifestation. Then immediately in the 25th verse, we dive into the evil dark part of eternity:

> *And this we saw also* [after seeing the Father and Son], *and bear record, that an angel of God who was in authority in the presence of God,*

Now, how do you get to that position? You get to that by doing the right things. Am I right? Do you become an angel of God in authority by doing the wrong things or by doing the right things?

> *who rebelled against the Only Begotten Son whom the Father loved and who was in the bosom of the Father, was thrust down from the presence of God and the Son,*

Now, here's my question for you: How did this powerful personage of light fall and become a devil? What happened there? Verse 26:

> *And was called Perdition, for the heavens wept over him—he was Lucifer, a son of the morning.*

*[27] And we beheld, and lo, he is fallen! is fallen,
even **a** son of the morning!*

Now, all those titles point toward a very high prestigious position in the councils of heaven that can only be obtained through righteousness. You don't go to that level by being a rebel and sinning against God. The question is: How did this powerful angel fall?

Student 1: Wasn't it pride at first?

Mike: Yes, but where did the enticement come? Where was the opposition? Because there has to be opposition, brothers and sisters. Where was the opposition that caused this personage to become prideful and fall?

Let me show you something else. Now, that's doctrine, okay? So, you have to ask yourself the question: what was the source of evil that caused this angel to make choices and fall from his position? What Brother Joseph is teaching is this: that evil exists, in eternity, always. When Lehi is giving his discussion in 2 Nephi 2:11 he says:

*For it must needs be, that there is an opposition
in...*

What?

*   **all** things.*

Now that word **all** things encompasses everything, everywhere, at **all** times, does it not? Does it exclude anything?

Student 1: In my mind, yes.

Mike: Okay. Go ahead.

Student 1: I think in my mind, that it excludes when we go and have eternal life because it says in the scriptures no evil can be there.

Student 6: Yeah.

Mike: Yeah, "no unclean thing can dwell in My presence." Correct.

Student 6: Yes.

Mike: But they can dwell *out* of His presence, and they do.

Student 6: But what about *the rest*? When we leave here, we go to a place of *rest*.

Mike: That's correct. And you have to ask yourself the question:

Why is it a place of *rest*? Is it because there's no evil there? Or, is it because you've obtained a status of spirituality that evil, even if it exists, has no power over you?

Student 6: So, people who are not righteous then...so not everybody will have *rest* there.

Mike: The *rest* that I think is the entering into *the rest of the Lord*, is that you become free, through the person that you've become, through the Atonement, holy, sanctified, complete and that Satan and any evil that continues to exist anywhere has no power over you. Think about the temple endowment. In the temple endowment, Elohim and Jehovah say this:

> We will **allow** Lucifer, our common enemy, to
> tempt and try man that they may learn by their
> own experience to choose the good over the evil.

Remember that? *"We will **allow**,"* and that's exactly what they do. This evil, according to Joseph, exists eternally in eternity. And the Fathers and Mothers in Heaven use this in order for their children to progress up through the various estates and rungs on the ladder, to progress and become as They are. There **has** to be opposition to all things. There **has** to be. But, just because there's opposition there, just because there's evil there, doesn't mean that it claims you.

Student 6: Okay, this is kind of a contradiction to me because we go there and it's supposed to be easier there. At least this is what I've been taught.

Mike: Go where?

Student 1: When we leave here, this earth. We leave here and go to Paradise, and many people will join the Church because it won't have the draw that this world has on us here. And yet, you're saying that there's still evil that exists and that there's opposition, so this is really confusing to me. What am I missing?

Mike: Well the point is that—yes, comment, go ahead.

Student 3: Doesn't *rest* just means God's light? I had a seminary teacher that said that.

Mike: *The rest of the Lord* is that you've entered into a position and become a person who has obtained promises and have been changed through the Atonement so that no matter what's happening around you, you have a promise of eternal life. You have a hope in Christ and the world and all of its downward tugs and pulls, temptations, addictions, and compulsions have no claim on you anymore. Let's look at the pattern for just a minute. We are taught in the Church that there are Paradise and the other place. You get the feeling like they are two different places and that there's some kind of physical or geographical barrier between the two. And that on one side you have people passing freely from one side to the other, but on the other side, they can't pass onto the *"rest"* or Paradise of God, unless something is done for them. That's a true principle. The pattern is this: Look at this life. Do we have walls that separate us from evil? Or are we separated from evil because we **choose** to be and evil will not come to us, and we will not go to it because of who we are? Is that the pattern?

Student 3: Yeah.

Mike: That's the pattern here. For example, I don't have to travel very far from my home—a dedicated home, where the Spirit will come, where angels feel comfortable, and where the Spirit of the Lord dwells—I don't have to go far to find a place that is a satanic stronghold. There are no walls, no chain link fences, and there are no gulfs that separate us. I just don't go there because I choose not to go there. And they don't come here because they're not comfortable coming here. Why is there no interaction between the two? Because of the persons they are. Not because there's a barrier, but because of the persons they are.

Go back to section 76 and let me show you one other thing here. This is something to ponder. These are things Joseph is talking about. If I were just surmising this, that would be one thing, but Joseph points out that there were tabernacled, evil beings in the premortal life that oppressed God's spirit children who had not yet come to earth. And the purpose for coming to the earth was to get a physical body—at least one purpose—so that they could be put on an equal footing or at least have a chance to overcome the oppression of these embodied, evil persons who existed in eternity and continue to exist.

Margie: Well, if there were no organized evil in the premortal life, there would be no agency, and there would have been no war, and there would have been no three parts or groups of people.

Mike: And that's another point! Agency is an eternal principle, and we all believe that. Agency exists everywhere. There is no place where it does not exist. It exists along with law, light, and life. It's always there. You can't have agency without opposition. You have to have opposites in order to have agency, or it can't exist.

So, let me now take you to Stroud chapter 23 verse 6. We're back in section 76:27, and in verses 25-27 we see the fall of Lucifer, a Son of the Morning. And notice at the bottom of verse 27 it says:

He is fallen! is fallen, even a son of the morning!

Exclamation point! Now, go to 28:

> *And while we were yet in the Spirit, the Lord commanded us that we should write the vision;* **for we beheld Satan**, *that old serpent, even the devil, who rebelled against God, and sought to take the kingdom of God and his Christ—*
>
> *[29] Wherefore, he maketh war with the saints of God, and encompasseth them round about.*
>
> *[30] And we saw a vision of the sufferings of those with whom he made war and overcame, for thus came the voice of the Lord unto us:*
>
> *[31] Thus saith the Lord concerning those who know my power,*

I'm going to contend that verses 25, 26, and 27 are talking about one person, and verses 28, 29, and 30 are talking about a whole different being. Now, I'm going to contend, and this is me, my opinion, that the person in 28, 29, and 30 is an embodied, evil, older, probably resurrected being, and **that** is the person that enticed Lucifer and caused his fall.

Student 4: Mike, we also had that lesson today, and one of the things Brother Oaks said that caught my attention was that he was cast down as an unembodied spirit in mortality. Satan and his followers tempt and seek to deceive and captivate the children of God. So, it is this evil one who oppresses and sought to destroy the Father's plan, who actually facilitated it because this opposition enables choices. It's the opportunity to make right choices that lead us to growth. That is the purpose of the Father's plan. If all the things you're saying are true and Satan is here as a disembodied spirit, well, we were given a spirit to protect us, as you've been telling us.

Mike: We're given a body to protect us, not a spirit.

Student 4: Yeah, a body, yeah, right.

Mike: And what I'm saying is that Satan and Lucifer are two different beings. Satan is a title. Lucifer is a name. There are many people in eternity, many men, and there will be many more, who have borne the title of Satan.

Student 6: I'm just trying to understand this. So, are you saying that Satan and Lucifer are two different people? Or are there many of them? Is that what you're saying?

Mike: I'm saying that in this case, in section 76, when it talks about an angel in authority that fell and was cast out of God's presence, his name is Lucifer and he is identified as a Son of the Morning. In the next verse, the Prophet Joseph Smith says, "While we [Joseph and Sidney] were yet in the vision, we were commanded to write it...and now we saw Satan!" I'm contending that this person they see in this verse is not Lucifer. This person in this verse is one of those that Joseph Smith is talking about. Let me read that quote again:

> God is good and all His acts are for the benefit of inferior intelligences. God saw that those intelligences [that don't have a lot of experience] had NOT power to defend themselves against those that had a tabernacle [this is all premortal], therefore the Lord calls them together in counsel and agrees to form for them tabernacles.

Why? Because all beings with bodies have power over those that do not. What I'm contending is that this Satan we are reading about here is an older, resurrected, embodied person from an ancient earth in the past and now fulfills the role of Satan. And

24

this man was the cause of Lucifer's fall.

Student 2: So, we are never, ever safely dead.

Student 6: That's right.

Mike: Yes, you are because you get to a point where you become a god or a goddess, and they just can't—they have no power over you. You can be in a state where they're powerless over you. That doesn't mean that they don't exist there. You have to have evil with good.

Student 2: Yes, but this resurrected being followed a pattern and lived on an earth, apparently. They had the pattern. He was resurrected. So, these resurrected beings came forth, and let's say he came forth in the **evening** of the second resurrection, and he still has power to come forward now and tempt sons of God?

Mike: Because of a resurrected body, he'll have power over spirits who are evil that never received a body. We have a scriptural example of this. Lucifer, or Satan—whoever it is— goes to Cain and talks to Cain about entering into a combination to kill, to introduce murder, how to murder and get gain and keep it a secret. He, as a spirit being, needs to have somebody with a body that he can begin the process of murder and mayhem. So, he makes a deal with Cain. "You do my bidding and here's the deal: in eternity, you will reign over me, and I'll be subject to you." Why? Because Cain will die and at some time resurrect and have a physical body, while Lucifer will not. So, in eternity, who's going to have more power: Lucifer or resurrected Cain?

Student 6: Resurrected Cain.

Mike: There's the principle we're talking about here. If you go back and look at the pattern, as it has existed in untold number of earths and worlds, then the pattern duplicates itself. So, not only do you have unembodied evil (those who've never been born i.e. Lucifer and the third-part who were cast out for rebellion) but also in eternity you have embodied, resurrected evil that exists and always will. My thinking is that it has to exist in order for agency to exist and flourish. Let's take the pattern. You're going to be a Mother and a Father in Heaven at some future time. You're going to have your own spirit offspring, and they're going to look to you, eventually, for salvation and exaltation.

You're going to create a world for them to go down upon and they're going to have an experience. So, where is the devil and where is the evil that will exist in **your** worlds after all these others have come and gone? If you have a child, a son, who rises up in princely power, but makes choices and falls because he is enticed, well who was the enticer?

Go over to 2 Nephi chapter 2 and let me show you. It wasn't enough in the Garden of Eden to have two trees, even though they stood in opposition to each other. Let's read verse 15 and think about all we've talked about. There has to be opposition in all things:

> *[15] And to bring about his eternal purposes in the end of man, after he had created our first parents, and the beasts of the field and the fowls of the air, and in fine, all things which are created, it must needs be that there was an opposition;*

Semicolon. Here it is:

> *even the forbidden fruit in opposition to the tree of life; the one being sweet and the other being bitter.*

The *forbidden fruit* is the sweet, and the *tree of life* is bitter. I know it sounds like it should be the other way around, but it's not. Now, here is your key:

> *[16] Wherefore, the Lord God gave unto man that he should act for himself.*

So, you've got the two trees in opposition. You've got a commandment where God says, "You can eat of all of these but that one," right? So, the opposition is there. You've got the commandments there, but look at the last part of verse 16:

> *Wherefore, **man could not act for himself save it should be that he was underlineenticed** by the one or the other.*

Now, look at what happens:

> *[17] And I, Lehi, according to the things which I have read, must needs suppose that **an angel of God**, according to that which is written, had*

*fallen from heaven; wherefore he became **a** devil,*

Not **the** devil; **a** devil:

having sought that which was evil before God.

So, who is the enticer? Once the stage is set, the props are up, and the commandment given, Lehi comes out and says that you could **not** choose one or the other unless there is an enticement. So, you have to bring in this third party. Always, there has to be an enticer. Who enticed Lucifer, a Son of the Morning, to sin and fall? That's what I'm saying. And what Joseph is teaching us here is a whole new paradigm of thought, and that's the purpose of this lesson tonight. He's teaching us that things in the premortal life were pretty much like things are right here on earth. Many think that it was a nice, easy-going place up there where we were in the presence of Heavenly Father, and everything was peace and roses, except for a war that didn't last too long. And then they were vanquished and cast out, and we continued with peace, happiness, and prosperity. According to what Joseph is telling us, that isn't it. There was oppression. There was persecution. And those spirits were persecuted and oppressed by evil, embodied, tabernacled beings. From where? From earlier earths and earlier times. Now, that all fits in with what we hear in the temple:

What are YOU doing here?

I'm doing that which has been done on other worlds.

So, we start putting all this together, and it's a marvelous picture. And then it answers, or starts to answer, questions like, just what is this *rest of the Lord*? Just what is Paradise in the spirit world? And when you start to get a feeling for some of these keys that Joseph gives us then you maybe get a different picture.

In closing, I want to quickly read the quote by Joseph Smith:

It is natural with the spirits that have the most power to bare down on those of lesser power.

That's one quote. Next quote:

All beings who have bodies have power over those who have not.

Third quote:

God is good and all of his acts are for the benefit

*of inferior intelligences. God saw that those intelligences had **NOT** power to defend themselves against those that had a tabernacle, therefore the Lord calls them together in counsel and agrees to form them tabernacles.*

And the last quote:

Before the foundation of the earth in the Grand Counsel, the spirits of all men were subject to oppression and the express purpose of God in giving it a tabernacle was to arm it against the power of darkness.

Those are little-known quotes taken right from the Prophet Joseph Smith in the Nauvoo period that give us a little different twist, a little different look on things, something to ponder and something to think about.

Student 1: It makes me wonder why we want to go there, to the eternal place. Now, we go there, and we still have to struggle or worry that there will be evil?

Mike: No, no, no. Not at all. You're NOT going to struggle, and you're NOT going to worry because in your progression you have gained supremacy over these things. Do you think that God the Father and Jesus Christ struggle and worry about evil that exists anywhere?

Student 6: Look at Lucifer. Look what happened to him. He was a Son of the Morning. How are we going to have the confidence to be Mothers and Fathers in Heaven?

Margie: It's all on what you focus on. If you focus on Satan and worry about that world attacking you, then you are going to have some worries. But why don't you focus on the Savior and say, "Hey, if He can do it, I can do it!" You know, there's your opposition once again.

Student 6: I'm just saying that the men were high and close to God. They were high in authority and righteousness, and THEY fell, so none of us... what I'm saying is it's possible for anyone to fall.

Mike: If you obtain a resurrected body that is an exalted, celestial, resurrected body, that is going to give you more power over these beings than a person who resurrects into a body that inhabits a telestial world. And we can concentrate on Lucifer's fall, but let's take a look at Joseph. Let's take a look at Abraham. Let's take a look at Isaac. Let's look at Moses. Let's look at all of those guys who obtained this high stature and **didn't** fall.

Student 2: So, that is why you constantly teach about the Second Comforter.

Mike: That's why I constantly teach about the importance of **knowledge** and that:

> *A man is saved no faster than he gets knowledge.*

Notice that quote. I've got it memorized. It's another one that backs up what we're talking about. No man can be saved without knowledge. Here's the whole quote:

> *A man is saved no faster than he gets knowledge, for if he does not get knowledge, he will be brought into captivity by some evil power in the other world, as evil spirits will have more knowledge, and consequently more power than many men who are on the earth. Hence it needs revelation to assist us, and give us knowledge of the things of God.*

Did you catch that? Because that spirit will have more knowledge and hence, more power than you do. So, it all ties in. We want to be able to obtain knowledge because it gives us power. The purpose of being tabernacled in this life, at least one that we've never thought of—I hadn't until recently, and these quotes bring this to mind—one of the grand purposes is to give us at least an equal edge over evil that has a body in eternity. Now, you take your body, and arm that with light, truth, knowledge, and a glorious resurrection and you have nothing to fear! You're in a position where you, like the Father and the Son, will say, "We will allow these beings, our common enemies, to tempt and try man that they may learn from their own experience to distinguish good from evil." It's all part of the plan. It's all a part of bringing His children, and eventually, you bringing your children up through this plan to come into contact with evil and to overcome it because of who you've become: a holy, sanctified, resurrected, glorious being! They continue to exist, but you have supremacy over them. You're in *the rest of the Lord*. You don't worry about it. They don't affect you. It's like when the devil comes up to our Father in Heaven, or comes up to the Lord in the first and second chapter in Job. They have this encounter. The Lord is in this council talking with the sons of God, and the devil comes up. And the Lord says,

"What are you doing here?"

And the devil says,

"Oh, well, I've been going up and down in the earth and walking to and fro in it."

And in 1 Peter he says he's like a *"roaring lion, [who] walketh about, seeking whom he may devour."* That's here in the telestial world. That's the evil who you come into contact with to have an opposition that refines you and polishes you and makes you a polished shaft in the quiver of the Almighty. And then the Lord says:

"Have you considered my servant Job, a perfect and just man?"

And then Lucifer sets up this deal and says:

"Yeah, because You protect him! You favor him! You cheat! You're not living up according to the deal! You let me have equal opportunity with him, and he'll curse You to Your face."

And the Lord says:

"Well, take everything he's got, but don't hurt his life. Take his property…"

You know the story. Job loses it all but does not sin. The second time the devil comes up, and the Lord says:

"What are you doing here?"

It's the same thing, and the Lord says:

"Have you considered my servant Job?"

And he says:

"Yeah, skin for skin! If You let me go at his physical body, he'll curse You to Your face."

The Lord said:

"Go at it, but don't kill him."

And then you go all the way back to the 42nd chapter after that whole deal, and we never read the 42nd chapter of Job. I want you to read that because in the 42nd chapter of Job, after all that contact with evil, it says that the latter end of Job was more glorious than the beginning.

And then he says:

[5] But now mine eye seeth thee.

He has a Second Comforter experience. He attains eternal life promises. And at that point, do you think Lucifer has any control over Job? And do you think Job gives a second thought about what he went through after he's obtained everything through the experience? See?

So, you have nothing to worry about. It just is the process for you to come up and be like the Mothers and Fathers, who, by the way, know that evil is there, and even confront it periodically. Otherwise, you can't say, *"We will allow Lucifer, our common enemy..."* That statement right there tells you that they confront evil, and of course they do because it's part of the plan to become as They are. But, it doesn't bother them. And who's in charge? They are. And how did They get to that point? By going against it, face to face, through eons of time, and gaining the victory just like we're doing here!

Student 4: We look at those with Joseph Smith: Oliver Cowdery and the five men that left—in every case they had seen angels, they'd seen these things, but they succumbed to carnal, sensual, and devilish ideas. And even some of them had problems with sexual sins and so forth, and left the Church. Not because all this stuff wasn't true, it's just that they fell because of appetites of the body. It's carnal, sensual, and devilish. Now, that's the opposition that was talked about today in Priesthood and Relief Society. It has to be there. These men had to be tested. Some of them arose out of it, and some of them didn't. And that's where we are. And what you've said this evening, that's where we all are, and we all have to keep pressing forward and overcoming this opposition and overcoming our sensual desires.

Mike: Everything that's going on in the temple, the whole temple endowment and all the temple blessings and priesthood blessings, are designed to give you power and supremacy over evil. In section 38 the Lord says:

> *[32] That ye should go to the Ohio; and there I will give unto you my law; and there you shall be **endowed with power** from on high.*

Power to do what? To overcome evil that exists in this world and provides the opposition for growth and sanctification. You cannot be sanctified and perfected without passing through hell and experiencing the fire. You can't do it. Every one of those who sits enthroned, the Elohim, have been through the fire and are refined because of it. It's the process. There is no other way. That's why Eve says:

> *Is there no other way?*

And Satan speaks a great truth right there when he says:

> *There is no other way.*

And it's true! This is the way. In fact, it's interesting that the ancient saints, and even the *New Testament* saints, referred to the Gospel of Jesus Christ, not as the Gospel of Jesus Christ, but they referred to it as *"The Way."* They weren't called Christians until later up in Antioch when Paul goes up there. Prior to that, during the Ministry of Christ, you know what they called themselves? They didn't call themselves Christians. They called themselves *Followers of the Way.* Now, that makes sense, in John 14, "...I am the way, the truth, and the light." See?

So, when Eve says, "Is there no other way?" No! There is no other way. And this is the path to the Elohim.

Anyway, something for you to think about. I'll post these quotes by the Prophet Joseph Smith so that you can have them. Interesting stuff! Causes you to come up with a lot of questions, doesn't it? But, we have to keep an open mind, and the biggest challenge for growth among the Latter-day Saints is to do away with false traditions.

Student 1: Now, let me ask you a question. I was teaching that class in Relief Society today.

Mike: Okay.

Student 1: I made a remark that some didn't agree with. I said, "Okay, we all know Heavenly Father is fair. Yeah? We all agree.

So, in other words, if that is the case, Satan has equal time and equal opportunity to influence us as Christ has influenced us for good." But some didn't feel that way. And I think that is fair. And then it's up to us which one we follow, right?

Mike: Right. I'm not surprised that there are some who didn't agree with you.

Student 1: So, you agree with me?

Mike: Absolutely.

Student 1: Okay.

Mike: Absolutely. That's an eternal law. You can't expect God to bless you with a **five** and only give Satan a number **two** opportunity. It doesn't work that way.

Student 1: I just don't want to teach false doctrine.

Mike: Yeah. Well, it's not false doctrine, just a doctrine that people have not heard. So, you are coming up against things that people have held for truth all of their lives, and when you present something that doesn't fit into that paradigm, they're going to resist change. You see, it's true; you just have to be careful who you speak it too and what you say. But, it's a true principle. Absolutely.

Well, thanks, brothers and sisters! Everything I've given you is doctrine <u>except for Stroud 23:6,</u> right? And I told you that's my opinion. And if you saw me and I were wearing a tie, I'd put my tie over my shoulder for a visual sign that I'm giving my opinion. Alright, thanks! Have a great week, and we'll see you next week.

References:
D&C 121:39-40
The Words of Joseph Smith, Ehat and Cook page 68 —for it is a
Natural thing with those spirits that has the most power to bore down
on those of Lesser power
D&C 76:25-31
2 Nephi 2:15-17
History of the Church, 4:588; from a discourse given by Joseph Smith on Apr. 10, 1842, in Nauvoo, Illinois; reported by Wilford Woodruff.
Job 42
D&C 38:32
(Pray that the Lord may strengthen my lungs, stay the winds, and let

the prayers of the Saints to heaven appear, that they may enter into the ears of the Lord of Sabaoth,)

Joseph Smith Statements on Tabernacled Evil
"It is natural...with those spirits that (have) the most power to bare down on those of lesser power."
(Joseph Smith; Words of Joseph Smith, p. 68.)

"All beings who have bodies have power over those who have not."
(Words of Joseph Smith, p. 60.)

"God is good and all his acts (are) for the benefit of inferior intelligences - God saw that those intelligences had NOT power to defend themselves against those that had a tabernacle, therefore the Lord calls them together in counsel and agrees to form them tabernacles."
(Words of Joseph Smith, p. 68.)

"Before (the) foundation of the earth in the Grand counsel...the Spirits of all men were subject to oppression and the express purpose of God in giving it tabernacle was to arm it against the power of darkness."
(Words of Joseph Smith, p. 62.)

Page 60 The Words of Joseph Smith
The world and earth are not synonymous terms. The world is the human family. This earth was organized or formed out of other planets which were broke up and remodelled and made into the one on which we live. The elements are eternal. That which has a begining will surely have an end. Take a ring, it is without beginning or end; cut it for a beginning place, and at the same time you will have an ending place. A key, every principle proceeding from God is eternal, and any principle which is not eternal is of the Devil. The sun has no beginning or end, the rays which proceed from himself have no bounds, consequently are eternal. So it is with God. If the soul of man had a beginning it will surely have an end. In the translation, "without form and void" it should read "empty and desolate." The word "created" should be formed or organized. Observations on the Sectarian God. That which is without body or parts is nothing. There is no other God in heaven but that God who has flesh and bones. John 5—26, "As the father hath life in himself, even so hath he given the son to have life in himself". God the father took life unto himself precisely as Jesus did. The first step in the salvation of men is the laws of eternal and self-existent principles. Spirits are eternal. At the

34

first organization in heaven we were all present and saw the Savior chosen and appointed, and the plan of salvation made and we sanctioned it. We came to this earth that we might have a body and present it pure before God in the Celestial Kingdom. The great principle of happiness consists in having a body. The Devil has no body, and herein is his punishment. He is pleased when he can obtain the tabernacle of man and when cast out by the Savior he asked to go into the herd of swine showing that he would prefer a swines body to having none. **All beings who have bodies have power over those who have not.** The devil has no power over us only as we permit him; the moment we revolt at anything which comes from God the Devil takes power. This earth will be rolled back into the presence of God and crowned with Celestial Glory.

Words of Joseph Smith Page 62
19 January 1841 (Tuesday). McIntire Minute Book Next Meeting
—Joseph said that before foundation of the Earth in the Grand Counsel that the Spirits of all Men ware subject to opression & the express purpose of God in Giveing it a tabernicle was to arm it against the power of Darkness —for instance Jesus said Get behind me Satan Also the apostle said Resist the Devil & he will flee from you.

28 March 1841 (Sunday). McIntire Minute Book Next Meeting Meeting on Sunday Joseph Reads the 38th Ch—of Job. in the book he says is a Great Display of human Nature—it is page 68 The Words of Joseph Smith
very Natureal for a man when he sees his fellow man afflicted his Natureal conclusion is that he is sufering the Rath of an angry God & turn from him in haste not knowing the purpose of God he says the spirit or the inteligence of men are self Existant principles he before the foundation this Earth—& quotes the Lords question to Job "where wast thou when I laid the foundation of the Earth" Evidence that Job was in Existing somewhere at that time he says **God is Good & all his acts is for the benifit of infereir inteligences— God saw that those intelegences had Not power to Defend themselves against those that had a tabernicle therefore the Lord Calls them togather in Counsel & agrees to form them tabernicles so that he might Gender the Spirit & the tabernicle togather so as to create sympathy for their fellowman—for it is a Natureal thing with those spirits that has the most power to bore down on those of Lesser power** so we see the Devil is without a tabernacle & the Lord as set bo[u]nds to all Spirits & hence Come the Saying thou son of David why art thou Come to torment us before the time, & Jesus Comanded him to Come out of the Man & the Devil besought him that he might Enter in a herd of swine Near by (for the Devil knew they

were a Coveitous people & if he Could Kill their Hogs that would Drive Jesus out of their Coasts & he then would have tabernicle enough) & Jesus— permitted him to Enter into the swine.

Chapter 7 Consequences Of Rejection

We previously learned that an individual can reject the knowledge of God through apathy, reluctance, or out right rebellion. Naturally the penalty for rejecting the word of God will vary according to the nature of the individual. Those who oppose God in open rebellion must suffer a more severe penalty than those who in affect reject His word because they are to apathetic to learn His word. Nevertheless, there are natural consequences for rejecting the knowledge of God regardless of the reasons for or circumstances surrounding the rejection. Wilford Woodruff recorded in his journal the following remarks made by Joseph Smith during the general conference in April of 1844. *"But if ye are not led by revelation how can ye escape the damnation of hell?* (Joseph Smith; April 7, 1844; Words of Joseph Smith, p. 345.) On other occasions the Prophet stated: *"The principle of knowledge is the principle of salvation. This principle can be comprehended by the faithful and diligent; and anyone that does not obtain knowledge sufficient to be saved will be condemned."* (TPJS, P.297.) *"Knowledge saves a man and in the world of spirits no man can be exalted but by knowledge."* (TPJS, P.3 57.) It becomes apparent that when individuals reject the knowledge of God which He tries to bestow upon them, whether their rejection be caused by apathy, reluctance, or rebellion the natural consequences are the same. They forfeit the exaltation they could have received and in its place receive condemnation or the "damnation of hell." God is a kind and loving Father. He gets no pleasure at condemning His children. Our condemnation causes Him pain and suffering just as earthly parents suffer pain when they watch their children suffer the natural consequences of their mistakes and follies. He knows the end from the beginning and, therefore, tries to guide us in order to protect and shield us from the consequences we experience from mistakes. He warns us, calls us to repentance, tries to teach us of the grave danger we are in unless we heed His voice of warning. But He cannot live our lives for us and wisely allows us to choose our own destiny. EM In order to more clearly understand why the acquisition of knowledge is so important, let us place our lives in their historical setting from an eternal perspective. Examining our pre-mortal existence, our present probationary state, and our post-mortal spiritual state we can understand how knowledge or the lack thereof can affect us. 7.1 Pre-Mortal Existence The traditional understanding of most Latter-day Saints is to think of our premortal existence as a place of extreme happiness and joy. We lived in the very presence of our Father in

Heaven. There was no contention or difficulty whatsoever, except for the rebellion of Lucifer. The nature of that rebellion is quite nebulous in our minds and is generally thought of being fairly short in duration. With that one exception our past lives for countless thousands of earth years, perhaps even billions of earth years, have been lives filled with peace and contentment, in which we prepared for coming to this probationary state. Though that picture serves a purpose, it is not entirely accurate. Joseph Smith made some statements which would indicate that perhaps life there was not all that different from life here. There were great difficulties associated with our pre-mortal existence; difficulties which were so severe that only knowledge and the obtaining of corporeal bodies could enable us to overcome them. While speaking upon the subject of our pre-mortal existence the Prophet said: *"It is natural... with those spirits that (have) the most power to bare down on those of lesser power.'* 1(Joseph Smith; Words of Joseph Smith,p.68.) In our pre-mortal life some beings had more power than others and that they used that power unrighteously to bear down on beings of lesser power. That sounds much like this mortal life of strife and power struggles. That God did organize his spirit children along ecclesiastical lines of some sort cannot be denied, but as soon as any of His leaders begin to exercise any degree of unrighteous dominion they would be immediately removed from their office, "Amen to their Priesthood," as it were, and thus eliminated the oppression they were causing. We see this same thing in wicked men upon this earth who unrighteously wield power and authority over individuals and nations due to their knowledge of science or technology, or their ability to manipulate circumstances both spiritualy and physicaly. Joseph Smith made another blanket statement regarding power when he explained: *"All beings who have bodies have power over those who have not."* (Words of Joseph Smith, p.60.) This is a concept readily accepted by most Latter-day Saints. It is for this reason that evil spirits have no power over us unless we permit them, because we have bodies and they do not. However, coupling this statement with the previous statement by Joseph can we deduce that there were tabernacled beings who dwelt in our pre-mortal state who exercised unrighteous dominion over our spirits sence they had bodies and we did not? Be not too hasty in rejecting this line of reasoning even though it flies against everything we have traditionally been taught. Addressing this very idea the Prophet Joseph taught the following: *"God is good and all his acts (are) for the benefit of inferior intelligences - God saw that those intelligences had NOT power to defend themselves against those that had a tabernacle, therefore the Lord calls them together in counsel and agrees to form them tabernacles."* (Words of Joseph Smith, p.68.) We, therefore, learn that in our pre-mortal estate, God called the counsel together to present a plan whereby those who did not have tabernacles could be provided with corporeal bodies. Joseph explained that the express purpose for granting tangible bodies to the children of God was so that they could defend themselves against the oppressions of an unrighteous group that already had tabernacles. It is generally understood that at the time of the grand counsel in heaven the only being to possess a corporeal body was God himself, all others being spirit entities only. This, however, is not entirely correct according to Joseph Smith. There were other beings - unrighteous, wicked individuals, who also possessed physical bodies. Inasmuch as they were not righteous let's call them children of the devil rather than children of God. **These physical bodied children of the devil lived among us in our pre-mortal state and caused such terrible oppression upon us that God called a counsel to put into action the eternal plan to protect His children from the onslaught of these wicked personages by arming His children with physical bodies.** Thus re-enacting the eternal drama and setting in motion that which has been done on other worlds. Joseph amplified upon this theme explaining: *"Before (the) foundation of the earth in the Grand counsel the Spirits of all men were subject to oppression and the express purpose of God in giving it a tabernacle was to arm it against the power of darkness."* (Words of Joseph Smith, p.62.) Clearly the oppressive tabernacled beings mentioned in the earlier quotes and the tabernacled powers of darkness Joseph mentioned in this passage are one and the same. They are the ones who oppressed us in our pre-mortal state and it is because of their oppression that God desired to extend to us the privilege of mortality. In other words, there were some wicked, evil tabernacled beings who resided in our pre-mortal existence who bore down upon and oppressed those who did not have bodies. God saw that this was not fair and so said in effect, *"I will organize an earth and allow men to take upon them tabernacles of flesh for the express purpose of placing them on equal footing with these wicked tabernacled beings who are oppressing my spirit children. Since all beings with tabernacles have power over those without tabernacles it is impossible for my spirit children to defend themselves against the more advanced wicked ones who emanate powers of darkness."* Thus clothed with a tabernacle, and gaining sufficient knowledge of how to use the tabernacle, we will be able to overcome the powers of darkness and go on to receive our exaltation. At present we are as infants and do not even begin to understand the powers within us by virtue of having a physical tabernacle. It is to this end that our search for knowledge must take us. 7.2 Mortal Probation It is very evident to all here upon the earth that knowledge is power. Because of knowledge our economic differences abound, one knows how to acquire material goods and another does not. Knowledge in the scientific field makes technological advances possible, thereby granting one society power over another that lacks those advances. Knowledge, in and of itself, brings with it certain associated powers regardless of the righteousness or wickedness to which the powers are applied. For example: mechanical forces can accomplish an amazing amount of labor but is quickly outworked by electrical power. Electrical power, however, is easily dwarfed by nuclear power. Knowledge of these forms of power grant to the user certain powers regardless of how righteous or wicked the user may be. A war fought between two countries, one armed with swords and spears and another with nuclear weapons would be no contest at all. In like manner we are engaged in an eternal war over our souls. During our pre-mortal existence the battle was very one sided. The powers of darkness possessed physical bodies (at least some did). This gave them a tremendous advantage. Here on earth we have been given a temporary reprieve against direct confrontation with these powers so that we might learn how to govern and control our bodies. When we gain sufficient knowledge of self mastery as well as other knowledge which God will grant us as we become prepared to receive it, we will be able to continue on with the fight until we eventually are able to triumph over the enemy completely. Ultimately the war must be won or lost on an individual by individual basis. No one can fight our battle for us. No one, no matter how much they love us, can win the war for us. We alone, each of us individually, must gain sufficient knowledge and strength of self to totally overcome the powers of darkness in the eternal battle for our souls. It is important that we take advantage of our time here in mortality, for when we leave this earth we will also leave the protective shield which momentarily prevents direct confrontation with the powers of darkness and affords us the opportunity to develop self mastery and to acquire the needed knowledge to overcome the adversary. Satan knows this so he tries to prevent us from gaining sufficient self mastery and the knowledge we need to triumph over him by side tracking us with the cares of the world or by interesting us in gaining knowledge about things which, though interesting, have no real consequence upon our eternal standing. The Lord has told us that: *"Whatever principle of intelligence we attain unto in this life, it will rise with us in the resurrection. And if a person gains more knowledge and intelligence in this life through his diligence and obedience than another, he will have so much the advantage in the world to come."* (D&C 130:18-19.) The Lord is not referring to scholastic learning or the acquiring of secular knowledge. A profound knowledge of hydro dynamics, electrical engineering or foreign languages will not give us any advantage in the next world. The kind of knowledge and intelligence the Lord refers to in this verse can, as He stated, only be obtained by "diligence" and "obedience". Thus "diligence" in keeping the commandments of the lord and "obedience" to the mind and will of the Lord are the schoolmasters we need to follow. The question then is, over what will we have advantage in the next world by gaining knowledge here in mortality? Let's consider the next world and see. 7.3 Post-Mortal State It is evident that one of the purposes for coming to this earth is to obtain a body and knowledge of how to overcome the powers of darkness we will encounter in the next world. Those who neglect their responsibility or reject the knowledge God desires to pour out upon them must suffer the natural consequences by being brought into captivity and oppressed by the powers of darkness in the next life. Joseph Smith taught that: *"A man is saved no faster than he gets knowledge, for if he does not get knowledge, he will be brought into captivity by some evil power in the other world, as evil spirits (and perhaps tabernacled beings too) have more knowledge, and consequently more power than many men who are on the earth. Hence it needs revelation to assist us, and give us knowledge of the things of God."* (TPJS, p.217.) Knowledge gained by personal revelation is the key that will unlock the door to freedom in the next world. Those who reject the key to their freedom must pay the price. As with every other principle of the gospel, disobedience to this one will bring about a wide variety of punishment, or subjection to the powers of darkness, depending upon the degree of rejection. Heber C. Kimball was shown the powers of darkness in vision and learned how they are organized in the spirit world, or the world into which we will pass when we leave this state. He saw that they there continue the war on the souls of men, particularly upon the righteous. He cautioned us lest we be overcome by them even in that estate. Said he: *"As for the departure from this state of existence (mortality), it is but for a moment; and though I have not tasted death, yet I have seen in vision the invisible enemies of God, and they were organized and arranged in battle against one or two men, simply because those men were going to proclaim the Gospel... and the devil did not like it... they will have great power in the last days (evil spirits), and if you do not overcome them, you will fall into the same spirit and you will be as liable to be deceived in that state of existence as you are in this... "*(Heber C. Kimbal; JD 4:5.) In referring to the future life of individuals who would not subject themselves to the powers of the Priesthood of God, but would rather subject themselves to the powers and influences of darkness in this life Orson Pratt said: "The whole spirit world in the lower orders is full of deception, and unless you have something to detect and understand the truth from the false you are liable to be led astray and destroyed. *"I do not know that I need to say anything further about these two powers, only that all evil powers will go to their own place; and, unless these men repent, the same being that has power over them here in the flesh will hold them in captivity in the next world; unless they repent, the same being who gives them revelation here will hold the mastery over them there, and will control them; and if they do not find a dictating and controlling power in the*

Priesthood, they will find it among those beings to whom they have yielded themselves subject to obey; and so will every other person that yields to false influences; they will be overcome and Satan will destroy them, unless they repent." (JD 13:74-75.) Partial rejection of the knowledge of God will exclude one from the presence of God and exaltation. These individuals will be assigned to some other kingdom of glory in which they will be held captive by the powers of darkness to a greater or lesser degree as determined by their knowledge. One comforting thought is that complete rejection of the word of God and open rebellion to his plan is simply not possible for most of us. To completely reject the plan one must first have had the heavens opened to him, know God, and receive the order of blessings and ordinances attending the visitation of the Second Comforter. (See Words of Joseph Smith, p. 347 & 396) To have enjoyed this blessing and then reject the higher knowledge would cause one to become a son of perdition. Those suffering this punishment will be cast into outer darkness where they will be turned over completely to the powers of darkness and made captive to them. It seems very clear that the punishment we will receive in the next world will be very closely linked to the amount of knowledge we gain in this world. Obviously the knowledge needed to overcome the powers of darkness is not the type of secular knowledge learned in the public school system but rather knowledge of righteousness, knowledge of faith, and knowledge of repentance which can only be gained by experience, obedience, faithfulness and diligence to the revealed word of God. Our Father knows the tremendous powers of subjugation possessed by the evil one, and is therefore eager to teach His children through the Light of Christ, the Gift of the Holy Ghost, living oracles, scriptures, and most importantly through personal revelation so that we can overcome those powers and win the battle for our soul.

Chapter Twenty-Six
Podcast 026 The Celestial World Part 1

We've talked about the telestial world, and we spent two lessons on the terrestrial world; so, guess what I'd like to talk about tonight?

Students: Celestial!

Mike: Yes, good guess! How did you know? Ha-ha! Let's go to *Doctrine and Covenants* 76 and look at a couple of things here. This section gives us a good launch pad to discuss these things. Verses 50-70 are all about the celestial world. I find it interesting that Joseph Smith said that what we have in 119 verses in section 76 is only one hundredth of what he saw. Think about that for just a minute. If we have 119 verses and it represents only one hundredth of what he and Sidney saw at the John Johnson farm that day (in what Church History calls "the vision"), imagine what he saw that he could have told us if we had been able to bear it. The only reason the Lord closes up visions or forbids prophets to continue to talk about or write about doctrinal subjects is that we're not ready for it. As we've talked about numerous times, the prophet spent all his life, right up to his martyrdom, trying to prepare the Latter-day Saints to receive what he had seen and had been taught from on high. By and large, the society of the Latter-day Saints couldn't handle it. And I say society because there were individuals that grasped this and got much more. Well, this week I had a discussion with a young man. I've had this discussion with several people, and it ties in with verse 53. I want to take just a minute and discuss this with you because it's a principle that's not well understood. We teach it, and it's just not good doctrine. I don't say "false doctrine" anymore; it's just not good doctrine. It's not that the Church teaches it, but somehow this has crept in as a tradition among Latter-day Saints. You'll recognize it. Verse 53 is talking about the celestial world. It says:

> *[These are they] who overcome by faith, and are sealed by the Holy Spirit of promise, which the Father sheds forth upon all those who are just and true.*

This *"sealed by the Holy Spirit of promise"* is the thing that we don't understand very well. Let's go over to *Doctrine and Covenants* 132:7. We see this term used again. This verse is the Lord's description of being sealed by priesthood power. The key to this whole thing is this phrase, *"the Holy Spirit of promise."* Let's look at verse 7:

> *And verily I say unto you, that the conditions of this law are these:*

Now, I want you to notice the first two words: *"**all** covenants."* The word is **ALL**. That doesn't leave out anything:

> ***All** covenants, contracts, bonds, obligations, oaths, vows, performances,*
>
> *connections, associations, or expectations,*

This includes ordinances performed in temples, performed in the Church, covenants, and laws, everything:

> *that are not made and entered into and sealed by the **Holy Spirit of promise**, of him who is anointed, both as well for time and for all eternity,*

That's talking about a person who holds this sealing power, at that time it was Joseph Smith:

> *and that too most holy, by revelation and commandment through the medium of mine anointed, whom I have appointed on the earth to hold this power (and I have appointed unto my servant Joseph to hold this power in the last days, and there is never but one on the earth at a time*

> *on whom this power and the keys of this priesthood are conferred),* **are of no efficacy, virtue, or force in and after the resurrection from the dead; for all contracts that are not made unto this end have an end when men are dead.**

Now, go back and read again and we're going to skip the middle part. It would read like this:

> ***All*** *covenants, contracts, bonds, obligations, oaths, vows, performances,*
>
> *connections, associations, or expectations, that are not made and entered into and sealed by the* ***Holy Spirit of promise****, are of no efficacy, virtue, or force in and after the resurrection from the dead; for all contracts that are not made unto this end have an end* ***when men are dead****.*

Student 1: Can I ask a question?

Mike: Yes, go ahead.

Student 1: The *Holy Spirit of Promise* is the Holy Ghost, right?

Mike: It is.

Student 1: I just wanted to make sure.

Mike: If you were to ask what the functions of the Holy Ghost are, you could probably put four or five top ones in there. He testifies of all truth. He testifies of the Father and the Son. He is the Sanctifier; so, men and women who obtain a state of sanctification in this world, do so by the power of the Holy Ghost. The Holy Ghost sanctifies. Sanctify means "to make holy." The Holy Ghost is a Purifier; so, when we read in the scriptures about men and women being made "pure," it's the Holy Ghost that does this. The other thing that He does is He places a seal on all covenants, ordinances, contracts, bonds, everything listed in that scripture. *The Holy Spirit of Promise* is describing the sealing, ratifying, certification, and any words that have to do with that, that this Man places upon all ordinances, vows, contracts, obligations, etc. In essence, when He places His ratifying seal and when he certifies this, which is one of his assignments, that ordinance, that contract, that bond, that vow is good not only in this life but in eternity. So, that seal by the *Holy Spirit of Promise* takes a relationship here in this world and allows it to continue as such in the world to come and into eternity. Now, there is something that has come up again this week, and it has come up several times in the last few months. Let's use the marriage ceremony for example since we're talking about the celestial world tonight. There are a lot of people, way too many people that have the feeling that once you go to the temple and you have a marriage ceremony performed by the sealer there, that that is all that has to happen to be sealed in eternity. We've all knelt at the altar, and we've all seen that and we've all heard the words. I have the sealing ceremony memorized. We're missing out on one little phrase in that sealing ceremony that makes that whole ordinance conditional. It's conditional, and I'm going to say that all ordinances performed in the temple that you and I are experiencing right now, are conditional in nature. Every ordinance that we see there, from the initiatory, to washings, anointings, to sealings in the sealing room that we do for the living and the dead, are ALL conditional, meaning there's an "out clause."

Student 1: It says that right there. You can hear it.

Mike: That's right! If you're listening to that, it says you have *the blessings of thrones, principalities, powers, dominions, exaltations, all the blessings of Abraham, Isaac, and Jacob, are sealed upon you* **according to your faithfulness***;* that's your clause. That clause and similar wording are placed upon all ordinances that are performed in the Church that you and I have experienced until you come up to a higher ordinance called a *second anointing*. That condition that you hear "according to your faithfulness," in the *second anointing* ordinance, that clause is removed. In the *second anointing* ordinance, it's not conditional.

Student 6: Are you saying that if you were to have that done in the temple, there is a script for that, and it's not in that script? I understand you're saying it in general, but I'm asking if there is actually a script.

Mike: You mean like the sealing script that is written down and kept in the temple presidency's safe, etc.? That kind of a thing?

Student 2: Yeah.

Mike: Yes, there is a script. There is a sheet of paper. If you're in the temple, and you have to evacuate the temple, there are certain people who are entrusted with gathering up all the written material on which the initiatory wording, the endowment ceremony, anything that is written down. You'll see ordinance workers and sealers, especially if they're new before they have it memorized, they'll refer to a written document. Now, those documents are to be gathered up in the case of an emergency, by a specified person, and they're entrusted to take those out of the temple and see that they are kept safe. The *second anointing* and any other ordinances that are performed in temples have a script. If you were to see the script for the *second anointing*, however, the difference on that would be that *"according to your faithfulness"* or any similar wording that makes it conditional is removed. That's why in the temple you hear, *"if you are true and faithful the day will come when you'll be chosen, called up and anointed kings and queens, priests and priestesses, **whereas you are now only anointed to become such.**"* That is the conditional part. The day comes when you are called up, and that condition is removed. What members of the Church don't realize is that when you have a temple sealing, you've had an ordinance performed that the efficacy of that ordinance depends upon your **subsequent faithfulness** while you're alive.

Student 6: You think that when members hear that they don't understand that?

Mike: You would be surprised. I came up against it again this week. There's a feeling, way too much in the Church, that once the ordinance has been performed and he says, "I seal you husband and wife for time and all eternity," that it's final. They don't hear the rest of it, and it's because that's what they've been taught. So, they leave the temple thinking that no matter what, they will always be a family unit, which was the case with the young man I was talking about. His parents were married in the temple, got divorced, and are now living apart with no desire to ever get together. The husband has remarried in the temple. This young man thought that in eternity, his mom and dad would get back together and they'd be a family unit. I sat down, talked to him about it and explained it all. He was very open, but it was definitely not his understanding that that's the way it was. Now, here's something else. Even if you have the *priesthood second anointing ordinance* performed in the temple, even though the wording takes out the conditional clause, even those promises must be sealed by the *Holy Spirit of Promise.* The *second anointing* is where you receive the *fullness of the Melchizedek Priesthood,* and you are no longer just anointed **to become** a king and a priest, a queen and a priestess, but you **are anointed** a king and a queen, a priest and a priestess. Even that ordinance is of no efficacy or force in and after the resurrection of the dead unless **it** is ratified by the *Holy Spirit of Promise.* The wording is taken out, but it still requires the *Holy Spirit of Promise* to place His seal, His certification, His ratification upon the ordinance for it to be binding in eternity. This is why people who receive their *second anointing* type blessing from an angel don't have to worry about the clause nor the sealing by the *Holy Spirit of Promise* because that angel isn't going to come under the direction of God, unless the Holy Ghost knows you are already right and He is already in tune with all of that. Unless He has already placed His seal on it, you are not going to have that ordinance performed by an immortal. That's why most people who understand this doctrine about having your *calling and election made sure*, being sealed up to eternal life, receiving the *fullness of the Melchizedek Priesthood*, etc., would rather have it performed by an angel, a translated being, or an immortal under the direct direction of God, than to have it performed as a priesthood ordinance in the temple. I'm not saying that it's not desirable to do that and my feeling is that we're going to see a whole lot more of that in the near future. The point is, when done under an immortal hand, under the direction of God, and not by mortals through an institution, that it is already in a condition of being ratified and in effect in eternity. Does that make sense? Now, you can lose this. Once it is done, you can lose this. It's possible to lose this.

Let's go back to section 76 again. Let's talk about a couple more things on that. Subsequent unrighteousness or subsequent sin voids that out. But, for those who have been sealed up to life under the hands of an immortal being and if you come out in open rebellion against that, after having received this—this is knowing God, not knowing "about God," but knowing God— then you put Christ to open shame, you crucify Him anew, and the result is that you become a Son of Perdition. Now, I don't believe you can become a Son of Perdition by stepping away from that *second anointing ordinance* that's performed in the temple unless it's ratified by the Holy Ghost and leads to an encounter with God, face to face.

Student 6: Say that again.

Mike: What I'm saying is this: Awhile back, on the internet, I read about a man from England who was a general authority, a mission president, and a member of the Second Quorum of the Seventy, etc. He was invited into the London Temple by Jeffrey R. Holland and received his *second anointing* blessings. He then fell away from the Church. He talks about the experience, and it's quite an interesting thing. But, here's the point. His feeling is, and he says of himself, "I'm a Son of Perdition." I don't believe he is. First of all, the *second anointing* blessing, to make your *calling and election sure,* is to lead you up to a point where you can receive a personal encounter with God Himself, with the Son. This is due to two things, and we've talked about this in detail. You converse with the Lord through the veil, you hear His voice, and obtain promises from Him. That is a step that leads to the next step where you enter into the presence of the Lord, and you see Him face to face, as one man sees another man. Now, when you get to that point, and you turn against that and come out in open rebellion, that's a Son of Perdition level. But, to have the ordinance of the *second anointing* performed in a temple by an apostle and it goes no further than that, makes it just an ordinance. In other words, it did not lead you to converse with the Lord through the veil. You did not have *the more sure word of prophecy* experience where the Lord talks to you, you hear His voice, and you obtain promises. Then that opens the door sometime after that to enter into His presence and have the *Second Comforter.* If you don't have that, then I don't believe you can become a Son of Perdition, even though that upper-level priesthood ordinance was performed in the temple by an apostle or a member of the First Presidency. Unless it leads where it's supposed to lead, and you sin against that, I don't think it's possible for you to be a Son of Perdition.

Student 6: Why would the gentleman think he was a Son of Perdition if he doesn't even believe in the anointing in the first place? Unless he is saying it lightly, like, "Ha-ha, I'm a son of perdition!"

Mike: This man believed in it in the first place. Both he and his wife believed in it, but they had questions about doctrinal things, and their questions were not answered satisfactorily by local authorities. So, they went up to a higher level, then to the General Authorities, and still didn't get answers. They felt that the Church was hiding something, etc., and so he apostatized away. When he originally went into the London Temple, they were full of faith and believing. I've read his whole story in detail because I wanted to see what he was thinking about. His whole problem is that he lacks doctrinal understanding. He does not have a doctrinal understanding even though he was a member of one the seventies quorums, a mission president, and a Church leader. Being a leader doesn't mean that you necessarily have a correct understanding of doctrine, and he does not.

Student 6: That's what I'm saying though. He's flippantly saying, "I'm a Son of Perdition," but if he doesn't believe the doctrine, there's no such thing as a Son of Perdition.

Mike: I think he's been told by others that with what he's done, after having received these ordinances, that that's his fate. So, whether he believes it or not, that's what somebody in authority is saying about him.

Student 6: Okay.

Mike: Here's the point. Very few people who are in mortality, in comparison to the numbers in the population, ever reach a point where they can even commit the sin against the Holy Ghost. To put the Son of God to open shame, you would have to know God in the purest sense of the word by Him revealing Himself to you, and you have that personal encounter with Him, and then you turn against Him in open rebellion. "Crucify Him anew," means that after knowing these things, and if you lived in the meridian of time, you would be in that group that would yell "crucify Him." So, can you see that level is pretty difficult to reach? To become a Son of Perdition, you have to have been pronounced a candidate for exaltation in the celestial world, and then you come out in open rebellion against that. I guess what I'm saying is that you can't fall that low unless you have ascended to that height.

Student 6: Elder Stroud, you have taught us that the *Book of Mormon* people were very favored of the Lord. Many of them had their *calling and election made sure*. Are you saying that they wouldn't have been to that level where they were actually Sons of Perdition, but to a level where the Lord wiped them away to send them to a new learning area?

Mike: I think there were many in the Nephite society who qualifies for perdition; I do. I think that they saw God and that they obtained promises. They had face to face encounters and then turned against it. I do believe that's what it's talking about when you read in Alma 9 about a society that was highly favored. "Highly favored" is pointing you in this direction.

Student 6: So, they would be Sons of Perdition!

Mike: They would be. But, comparatively speaking, the numbers are few because, with population numbers of the earth at any given time, those who will obtain exaltation in the highest degrees of heaven are also relatively few. Now, those few could number into millions when you consider the billions that have been here. So, there are Sons of Perdition. I believe there are probably some who qualified for that in the early history of the Church that were contemporaries of Joseph Smith. There were some people there that had some pretty potent encounters. In the bottom rung, when it's all said and done, Christ will be the judge as to who qualifies for this nefarious reputation, right? Nonetheless, I think we will be surprised. We have an old tradition in the Church that says that you can count the Sons of Perdition on one hand. I don't know about that because there have been, in all dispensations, times when men and women have obtained glorious stature. In the *New Testament*, Paul comes out and says that the Hebrew Church obtained the *Church of the Firstborn*. To obtain the *Church of the Firstborn* means that you have had the heavens opened. Let's go over to *Doctrine and Covenants*, and I'll show you what it means to have the *Church of the Firstborn*. Section 107 gives a pretty good description of that. We want to go to verse 18. This is a description of celestial *Church of the Firstborn* inheritors:

> *The power and authority of the higher, or Melchizedek Priesthood, is to hold the keys of all the spiritual blessings of the church—*

> *[19]* *[#1]* *To have the privilege of receiving the mysteries of the kingdom of heaven, [#2] to have the heavens opened unto them, [#3] to commune with the general assembly and church of the Firstborn,*

In our case, that would be the Church of Enoch because that's the *Church of the Firstborn* that deals with us. Messengers who are on earth that look like us and can disguise themselves as mortals, but in reality are translated beings, are coming from Enoch's society. They're ministering to us because we are their family, we are their children. Our heritage, if we dig into it, those of us who are enjoying the blessings of the gospel and the temple and the priesthood are descendants of Enoch's society. We can take our genealogical lines back through patriarchal blessings to the House of Israel, but you know it goes back to Jacob/Israel, to Isaac, to Abraham, to Noah and back through all the Patriarchs, back to Enoch. So, if you run it back, you're going to find out that your lineage is tied with these people. These are your fathers. So, the *Church of the Firstborn* ministers to us in this telestial world and they minister to those who are heirs of exaltation. This means that if you have these blessings and you're enjoying some of these things, this is the society of people that come and minister to you. And then [#4]:

> *and to enjoy the communion and presence of God the Father, and Jesus, the mediator of the new covenant.*

So, you see, that's all of these blessings. That's what we're shooting for. When you get to this category, if you are living in this world, and you obtain these blessings, you are a celestial being. You just haven't obtained a celestial resurrection, a celestial inheritance, nor have you been authorized to propagate spirit offspring, to command the elements to create worlds, and to begin the process where your children will one day look to you for redemption and salvation, and worship you as their Father and Mother. You're not up to that point, but you've obtained the promises from God that you will be and that's what we're talking about here. Now, if you turn against that in this life, then you've sinned against great light. Does that make sense?

All of these podcasts and the things that we've talked about are like various jigsaw puzzle pieces on a table. You have listened to enough of this that when you read the scriptures you can put it together and you should see a pattern that emerges from that. You can now understand things in the scriptures that before would have kept you veiled because you didn't understand certain doctrinal principles. Let's go back to section 76. I'll show you another little secret. We'll probably have to take two lesson periods for this lesson on the celestial world. I want you to notice that starting in verse 53, through verse 58 that it's interesting wording when the Lord describes this. Look at 53:

> And who overcome by faith, and **are** sealed

I want you to notice the word "**are**." You may want to circle that. Go to verse 54:

> They **are** they who are the church of the Firstborn.
> [55] They **are** they into whose hands the Father **has** given all things—

They are either present in this telestial world, or have been obtained in the telestial world:

> [56] They are they who **are** priests and kings, who **have** received of his fulness, and of his glory;

Notice all this is pointing toward what happens in this world:

> [57] And **are** priests of the Most High, after the order of Melchizedek, which was after the order of Enoch, which was after the order of the Only Begotten Son.
> [58] Wherefore, as it is written, they **are** gods, even the sons of **God**—

Notice the small **g** and capital **G**. This is all referring to men and women who have obtained these blessings in this life. These people here, when it says "**are**" and "**have**," obtained these in this life. Now, go to verse 60 and let me show you the difference.

> [60] And they [talking about the same group] **shall** overcome all things.

What's that? That's future:

> [61] Wherefore, let no man glory in man, but rather let him glory in God, who **shall** subdue all enemies under his feet.

> *[62] These* [talking about all the people in verse 50]
> **shall** *dwell in the presence of God and his Christ*
> *forever and ever.*
> *[63] These are they whom he* **shall** *bring with*
> *him, when he* **shall** *come in the clouds of heaven*
> *to reign on the earth over his people.*
> *[64] These are they who* **shall** *have part in the*
> *first resurrection.*

And it goes on and on like that. What this is doing is pointing in the direction of what can be and should be sought for in this life. We shouldn't postpone these things and wait for them. I gave a lesson today in Priesthood. The name of the lesson was "The Temple—The Great Symbol of our Membership." It was from President Howard W. Hunter's talk. Getting to the temple is becoming more easily done because temples are now throughout the world and most of the population of the earth is within 300 miles of a temple. I can remember when I lived in Arizona in the 1970's and the people in South America, Mexico, and Central America had to come to Mesa, Arizona to get their temple blessings. It's not been too many years since that was the case. One of the things that I said in my lesson was that the importance of the temple is such that members who have a reasonable opportunity to get to the temple and for whatever reason, choose not to do so, the purpose of their membership in The Church of Jesus Christ of Latter-day Saints is frustrated and largely futile. I just read it again today: everything that the Church is trying to do as an institution is to take families and to perform ordinances that will make family units eternal. Now, in our day, that can't be done on mountain tops, and it can't be done outside the institution of the Church of Jesus Christ of Latter-day Saints. It has to be done in temples. So, if you are not getting to the temple, you are forfeiting eternal life, exaltation, and a celestial inheritance. Remember, there are no covenants or ordinances required for a telestial or a terrestrial world. All ordinances, beginning with the initial ordinance of baptism, are to open the gate, unlock the door, and give you the opportunity to move into the celestial world. All Church ordinances pertain to the Celestial Kingdom of God, everything. Nothing points to the terrestrial world.

Let's talk about this celestial world for just a minute. One of the things I taught in that class today was some standard mainstream doctrine about temples, the purpose of them, redemption of the dead, etc. I went over the temple recommend questions with the brethren in there, we discussed that, and then I made the statement, "In the temple ceremony, in the allegory of the temple, no mention is made of physical, mortal death. Physical, mortal death of the telestial world is not even mentioned in the temple endowment allegory. It's not mentioned. The closest it comes is when the garment is placed upon you, and they say that it will protect you until you have finished your work on the earth. That's the closest it comes to that. But, in reality, physical, temporal, mortal death is not a part of the temple ceremony." No one had thought about that, but once they were processing that, they were processing two things. First, if your membership in the Church doesn't get you to the temple, your membership is frustrated. That was a big thing to process for them. They didn't know if they liked the word *frustrated*. The word *frustrated* bothered them. Well, I told them that they could use whatever word they wanted, but if they don't make it to the temple and they've had a reasonable opportunity, the purpose of their membership is void because the purpose of Church membership is to get us to the temple. If you don't get there, what is the purpose of your membership? You basically have functioned in an Aaronic Priesthood organization. You have not graduated into a Melchizedek Priesthood order. You're functioning and officiating in an Aaronic Priesthood order in The Church of Jesus Christ of Latter-day Saints. Its sacred ordinances are Aaronic in nature, even the ministry of angels, which is the first thing that Adam wants when he leaves the garden and offers up a prayer at an altar. Then he has a confrontation with the dark side.

That guy says, "What do you want?"

And Adam says, "**I'm looking for messengers**."

So, that is Aaronic Priesthood. Did you know that? Receiving heavenly messengers is an Aaronic Priesthood function. That's not Melchizedek. How do I know that? Well, John the Baptist appears to Joseph and Oliver and says:

> *Upon you my fellow servants... I confer the Priesthood of Aaron, which holds the keys of **the ministering of angels**...*

You can't even detect true from false angels until you obtain an Aaronic Priesthood sign and token. That sign and token are given in the world before mortality. So, in the premortal world, which is before *"the lone and dreary world"*—call it the Garden if you want, but it's before the Fall—you receive two covenants: a covenant of obedience and a covenant of sacrifice, and you receive a token and a sign. That's all before the Fall. For what purpose? Why did you receive that token and sign before the Fall? Because God knows that when you fall into this world, the first thing that He wants you to do is to pray for and receive messengers to teach you about the Father and the Son. He also knows that when you pray in a certain way, the veil opens and those messengers come, both dark and light. So, you need to have something that was given to you before you fall into *"the lone and dreary world."* You must have access to a token and a sign so that you can detect false messengers, and boy, they're all around us! They are all around us. We're now at a stage where Helaman 13 says that *"we are surrounded by demons."* We're surrounded by them, and we need to be able to carefully discern between them. So, that sign and token you receive before you come into *"the lone and dreary world,"* in the premortal life, is to help you detect true from false messengers while you're in this world. If you can't detect them in this world, then how do we ever expect to be successful in getting into the world to come, let alone, the Celestial Kingdom? The whole purpose of false messengers is to deceive you and set you off on a false course.

Student 6: Is that to do with the Spirit of Christ? If it isn't, then it's a different sign and token that we were given before we came here.

Mike: That sign and token is the first token of the Aaronic Priesthood.

Student 6: So, we really did receive it before we came here to this second estate?

Mike: Look at what your temple endowment is teaching you. It's teaching you. Whether you received it, whether you knew about it, etc., etc., but when you receive that in the temple allegory, you receive it before. Adam and Eve are us, right? I'm Adam; you're Eve. They received that in the Garden of Eden. They already have that token and sign when they find themselves in *"the lone and dreary world."*

Student 6: So that token and sign are separate from the Light of Christ?

Mike: Well, the Light of Christ is certainly given to everybody, but because of the covenants we Latter-day Saints make, we have more available opportunities—more truth and more light. Let me tell you this. This is something interesting that I was pondering on the other day. This is an Aaronic Priesthood privilege to receive the ministering of angels. Yet, we tend to think of Aaronic Priesthood as these young men from ages twelve up to eighteen, right? I can tell you that none of those boys are going to receive a visitation from an angel. Not a one of them is ever going to have that happen.

Student 6: Okay, so Elder Stroud, was that a literal priesthood ordination or priesthood function, if you will, that we received before we came here if we were of the House of Israel and that was our desire?

Mike: If we follow patterns and we look at the temple allegory, yes.

Student 6: Okay.

Mike: Now, I can't find anything on that, but if you follow patterns, yes. Joseph Smith said that men who have the priesthood in this life were ordained to that very priesthood before they came here. Alma 13:9 talks about men receiving the holy order of the Melchizedek Priesthood before they are born into this world. Then verses 10 to about 15 talks about having that priesthood ordained again on them after they are **in** this world.

Student 6: Alma 13?

Mike: Yes. Alma 13: 1-9 talks about obtaining these kinds of things in the world before we were born. Then verse 10 on through to about 15 talks about having these keys and priesthoods and blessings **after** entering this world.

Student 6: Okay.

Mike: What I wanted to ask was why aren't these Aaronic Priesthood boys going to have these visitations of angels before they go to the temple? Now, they can have the ministering of these angels. They can have these angels whisper to them, guard them, direct them, be on their right hand and on their left hand, go before them and behind them, and bear them up. They can have that, but they are not going to have angels come through the veil and have a visitation before they go to the temple. Why not?

Student 3: They don't know how to detect them.

Mike: That's right! They can't detect them. The Lord is not going to put these young men in a position where you have an angel of the devil appear as an angel of light to say, "I'm from God and have a message for you." They've never been to the temple and received any correspondence or any kind of instruction on how to detect them. You have to know how to detect these people.

Student 3: In the *Doctrine and Covenants* they allude to that exchange a little bit.

Mike: Yeah, and we'll go into the *Doctrine and Covenants* in just a minute, but let me read to you a quote by the Prophet Joseph first:

> *We may look forward for angels and receive their ministration, but we are to try the spirits and prove them,*

Key words here: ***try*** *the spirits and* ***prove*** *them.*

> *For it is often the case that men make a mistake regarding these things. God has so ordained that when he has communicated, no vision is to be taken but what you see by the seeing of the eye, or what you hear by the hearing of the ear. When you see a vision, pray for the interpretation; if you get not this, shut it up; there must be certainty in this matter. An open vision will manifest that which is more important. Lying spirits are going forth in the earth. There will be great manifestations of spirits, both false and true.*

That was given by the Prophet Joseph in the Kirtland era. If they were having that kind of discussion then, what do you think is going on now?

Student 6: I was going to say, that is why we are always to offer our hand.

Mike: Yes, and we have a misunderstanding on that. Let's look at that for just a minute. Go over to section 129:4. I've just learned this of late, so we're all learning together. Let me show you what I've learned. The first three verses talk about angels and ministering spirits, spirits of the just, or what the scriptures call *"just men made perfect."*

> *[4] When a messenger comes saying he has a message from God, offer him your hand and request him to shake hands with you.*
>
> *[5] If he be an angel he will do so, and you will feel his hand.*

Keep in mind that this was given February 9, 1843. The first endowments were given in May of 1842. So, the first tokens of the Aaronic Priesthood, the detection token, had been given by the time section 129 comes. That's knowledge. Joseph Smith was saying, "I have things I have to teach you, but I can't teach until we get into the temple. You must be able to discern by seeing, hearing, and **handling** something." Handling something. Now that was before May of 1842 when the Lord revealed these detection signs. In section 129, that's now been revealed. So, they understand the first token of the Aaronic Priesthood. They understand the token, sign, and name; they understand all that.

Student 6: Okay!

Mike: You need to know that context of how that was given. Now, go to the next one. It says:

> *[5] If he be an angel he will do so, and **you will feel his hand**.*

I want to tell you that just feeling the hand of that person isn't enough. You have to feel the hand in a certain way. There must be a token exchanged, and you must feel that exchange in that handshake. Just feeling the hand is not enough. Do you see what I'm saying?

Student 6: Yes.

Mike: I used to teach this for years by saying, "Oh, well that way you can tell he's a true messenger because he's got a body, so he must be a true messenger, and you can feel his body." There is more to this:

58

> *[6] If he be the spirit of a just man made perfect*
> *he will come in his glory; for that is the only way*
> *he can appear—*
> *[7] Ask him to shake hands with you, but **he will***
> ***not move**,*

That's a key and you should triple underline ***will not move***. This man stands utterly immobile:

> *because it is contrary to the order of heaven for a*
> *just man to deceive; but he will still deliver his*
> *message.*

That's a good one. Now, you ask him to shake hands, and he does not move. There is no extension of a hand; there's nothing. Another thing is that he appears in glory. There's a glory about him because he's a disembodied person. This is a person that has been on the earth and is now qualified for a celestial inheritance. When you see him as a spirit, he will appear in celestial glory. You may even have to be changed to abide that glory and survive the encounter. But, he has no body, so he can't control the glory. So, that's the only way these celestial men and women can appear, without bodies. See, they are in-between. They haven't resurrected. They are deferring their resurrection, so that they may obtain a better resurrection. They do that by choice.

> *[8] If it be the devil as an angel of light, when you*
> *ask him to shake hands he will offer you his hand,*
> *and you will not feel anything; you may therefore*
> *detect him.*

You know, when I taught that for years, I said, he doesn't have a body, and I would even show the kids. I would put out my hand to them and say, "shake hands," and make it seem as if my hand went through his hand, even though you could see the hand. There wasn't one there because he was a spirit. I've since learned that it means, ***you will not feel anything*** because you will not feel the token. These spirit beings have the ability to interact with physical mortals. In the Church, we've got a belief that we think is doctrine, and it says that if you're a spirit personage, you cannot interact with mortals. That is NOT true, obviously. Look at Joseph Smith in the Sacred Grove. Look at Heber C. Kimball and the brethren in England. And I can't tell you how many people I've blessed and had an opportunity to minister to, who were physically attacked by spirits.

Student 6: But, why would they not know the token, when you have people putting things online about it?

Mike: They **do** know the token. The devils do know the token, but they are barred from giving it.

Student: Ok, so they do not have the physical power to actually give it.

Mike: They CAN'T give it because there are laws that say that devils cannot give these true tokens, especially the token of detection. Otherwise, what?

Student 6: I see. There would be deception.

Mike: You bet! None of us would have any hope. One of the things that Joseph Smith said was that when you ask him to shake your hand, a *just man made perfect* will stand perfectly still. Remember that? One of the things the devil will do, as an angel of light, is that he will shrink back. In other words, there will be a movement. It will be like, "Oh my gosh. I've been detected!"

Student 6: Is it like if you raise your hand to the square, they will shrink back?

Mike: They will do that. If you raise your hand to the square, they will depart. There's a difference between shrinking back and departing. If shrinking back, he's not going to depart. It's just that when you ask him to offer his hand, Joseph says he will "shrink back, but still offer you his hand, and you will not feel the token." Now, whether you don't feel the token because he has a spirit body and not a physical body, or if you're allowed to feel that token, as a spirit, if he could do that, you would feel it. But the point is, you don't feel the token. You don't see it; you don't feel it; it is not experienced.

Student 6: So, that is the whole purpose of the first token. It is a detection tool.

Mike: I won't say that's the whole purpose because I've learned that there are so many different levels to things that our Father gives us. But, I will tell you it's the main purpose it was given to Adam.

Student 6: Okay.

Mike: The Lord knew that in *"the lone and dreary world,"* he was going to be looking for messengers as commanded: *"I'm looking for messengers from my Father. I'm looking for messengers to give me further light and knowledge that my Father promised to send me."* See all that stuff? And we've talked about how when the veil opens; it opens to both sides. That's just an eternal law. So, you've got to be able to do that. I would say that if you ever reach a point where you have a visitation, the dialogue in the temple would be a very good thing to have memorized. True messengers come, and Adam says, "How do I know that you are who you say you are?" Then there's a dialogue that takes place.

Student 6: You're saying that when the veil opens, it opens for the opportunity to receive further light and knowledge, but also, you can be open to powers that are not on the light side?

Mike: When you part the veil, when you use the knowledge that the temple is teaching us to part the veil, be prepared for it to part, but the one who comes through is not always from Father. Look at the temple. When Adam prayed there in that way, he opened the veil and who came through? But the point is, that's the purpose of the detection tokens and signs. I would say that you follow that dialogue because it's not just that token that is given, there's also a sign and there's verbiage that goes on. There's a communication that goes on, and I've memorized it, so if I ever need to, I can carry on that exact conversation word for word. Joseph said that one of the worst things that can happen to us in this world is to receive a message from a false messenger, think it's from God, and zealously act on that message. That's one of the worst things that can happen to us here. Let me show you another interesting thing. In section 110, it's talking about messengers who come to the Kirtland Temple. In verse 13 it talks about Elijah coming and appearing there. You know that. Now, that's where the actual appearance takes place. But let's go back to the early history of the Church in section 2 in the *Doctrine and Covenants* where the Angel Moroni is quoting a scripture from the *Old Testament* that is anticipating Elijah's future visit. Notice this is given in September of 1823 and Elijah comes in April of 1836 in the Kirtland Temple. Now watch, here's a little mystery. There are only three verses here:

[1] *Behold, I will reveal unto you the Priesthood,
by the hand of Elijah the prophet, before the
coming of the great and dreadful day of the Lord.*

Now, how many times have you read that? Now, with what
we've talked about, stop and read it again. Notice it says, *"I will
reveal unto you the Priesthood **by the hand** of Elijah..."* You
follow where I'm going? When Joseph and Oliver see this
person who is standing above the Melchizedek Priesthood pulpit,
three feet off the ground and says he is Elijah, how are they
going to know that it is Elijah?

Student 6: But this was just prepping them before because at
that time they had no idea that it was the literal hand.

Mike: That's correct. Remember that in section 76, which takes
place long before the temple endowment is revealed in Nauvoo,
Joseph says, "What I'm giving you here in 119 verses is only one
hundredth of what the Lord has shown me." There is some
indication that when Joseph prayed in the Sacred Grove, he knew
something about what we call *"the true order of prayer."* There
is some indication there that when he prayed, he prayed with
uplifted hands, which is a sign, one of the keys, to open the veil.
Every depiction we see of Joseph Smith in the grove, do we see
him kneeling with his arms folded? What do you see? He's got
his arms up. Has he been instructed even at age fourteen? Does
he know some things that we don't know?

Let me give you another one. Let's go over to Luke chapter
24. This is after the resurrection of the Savior. He appears to the
Twelve in an upper room and doesn't open the door. He's just
standing there. The door was shut. He comes right through the
door because He's a resurrected being, and it just startles the
heck out of them. It's interesting, and it appears that He doesn't
look exactly like what He looked like when they knew Him
before His resurrection. It appears that as a resurrected being,
there's a difference in the way He looks from the way that they
knew Him during three years of His ministry. When they see
Him standing there, they thought it was a spirit. Is that maybe
just because He came through the closed door: Let's go to Luke
24:36:

And as they thus spake, Jesus himself stood in the midst of them, and saith unto them, Peace be unto you.

[37] But they were terrified and affrighted, and supposed that they had seen a spirit.

Now, was that because they didn't recognize who He was, or is it because he entered the room without opening the door? Their knowledge was that only spirits could do that because people with bodies can't.

Student 6: Or, maybe because they know He's dead and they figure it has to be a ghost.

Mike: Yeah, there's another thing, see? Watch:

[38] And he said unto them, Why are ye troubled? and why do thoughts arise in your hearts?

*[39] Behold my hands and my feet, that it is I myself: **handle me, and see**;*

I would submit that He's probably offering them a special handshake. If this is a true principle, it goes back into eternity, and surely the New Testament Church, who had obtained the *Church of the Firstborn* and *the spirits of just men,* understood these priesthood principles. They understood that. And what they didn't understand in detail, in the next 40 days that Jesus is with them, He will instruct them in-depth in the endowment, in the initiatory, and especially in the prayer circle. All of the apostles and their wives joined Jesus in the prayer circle with their priesthood robes on, holding hands, He kneels in the midst of them—they formed a circle around Him—and He offers up a prayer, and they all repeat the words of the prayer after Him. That takes place in the 40-day ministry. So, there are marvelous things.

We've barely touched the celestial world. Let me just say that all these things that we're talking about here, these keys, tokens, signs, names, covenants, ordinances, and laws, all pertain to the celestial world. None of these things pertain to anything else. I just gave you a little something to think about. All the ordinances of the temple are ordinances of the *Church of the Firstborn.* Nothing in the temple is pointing in any direction other than the celestial world. Every ordinance in there has to do with the *Church of the Firstborn.* And the *Church of the Firstborn* talks about the City of Enoch, the society of Enoch, and eventually, the society of the Gods in the celestial world, the Elohim. The Church of Jesus Christ of Latter-day Saints is the platform, the springboard, the training wheels, the preparatory step for something greater that could only be obtained in the temple of the Lord. When there are temples available, these ordinances can only be obtained in the temple. When there were no temples, it could be obtained in deserts, on mountain tops, and in solitary places. Next week, what we'll do is actually talk about the Kingdom. This gives us a feel for what we need to be involved with if we want an inheritance in that world. *"A man is saved no faster than he gets knowledge,"* Joseph said. I quote that all the time. This is the kind of knowledge we need to have. Once you get this knowledge and it distils upon you as truth, and the Spirit testifies to you, then you are required to act on it. Until that testimony settles in, until the Spirit bears witness to you of its truth, you're not required to take much action. In fact, you need to know of its truthfulness first, and then act on it.

Student 6: Elder Stroud, are there souls that are so pure and guileless that they, by their faith and purity, are not required the same level of knowledge because of their purity?

Mike: All of this knowledge is required, no matter who you are. You must obtain this kind of knowledge. <u>This is my opinion, ok?</u> If you're at a level of innocence and purity, you'll find that accessing this knowledge is easier, more readily available to you, than if you have to overcome natural man and all of its grossness and that. This is one reason that I feel that women have an advantage over men. Women are more refined spiritually, and hence, this knowledge comes to them. An interesting phenomenon is that once they learn it, however, in this world women have a hard time retaining it and they forget things. I hear this complaint. Margie has taught this to sisters many times and put their minds at ease. You'll hear this over and over by women: "I hear these things, but I just can't remember them. I can't remember that. I'm so frustrated. It goes in one minute, and the next minute it's gone." Let me just tell you that when you hear these things and the Spirit testifies to you, it is engraved in your spirit. You have it. Even though the physical body may provide an impediment for recall, know this, that no divine truth, accompanied by the Holy Ghost, needs to be relearned by you. It's there.

Student 6: Okay, so you don't have to be able to regurgitate it?

Mike: Women are not in that situation where they need to do that, but men are because men are responsible for the blood and sins of the generation in which they live. Being responsible for that makes them preachers of righteousness. They have a responsibility to testify boldly and fearlessly in order to rid their garments of the blood of the generation in which they live. Women do not have that.

Student 6: Okay.

Mike: Next week, we'll finish the celestial world. Today we talked a little bit about the type of people you need to be to inherit it. Next week, we'll talk about that Kingdom, that planet, that world; and there are lots of interesting things about it that we can discern on that.

Thank you for your questions. Thank you for your comments. We are past the time, so have a great week, and we will see you next week!

Student 6: Thank you so much! Know that you are making a difference.

Mike: I appreciate that. Thank you.

References:
D&C 76:50-70
D&C 76:53
D&C 132:7
D&C 107:18-19
D&C 76:53-64
Teachings of the Presidents of the Church: Howard W. Hunter, chapter 13 "The Temple—The Great Symbol of Our Membership."
"The Great Symbol of Our Membership" by Howard W. Hunter; General Conference, Oct. 1994
D&C 13:1 "Upon you my fellow servants...I confer the Priesthood of Aaron..."
Helaman 13:37 "...we are surrounded by demons..."
Alma 13:1-9 referring to men being ordained to the priesthood **before** being born; pre-mortally
Alma 13:10-18 referring to men being ordained to the priesthood **after** being born; mortally
Joseph Smith in the Journal of Discourses Vol. 6 page 240
D&C 129:4-8

D&C 110 messengers appearing to Joseph Smith and Oliver Cowdery; return of Elijah
D&C 2:1
Luke 24:36-39
Joseph Smith instructs the Twelve on priesthood, in the vicinity of Commerce, Ill., July 2, 1839, HC 3:391-92

Chapter Twenty-Seven
Podcast 027 The Celestial World Part

This last week has really been interesting. Last Sunday night we talked about the *Holy Spirit of promise*, and it seems like that has come up this whole week, and again today in Church. I'm surprised at how many people don't have a correct understanding about that. We read that last week, so we won't go into it. On the subject of marriage, I was talking to a man who came to our home the other day. He is divorced and wanting to get married again, and the gal he wants to marry is divorced. They both had temple marriages. They were concerned that they were breaking commandments by even seeing each other. It all boiled down to this misunderstanding on temple sealings and the *Holy Spirit of promise*. With this lesson, I have a handout by various Brethren—general authorities, apostles and prophets—who have spoken on this. I'd like to briefly hit two or three areas that I've highlighted, and then we'll leave it. Joseph Fielding Smith says:

> *If they are not faithful, then the Holy Spirit will withdraw the blessing, and then the promise comes to an end.*

David Bednar said:

> *This sealing can be forfeited through unrighteousness and transgression.*

Richard G. Scott said:

> *Realize that a sealing ordinance is not enduring until after it is sealed by the Holy Spirit of*

67

Promise. Both individuals must be worthy and want the sealing to be eternal.

James E. Faust said:

The inherent blessings will be obtained, provided those seeking the blessing are true and faithful.

He also said:

It is also important to remember that if a person undertakes to receive the sealing blessing by deceit, 'then the blessing is not sealed, notwithstanding the integrity and authority of the person officiating.'

What it all boils down to is that these blessings are void if the persons are not worthy or are unrighteous. Harold B. Lee said this:

By the laying on of hands we get the promise of power and authority, but it will not be ours— worlds without end—unless we keep our part of the covenant.

Bruce R. McConkie had a whole section to say about it:

The ratifying seal of approval is put upon an act only if those entering the contract are worthy as a result of personal righteousness to receive the divine approbation. They 'are sealed by the Holy Spirit of promise, which the Father sheds forth upon all those who are just and true.' If they are not just and true and worthy the ratifying seal is withheld. When any ordinance or contract is sealed by the Spirit, it is approved with a promise of reward, provided unrighteousness does not thereafter break the seal, remove the ratifying approval, and cause the loss of the promised blessing.

Seals are placed on contracts through righteousness. Bruce R. McConkie continues:

If both parties are "just and true," if they are worthy, a ratifying seal is placed on their temple marriage; if they are unworthy, they are not justified by the Spirit and the ratification of the Holy Ghost is withheld. Subsequent worthiness

will put the seal in force, and unrighteousness
will break any seal.

So, it's kind of what we talked about there: that sealing is only in place, first and foremost, if those entering the covenant like each other. I mean, the minimum requirement is that a man and woman like each other. And then it goes from there on up. If you work together and you're both striving with all your heart to be obedient and to keep your covenants which you've made at the time you went to the temple, and you die in that state, then the Holy Ghost places that seal, and you're okay. Enough said about that, but I'm just amazed at how poorly understood that is. I taught it again in our High Priest's Group today, and when I said that if you don't get along with your wife, if there's contention, if there's bickering, if you don't like each other, then that's enough to void the contract. You need to repent. Then we went over *Doctrine and Covenants* 121 and read to the brethren the following criteria to see how a seal is placed upon a marriage, and the whole section talks about what you need to do for the priesthood to be effective in your life. Verse 41:

> *No power or influence can or ought to be*
> *maintained by virtue of the priesthood,*

And here are the attributes that need to be in a marriage in order for them to be sealed by the *Holy Spirit of promise*:

> *only by persuasion, by long-suffering; by*
> *gentleness and meekness, and by love unfeigned;*
> *[42] By kindness, and pure knowledge, which*
> *shall greatly enlarge the soul without hypocrisy,*
> *and without guile—*

See, all those things have to be there, or the Holy Ghost will not ratify that temple sealing that took place when they went through. So, I hope that helps. I knew it was misunderstood, but these last two weeks it's just been amazing to me to see how people think. It's almost like the "saved by Grace" doctrine. Many "born again Christians" believe that once they accept Jesus Christ as their Savior and ask Him to come into their life, they are saved. They remember the date that they do that and take it and say that on that date they were saved. They believe they are saved, and no matter what happens after that, they are still saved. Like the "saved by Grace" doctrine, many who are sealed in the temple think that afterward, they can do anything they want and it doesn't matter, that sealing is still in place forever.

Anyway, I want to talk a little about the celestial world tonight. The Hubble Telescope is now sending back images of the galaxies that surround the Milky Way. We can't see our galaxy because we are in the middle of it, but we can peer out and see similar. These are great spiral galaxies. If you look at them on their side, they look very thin. If you look at them from the top or bottom, then they are these great pinwheel discs that go hundreds of thousands, if not millions of light years across from one side to the other. Right in the center of every one of these galaxies is a huge galactic light-bulge. They've determined that this light-bulge is a conglomeration of stars. We don't know how many of them there are in the center of each galaxy, but this is the source of light for all of life within that galaxy. It comes from the center of the galaxy, from this galactic light-bulge. Let me show you something interesting that Joseph Smith taught. Go over to Abraham in the *Pearl of Great Price*. The Prophet Joseph Smith wanted to tell us much more about this but was killed before he could give us more information. If you go to the end of chapter 3, to facsimile #2 (the drawings), and look under Explanation, you'll see Figure 5. It says:

> Is called in Egyptian Enish-go-on-dosh; this is one of the governing planets also, and is said by the Egyptians to be the Sun, and to borrow its light from Kolob through the medium of Kae-e-vanrash, which is the grand Key, or, in other words, the governing power, which governs **fifteen other fixed planets or stars**,

I'm going to interpret that, and <u>this is Mike Stroud now</u>. In the center of our galaxy, which we call the Milky Way Galaxy, there are a number of large stars or planets or suns. The number fifteen is mentioned here. I find it very interesting that fifteen planets govern this galaxy. I find it interesting that there are fifteen men that govern The Church of Jesus Christ of Latter-day Saints. Those fifteen are divided up into two groups; three in the First Presidency, and twelve in the Quorum of the Twelve. This is the dwelling place of the Elohim, who dwell in our galaxy. <u>This is my opinion now</u>, but I believe this is where our Father in Heaven resides. This is His home, and He resides on a planet nigh unto the largest of these governing planets, which is called Kolob. He doesn't dwell on Kolob, but He lives on a celestialized earth, nigh unto Kolob. This galaxy is a great pinwheel disc that rotates in a circle. All of the times and seasons and everything that measures any kind of progress in this galaxy has its origins in the center of the galaxy, and with these fifteen governing planets, according to the book of Abraham. Now, why did we go into this? From what I understand, and I'm giving my opinion here, every one of these planets that are in the center of this galaxy was at one time a telestial earth, and climbed, step by step, through a process that is duplicated throughout the universe. I do not believe there are multiple plans and different ways for these things to happen. I believe that there is one way, one plan. This earth that we are on right now is a pattern for what we see in the center of the galaxy. So, all of these glorified, exalted, perfected, resurrected planets have come to that point in the center of our galaxy, the abode of the Elohim, through the same process that the earth we are on is going through. The scriptures seem to bear that out. There are a few things I'm inferring here, but I'm making the inferences based on things that I see in the scriptures.

Let's take a look at a couple of things. Everything in the eternities moves in a circular way. The circle is the geometric symbol for eternity. We can look at things moving in a circular pattern. For example, let's take our Milky Way Galaxy. When this earth was first created, it was created near the throne of God. If what we are inferring here is correct, this earth that we are on, at one time in the past, was organized near where God dwells. That means that when it was organized in that manner, it was not a telestial world because anything that is nigh unto God is not telestial, nor is it terrestrial, it's celestial. So, this earth, when it was first organized, was organized in a celestial realm. I want to show you a few things about the earth that are kind of exciting. Let's go over to *Doctrine and Covenants* 88:17-31. It is talking about the spiritual progress of our earth. Verse 17 gives us some little keys:

> *[17]And the redemption of the soul is through him that **quickeneth** all things,*

71

To *quicken* means to *give life*. When a mother feels the spirit entering the body of her baby, in her body, the word that is used is *quickening*. So, when you have something that is organized out of chaos, and there is no life in it yet, it's just organized matter. Then the Lord quickens it and gives it life. The quickening of Adam in the temple was when the Lord says, *"We will put into this man his spirit, the breath of life, that he may become a living soul."* That's a quickening. So, the word *quicken* that you see mentioned all through these verses multiple times means *to give life to*:

> And the redemption of the soul is through him
> that quickeneth all things, in whose bosom it is
> decreed that the poor and the meek **of the earth**
> [there is the center point] *shall inherit it.*

Now, that's taken from the Beatitudes in Matthew and also from 3 Nephi. *"Blessed are the **poor** in heart, for they will inherit the earth."* The poor and the meek:

> *[18] Therefore, **it***

Now, we're talking about the earth in verse 18. Notice the last words in verse 17, *"the meek of the earth shall inherit **it**."* **It** is the earth:

> *[18] Therefore, **it** [the earth] must needs be*
> *sanctified from all unrighteousness, that **it** may be*
> *prepared for the **celestial glory**;*

So, this is earth's destiny, and for that matter, I assume that every created earth's destiny is to become a celestial world and to move to the center of the galaxy in which it was organized. Let's go a little bit further:

> *[19] For after it hath filled the **measure of its***
> ***creation**, it shall be crowned with glory, even with*
> *the presence of God the Father;*

What is the measure of the earth's creation? *"The measure of its creation"* is another way of saying, "for what purpose it was." If you can identify what the purpose of the creation/organization of the earth is, then you can identify *"the measure of its creation."* We know it has several purposes. One is to provide a testing place. The telestial world is a schoolhouse, and then you have the terrestrial earth, and then the celestial earth. They are all the same planet. This is the important part. Let's skip down to verse 25:

> *[25] And again, verily I say unto you, the earth abideth the law of a celestial kingdom, for it filleth the measure of its creation,* [and this interesting statement] ***and transgresseth not the law—***

Now, the earth, our planet is alive. It is a living soul. The definition of soul is over in section 88:15. Go back and look at that:

> *[15] And the spirit and the body are the soul of man.*

We were reading in Alma 40 today in our Gospel Doctrine class. In Alma chapter 40, Alma didn't have a clear understanding of the doctrine, and he kept referring to the spirit as the soul. Here, the *Doctrine and Covenants* teaches us that *"the spirit **and the body** are the soul of man."* That ties in also when the Lord puts Adam's spirit into his body *"so that he may become a living soul."* When you take the spirit and the body and put them together, by definition that is the soul. Throughout the Christian world, the word soul is used to refer to the spirit. Here the Lord is giving us a little pearl, a little gem, a doctrinal pearl to teach us what the soul is. So, the earth is a living soul, meaning that it has a spirit and it has a body. We now reside upon the physical body of this earth.

Student 1: So, we are residing on the earth's body.

Mike: We are. And when you die, your spirit goes where? It goes into the spirit of the earth. We call the spirit of the earth the *Spirit World*. So, it makes sense; as long as we have physical bodies in this telestial world, we're going to reside upon the physical body of the telestial earth. We also know that the earth is female; it has gender. The scriptures refer to the earth as female and refer to the sun as male. Also, the moon is referred to as female. Let me show you where we get that from. Go over to Moses 7. All of this is to try and get a picture of this earth because the celestial world, the Celestial Kingdom, is this earth. Moses 7:48. This was in the day of Enoch:

> *[48] And it came to pass that Enoch looked upon the earth;*

This is the earth in its telestial station. This was 5,000 years ago, but it's the telestial earth like it is now, the lone and dreary world:

> *and he heard a voice from the bowels* [of the earth] *thereof, saying: Wo, wo is me, the mother of men; I am pained, I am weary,* [this is the earth speaking] *because of the wickedness of my children. When shall I rest, and be cleansed from the filthiness which is gone forth out of me? When will my Creator sanctify me, that I may rest, and righteousness for a season abide upon my face?*

We can answer that question because the world that is coming, that we're on the cusp of, the terrestrial, millennial world that we talked about a few weeks ago is the world that the earth is desiring in verse 48. Notice where it says, *"When will my Creator sanctify me?"* The earth will be sanctified by fire, which will be the glory of the resurrected Christ. It will burn off everything that is telestial and preserve only that which is terrestrial. Then it says when that happens *"that I may rest, and righteousness for a season* [1,000 years] *abide upon my face?"* That's describing the earth longing for the great millennial, terrestrial, third estate world, which is coming. Isn't that interesting? So, what happened is that when the earth was created, *"nigh unto the throne of God,"* it began at that point to move out from the center of the galaxy. The earth, the planet, it moves out so that when we get in the Garden of Eden state, we're in a terrestrial/paradisiacal glory. That's another name for the Garden of Eden anciently, and all ancient documents refer to it as a paradise. That paradise world is out a distance from the center of the galaxy. It has moved from a celestial place, downward and outward to a terrestrial/paradisiacal place. That's where the earth is when we have the Garden of Eden scenario.

So, if you were to measure it, the earth is moving out in three steps. Step one is where it was created. Step two is at a terrestrial level, and it's beginning to move out and down. Then step three is into a telestial level. It's interesting that the further you move away from the center, the more difficult it is to have light and life. So, when we get into the telestial area, we are so far out from the center of that galactic light-bulge, that the Gods have to create an artificial light in order for us to have life in this world. That light is *"the greater light to rule the day;"* it's a sun. In the terrestrial, millennial, third estate, there will be no need for a sun. But, we have need of one where we are now because we are at such a distance from the center that there is a veil of cosmic dust that blocks the light from the center of the galaxy. In order for us to have life in the telestial world, we need to have light. So, the Lord, in the creation process, provides light for us, a sun. And that sun gives us light and life. Does that make sense?

Student 1: I read once that if the sun would be just a little bit further out we would freeze to death, and if it would be a little closer we would burn.

Mike: Of course, all of that is just by coincidence, right? The atheists say, "Well it just happened that way."

Now, the sunlight that we have as we look up in our atmosphere, into our heaven, the sunlight derives its light from the Light of Christ. The source of all light, all energy, all life, everything in the galaxy, is what we call the Holy Spirit. The sunlight that comes down and gives light to this earth derives its power from the Holy Spirit/The Spirit of Christ. All the laws that make it possible for us to dwell successfully on this earth—the laws of magnetism, laws of gravity, all of the laws of physics— derive their power from the Holy Spirit. Remember, the Holy Spirit can be defined as the 3 L's: light, life, and law. That's section 88:13:

> *The light which is in all things, which giveth life*
> *to all things, which is the law by which all things*
> *are governed, even the power of God who sitteth*
> *upon his throne, who is in the bosom of eternity,*
> *who is in the midst of all things.*

Light, life, and law. So, here we find ourselves on this planet, which is going through the same or similar experiences we are, in order to **return**. So, here's the point. This earth is in a circular motion. It has gone to its outermost area; it's in a schoolroom. The earth **is** the school, and it's being schooled. Notice back there in Moses 7 where it says, *"When shall I rest, and be cleansed from the filthiness which is gone out of me?"* The earth is learning some things. One of the things the earth learns is that the choices made by God's children on her face affect her. So, the earth is affected by God's children on its face, and how they use their agency. If you have enough of God's children who choose right and choose light and life and love, then you have an earth that prospers. There are no curses upon its face. The more that the children of God exercise their agency in a negative way, the more the earth becomes darkened because the Spirit of the Lord withdraws. It's that simple. When we make wrong choices, the Spirit withdraws, and as the Spirit withdraws it affects the earth. That's why the Lord, in the *Doctrine and Covenants*, says that the whole earth is covered in darkness and *"groans under the weight of its iniquity."* The whole earth is covered in darkness. You can't have life in darkness. Is it any wonder that right now we're experiencing natural upheaval on the earth in the form of tidal waves, volcanoes, earthquakes, and drought, etc.? All of these natural upheavals, in my opinion, are a result of the earth struggling to stay alive in a darkening condition. The earth needs light also. Light gives life. Where darkness prevails, light gives way to death. I believe that our earth is struggling right now because of the choices that God's children are making upon her face. The natural upheavals are the symbols or outward signs of that struggle. Anyway, it's something to think about. We struggle! The pattern is that God's children struggle when things become darkened. We can feel it. It affects us. You can see huge numbers of the population struggling with anxiety, discouragement, and depression. The suicide rate is up higher than it's ever been in my lifetime. That all comes when light diminishes and darkness increases. There begins to be a struggle. The earth is experiencing that same thing because the earth is on a path to come back into the presence of the Lord and be glorified, the same as the children of God. It's an interesting pattern.

Notice that before we can enter the celestial world, we need to have a baptism of water. The telestial world is a water-based world. That's why the second booth in the initiatory has a little fountain in there. The second booth in the temple initiatory represents the telestial, second estate, mortal world. This world is water-based. Look at this: nothing in this world survives without water—nothing! And spiritually, we require water to be washed clean in this world. This is a world where you obtain a forgiveness, followed by a remission of your sins. The door to remission of sins is opened through an ordinance that has to do with water: baptism, followed by the baptism of fire and the Holy Ghost. Well, the earth is doing the very same thing. So, in the days of Noah, Mother Earth had to experience a water baptism. Why? Because she became filthy. From the day of Adam, on up through seven patriarchs to the day of Noah, the earth obtained a state of filthiness. Not because the earth made poor choices, but because God's children upon her face created such gross immorality and violent crime that it affected the earth. Like we've just seen, the earth cries out, *"Wo, wo is me."* So, there had to be a baptism of water, and we see that with the universal flood in the day of Noah. So, here we go! Here's the earth in the telestial world and it's going through the very same steps that we are. You and I are interested in obtaining a celestial world and the destiny of the earth, according to *Doctrine and Covenants* 88, is to become a celestial world. Therefore, the earth had to be baptized with water. It also has to obtain the *baptism of fire and the Holy Ghost. The baptism of fire* for the earth will come when the Lord, Jesus Christ, comes in glory and the earth is burned.

Let's go back to your Articles of Faith in the *Pearl of Great Price*. Let's look at Article of Faith #10:

> *We believe in the literal gathering of Israel and in the restoration of the Ten Tribes; that Zion (the New Jerusalem) will be built upon the American continent;* [this part right here] ***that Christ will reign personally upon the earth;***

He does not do that in the telestial world. You don't see Christ come into the Initiatory until the third booth. He does leave the third booth and come down to the second booth in order to perform the *baptism of fire and the Holy Ghost.* That's the ordinance worker that leaves the third booth, comes through the veil and seals the washing with an ordinance. Then, you are invited into the third booth, which is the great millennial, terrestrial world. The person who reigns in that world is the Lord, Jesus Christ. That is His world. The 10th Article of Faith continues:

and, that the earth will be renewed and receive [again] *its*
paradisiacal glory.

Paradisiacal is another word for terrestrial. And also, another
word for it is Edenic. So, what does that tell us? You can see the
world, the earth we're on, is moving in a circular, cyclical
motion. Right now, we're about as far out as we're ever going to
be. From this point on, it begins to move back to where it was.
Student 1: So, now it goes from out, inward?
Mike: Yes. So, when it is all completed, and the earth goes back
and is sanctified, like it says in section **88**, and receives a
celestial glory, what you will see is that this earth has completed
a circular path. It also fits in with the total theme of the *Book of*
Mormon that all of us go through three phases: creation, fall, and
atonement. You can see the same thing in the earth; everything is
happening.

Section 88 is really interesting. Let's go back there for a
moment. There's a little thing in there that I find intriguing, and
it fits in with this idea that the earth is alive, has a voice, can
make decisions, and that it can exercise agency. Go to 88:25:

> *And again, verily I say unto you,* **the earth**
> **abideth the law** *of a celestial kingdom, for it*
> *filleth the measure of its creation,*

Notice the word *abideth.* "The earth abideth the law." That
seems to indicate that it keeps the law. And it doubles down on
that at the end where it says:

> *for it filleth the measure of its creation,* **and**
> **transgresseth not the law—**

Now, that little statement right there is very intriguing because it
seems to infer that there are planets that are living souls, that are
not faithful, that do not fulfill the measure of their creation, and
violate the law. Interesting little statement. Look at the first word
in the next verse:

> *[26] Wherefore,*

This means, "because of this." Because of what it said—because
the earth abides the law of the Celestial Kingdom, fills the
measure of its creation, doesn't break the law— because of this:

> *it shall be sanctified; yea, notwithstanding it shall*
> *die, it shall be quickened again,*

And where the earth dies is not at the *Second Coming*. That's a quickening at the *Second Coming*; it's a renewal. That's what the 10th Article of Faith says. So, the earth is going to receive its *baptism of fire* with the *Second Coming* of Christ. That completes the baptismal ordinance for Mother Earth.

Student 1: Did you say that the Second Coming is not the *baptism of fire*?

Mike: The *Second Coming* **is** the *baptism of fire*. It's not a death. The baptism of fire is not a death. In verse 26 it says, *"Not withstanding it* [the earth] *shall die..."* The earth does have to die. The death of the earth takes place at the **end** of the Millennium where there's another fire. So, fire does two things to the earth. Fire renews and cleanses the Earth and moves it from a telestial to a terrestrial, millennial estate. That happens by fire. Then, at the end of the Millennium, there's going to be another fire, another burning, and in this burning, the earth "dies." In order for the earth to resurrect, there needs to be death. Let's finish verse 26:

> *notwithstanding it shall die, it shall be quickened again,*

Even though the earth shall perish in a physical death, similar to what we do, it will be quickened again:

> *and shall abide the power by which it is quickened, and the righteous shall inherit it.*
> *[27] For notwithstanding they die* [meaning the righteous], *they also shall rise again, a spiritual body.*

And then it talks about that. All of this is interesting about Mother Earth. So, I guess the most important part is that the planet that we are on is faithful, it's obedient, it doesn't transgress God's laws, and in fact, it abides the law of a Celestial Kingdom. The law of a Celestial Kingdom is simply this: you keep **all** the commandments, and you live by every word that proceedeth forth out of the mouth of God. That is the law of the Celestial Kingdom. You keep the commandments, and when you break one, you repent. You strive for the atoning power of Christ to transform you so that you won't break that law again because the atonement changes you. Well, the earth does that.

Let's go over to Section 77 and take a look at what it says about the earth. This is the Celestial Kingdom. So, where is this earth headed? It's headed towards the center of this galaxy where it will be a source of light. *Doctrine and Covenants* 77:12:

> *Q. What are we to understand by the sounding of the trumpets, mentioned in the 8th chapter of Revelation?*
>
> *A. We are to understand that as God made the world in six days, and on the seventh day he finished his work, and sanctified it, and also formed man out of the dust of the earth, even so, in the beginning of the seventh thousand years* [which is the beginning of the Millennium] *will the Lord God sanctify the earth, and complete the salvation of man, and judge all things, and shall redeem all things, except that which he hath not put into his power* [which are the Sons of Perdition], *when he shall have sealed all things, unto the end of all things; and the sounding of the trumpets of the seven angels are the preparing and finishing of his work, in the beginning of the seventh thousand years—the preparing of the way before the time of his coming.*

We are living in that day right now. Any questions or comments?

Student 1: No, I need to think about all of this. It starts to make sense, but then I don't understand all of it.

Mike: Let's go to section 77, question 1:

> *Q. What is the sea of glass spoken of by John, 4th chapter, and 6th verse of the Revelation?*

In the Book of Revelation, John sees a *"sea of glass."* Joseph has asked, *"What is the sea of glass spoken of?"*

> *A. It is the earth, in its sanctified, immortal, and eternal state.*

So, the earth has completed its cycle, becomes celestialized, dies, is resurrected, brought back into the presence of her Creator, and enjoys a place in the center of the galaxy with these other celestialized, resurrected planets. I assume that the earth upon which our Father in Heaven dwells is the earth that He, at one time, lived upon as a mortal man. That's the pattern. So, the pattern is, if I inherit this earth in its celestial state, in other words, if I stay with Mother Earth, if I continue with her, if my progress matches hers, then in the celestial worlds I won't reside on another planet. I will reside on this planet. This planet will be my celestial world. I assume that the planet whereon our Father dwells was His mortal world, which went through this same cycle, came back full circle, and is now His residence in a celestial, resurrected, glorified, exalted state.

Student 1: What about Jesus Christ? Where will He dwell?

Mike: Since He lived on this world, I assume that this will also be His residence in the celestial center of things. Now, at some future time, you're going to have children, spirit offspring that will go onto an earth that you've created for them. That earth, then, begins the same process. If that earth is faithful and abides the law of the celestial world and doesn't transgress the law, it will come back into your presence with the rest of these glorified, sanctified, exalted, eternal worlds, and your children will dwell upon that earth.

Student 1: Oh, I guess that makes sense.

Mike: So, there's a pattern there; I guess we can look at patterns and that helps us try to understand it.

Now, in closing, I have just a couple of statements here. All of the ordinances of the Church of Jesus Christ of Latter-day Saints are geared toward the celestial world. The ordinance of *baptism*, the ordinance of *confirmation*, and the ordinance of the *baptism of fire and the Holy Ghost*, which is all of those three things together: water, confirmation, and fire. All of those three things are the baptismal ordinance.

Every person, if they want a celestial inheritance, needs to have everything that the earth needs to have—that ordinance performed—in order to enter into the celestial world. When you go to the temple, what you're doing is you're coming up a notch in ordinances that are also necessary for the celestial world. The Initiatory and the Endowment have nothing to do with the telestial or terrestrial world, nothing. The Initiatory and the Endowment are teaching you, symbolically and literally, the steps that you need to follow in order to stay up with Mother Earth as she rolls back into the presence of her Creator. All of the ordinances—the ordinance of sealings, marriages, the ordinances of the *Second Anointing, calling and election made sure*, the *Church of the Firstborn*—all these things we've talked about over the months, all pertain to the celestial world.

Student 3: So, the Lord is always preparing us for the celestial.

Mike: Yeah. All you have to do is live the celestial law. If you want as short a definition as I can give you of what it means to live or keep celestial law, it's that you seek and strive to live by every word that proceedeth out of the mouth of God. That is the celestial law. If you do that, you will become one with the Father and with the Son, and They, through the Holy Spirit, will dwell in you, and you will dwell in Them. You'll be perfected in Them, sanctified in Them, and eventually, glorified in Them. These are all stair-steps. *Justification* is a lower step. It's a step that leads towards exaltation. You need to be *justified*. Then you need to be *sanctified*. Moroni puts this in perspective: you need to be *perfected in Christ*. We've talked about that. We've had lessons about what that means. Eventually, what comes next, and I'm going to talk about this in a future lesson, is a process that's called *Glorification*. What does it mean to be glorified? That's the final step. You get to a point where you're glorified. If you are glorified with the law of the celestial world, then you will inherit the Celestial Kingdom because you now have a glorification, a glorified body; you are a celestial person. That's where you'll go. You're going to end up going to a place that matches the person you are.

So, the whole name of this process is to be **changed** from who we are into something more noble, more glorified, more exalted, and more holy. I like the song we sing in church, "More Holiness Give Me." The word throughout the whole hymn is *more* of this, and *more* of that, etc. Now, that's a great song that talks about this process. You cannot get where They are and remain where you are. That's the bottom line. We are a long way out. If you'll notice in 3 Nephi, when the Lord appears to the Nephites, He calls three times. There is a voice that is heard three times, but nobody recognizes it until the third time. We're two-thirds of the way out from the center of this galaxy. Symbolically, it takes calling us three times to show the distance of where we are. You can go on the internet and find something interesting. They will take a model of the Milky Way Galaxy and show where we are, where our earth is in one of those great pinwheel arms. And, we are way out from the center. During the Millennium this earth will move one-third of the distance that it is now—total distance—it will move a third of the way back. So, if you look on Google, or wherever, at where the earth is in this pinwheel galaxy, and just kind of measure from the center and then find half way between where we are and the center, and that's approximately where we're going to be in the world to come. Isn't that interesting?

Student 1: How do I google that? The Milky Way?

Mike: Just type into Google, "Where is the earth in the Milky Way Galaxy?" Look at that; it's fascinating. We're so far out that the light from the center can't reach us, so the Fathers and Mothers have created for us a sun in this fallen state. Isn't it interesting that the sun is symbolic of The Son? It's the Lord's source of light and life. Over in Moses, it says, *"all things...bear record of me."* Everything. So, if you look at that, the Savior and the Father said, "Everything that you see around you, whether it's a bird, a fish, an insect, a planet, or a galaxy, everything testifies of Me." You'll find Christ in everything if you're looking for it. It's just fascinating! Whether it's a butterfly coming out of a cocoon, or whatever you want to find in nature, it all testifies of Christ.

That's the celestial world. That's this earth in its sanctified, glorified, resurrected and exalted state.

References:
D&C 121:41-42
Pearl of Great Price ch 3 Figure 5
D&C 88:17-31
Moses 7:48
Abraham 3:9 "...nigh unto the throne of God..."
Genesis 1:16; Moses 2:16; Abraham 4:16 "...the greater light to rule the day..."
D&C 123:7 "...the whole earth groans under the weight of its iniquity."
D&C 88:13:13
Article of Faith 10
D&C 77:12 and 1
Revelation 4:6 "...sea of glass..."
3 Nephi 11:3-6 (a voice out of heaven heard three times)
Moses 6:63 "...all things...bear record of me..."

Selected Teachings on
The Holy Spirit of Promise

Joseph Fielding Smith (*Quorum of the Twelve*)
I will make an explanation of the expression, "Sealed by the Holy Spirit of Promise." This does not have reference to marriage for time and all eternity only, but to every ordinance and blessing of the gospel. Baptism into the Church is sealed by this Spirit, likewise confirmation, ordination, and all ordinances as well as marriage for time and all eternity.
The meaning of this expression is this: Every covenant, contract, bond, obligation, oath, vow, and performance, that man receives through the covenants and blessings of the gospel, is sealed by the Holy Spirit with a promise. The promise is that the blessing will be obtained, if those who seek it are true and faithful to the end. *If they are not faithful, then the Holy Spirit will withdraw the blessing, and the promise comes to an end.* (*Doctrines of Salvation*, 2:94-95)

David A. Bednar (*Quorum of the Twelve*)
The Holy Spirit of Promise is the ratifying power of the Holy Ghost. When sealed by the HolySpirit of Promise, an ordinance, vow, or covenant is binding on earth and in heaven. (See D&C 132:7.) Receiving this "stamp of approval" from the Holy Ghost is the result of faithfulness, integrity, and steadfastness in honoring gospel covenants "in [the] process of time" (Moses 7:21). However, *this sealing can be forfeited through unrighteousness and transgression*. (*Ensign*, May 2007, 22)

Richard G. Scott (*Quorum of the Twelve*)
Realize that a sealing ordinance is not enduring until after it is sealed by the Holy Spirit of Promise. *Both individuals must be worthy and want the sealing to be eternal.* ("Temple Worship: the Source of Strength in Times of Need," *Ensign*, May 2009)

James E. Faust (*First Presidency*)
I wish to say a word about the Holy Spirit of Promise, which is the sealing and ratifying power of the Holy Ghost. To have a covenant or ordinance sealed by the Holy Spirit of Promise is a compact through which the inherent blessings will be obtained, *provided those seeking the blessing are true and faithful* (see D&C 76:50-54).
For example, when the covenant of marriage for time and eternity, the culminating gospel ordinance, is sealed by the Holy Spirit of Promise, it can literally open the windows of heaven for great blessings to flow to a married couple who seek for those blessings. Such marriages become rich, whole, and sacred. Though each party to the marriage can maintain his or her separate identity, yet together in their covenants

they can be like two vines wound inseparably around each other. Each thinks of his or her companion before thinking of self.

One of the great blessings available through the Holy Spirit of Promise is that all of our covenants, vows, oaths, and performances, which we receive through the ordinances and blessings of the gospel, are not only confirmed but may be sealed by that Holy Spirit of Promise. However, that sealing may be broken by unrighteousness. *It is also important to remember that if a person undertakes to receive the sealing blessing by deceit, "then the blessing is not sealed, notwithstanding the integrity and authority of the person officiating"* (Joseph Fielding Smith,*Doctrines of Salvation*, comp. Bruce R. McConkie, 3 vols., Salt Lake City: Bookcraft, 1954-56, 2:98-99).

To have a covenant or ordinance sealed by the Holy Spirit of Promise means that the compact is binding on earth and in heaven. ["The Gift of the Holy Ghost--A Sure Compass," *Ensign*, Apr. 1996, pp. 5-6]

Melvin J. Ballard (*Quorum of the Twelve*)
We may deceive men but we cannot deceive the Holy Ghost, and our blessings will not be eternal until they are also sealed by the holy spirit of promise, the Holy Ghost, one who reads the thoughts and hearts of men and gives his sealing approval to the blessings pronounced upon their heads. Then it is binding, and of full force, (*Sermons and Missionary Service of Melvin J. Ballard*, Deseret Book Co., 1949, p. 237.)

Harold B. Lee (*Quorum of the Twelve*)
I shall inject here another phrase that is oft discussed (and I think is misunderstood) and to which we try to attach some mysteries. This phrase, where the Lord directs that all of these things are to be eternal, is: "must be sealed by the Holy Spirit of promise." Let me refer first to the 76th section of the Doctrine and Covenants. Speaking of those who are candidates for celestial glory, the Lord says:

"They are they who received the testimony of Jesus, and believed on his name and were baptized after the manner of his burial That by keeping the commandments they might be washed and cleansed from all their sins and receive the Holy Spirit by the laying on of the hands . . . And who overcome by faith, and are sealed by the Holy Spirit of Promise, which the Father sheds forth upon all those who are just and true" (D&C 76:51-53.)

In other words, baptism is only efficacious, and the initiary ordinance is applicable, when it is sealed by the Holy Spirit of Promise. We have that same phrase repeated in section 132, verse 19, for the Lord is speaking now of celestial marriage.

". . . if a man marry a wife by my word and it is sealed unto them by the Holy Spirit of Promise, they shall pass by the angels, and the gods, which are set there, to their exaltation and glory in all things. . . ."

And with reference to the priesthood, when the Lord discusses in the 84th section the oath and covenant, exactly the same principle is implied*. By the laying on of hands we get the promise of power and authority, but it will not be ours -- worlds without end--unless we keep our part of the covenant. (Stand Ye In Holy Places, p.53)*

Bruce R. McConkie (*Quorum of the Twelve*)
One of the functions assigned and delegated to the Holy spirit is to seal, and the following expressions are identical in thought content:
> To be sealed by the Holy Spirit of Promise;
> To be justified by the Spirit;
> To be approved by the Lord; and
> To be ratified by the Holy Ghost.

Accordingly, any act which is sealed by the Holy Spirit of Promise is one which is justified by the Spirit, one which is approved by the Lord, one which is ratified by the Holy Ghost....
As revealed to Joseph Smith, the Lord's law in this respect is: "All covenants, contracts, bonds, obligations, oaths, vows, performances, connections, associations, or expectations, that are not made and entered into and sealed by the Holy Spirit of promise, of him who is anointed, both as well for time and for all eternity, and that too most holy, by revelation and commandment through the medium of mine anointed, whom I have appointed on the earth to hold this power (and I have appointed unto my servant Joseph to hold this power in the last days, and there is never but one on the earth at a time on whom this power and the keys of this priesthood are conferred), are of no efficacy, virtue, or force in and after the resurrection from the dead; for all contracts that are not made unto this end have an end when men are dead." (D. & C. 132:7.)
By way of illustration, this means that baptism, partaking of the sacrament, administering to the sick, marriage, and every covenant that man ever makes with the Lord—plus all other "contracts, bonds, obligations, oaths, vows, performances, associations, or expectations"—must be performed in righteousness by and for people who are worthy to receive whatever blessing is involved, otherwise whatever is done has no binding and sealing effect in eternity.
Since "the Comforter knoweth all things" (D. & C. 42:17), it follows that it is not possible "to lie to the Holy Ghost" and thereby gain an unearned or undeserved blessing, as Ananias and Sapphira found out to their sorrow. (Acts 5:1-11.) And so this provision that all things must be sealed by the Holy Spirit of Promise, if they are to have "efficacy, virtue, or force in and after the resurrection from the dead" (D. & C. 132:7), is the Lord's system for dealing with absolute impartiality with all men, and for giving all men exactly what they merit, neither adding to nor diminishing from.

When the Holy Spirit of Promise places his ratifying seal upon a baptism, or a marriage, or any covenant, except that of having one's calling and election made sure, the seal is a conditional approval or ratification; it is binding in eternity only in the event of subsequent obedience to the terms and conditions of whatever covenant is involved.

But when the ratifying seal of approval is placed upon someone whose calling and election is thereby made sure—because there are no more conditions to be met by the obedient person—this act of being sealed up unto eternal life is of such transcendent import that of itself it is called being sealed by the Holy Spirit of Promise, which means that in this crowning sense, being so sealed is the same as having one's calling and election made sure. Thus, to be sealed by the Holy Spirit of Promise is to be sealed up unto eternal life; and to be sealed up unto eternal life is to be sealed by the Holy Spirit of Promise. And of this usage of terms, a usage which is wholly misunderstood unless the whole concept of the sealing power of the Spirit is understood, the scriptures and other prophetic utterances bear repeated witness. (*Doctrinal New Testament Commentary*, 3:335-336)

One of our revelations speaks of "the Holy Spirit of promise, which the Father sheds forth upon all those who are just and true" (D&C 76:53), meaning that every person who walks uprightly, does the best that he can, overcomes the world, rises above carnality, and walks in paths of righteousness will have his acts and his deeds sealed and approved by the Holy Spirit. He will be, as Paul would have expressed it, "justified ... by the Spirit" (See 1 Cor. 6:11)....

In order to get a proper marriage one must do this: first, search for and seek out celestial marriage—find the right ordinance; second, look for a legal administrator, someone who holds the sealing power—and that power is exercised only in the temples that the Lord has had built by the tithing and sacrifice of his people in our day; and third, so live in righteousness, uprightness, integrity, virtue, and morality that he is entitled to have the Holy Spirit of God ratify and seal and justify and approve, and in that event his marriage is sealed by the Holy Spirit of promise and is binding in time and in eternity. ("Celestial Marriage," *New Era*, June 1978, pp.16-17)

To seal is to ratify, to justify, or to approve. Thus an act which is sealed by the Holy Spirit of Promise is one which is ratified by the Holy Ghost; it is one which is approved by the Lord; and the person who has taken the obligation upon himself is justified by the Spirit in the thing he has done. The ratifying seal of approval is put upon an act only if those entering the contract are worthy as a result of personal righteousness to receive the divine approbation. They "are sealed by the Holy Spirit of promise, which the Father sheds forth upon all those who are just and true." (D. & C. 76:53.) *__If they are not just and true and worthy the ratifying seal is withheld__*.

When any ordinance or contract is sealed by the Spirit, it is approved with a promise of reward, *__provided unrighteousness does not thereafter break the seal, remove the ratifying approval, and cause loss of the promised blessing.__* (Doctrines of Salvation, vol. 1, p. 55; vol. 2, pp. 94-99) *__Seals are placed on contracts through righteousness.__*

The operation and power of the Holy Spirit of Promise is best illustrated by the ordinance and contract of baptism. An unworthy candidate for baptism might deceive the elders and get the ordinance performed, but no one can lie to the Holy Ghost and get by undetected. Accordingly, the baptism of an unworthy and unrepentant person would not be sealed by the Spirit; it would not be ratified by the Holy Ghost; the unworthy person would not be justified by the Spirit in his actions. If thereafter he became worthy through repentance and obedience, the seal would then be put in force. Similarly, if a worthy person is baptized with the ratifying approval of the Holy Ghost attending the performance, yet the seal may be broken by subsequent sin.

These principles also apply to every other ordinance and performance in the Church. Thus *__if both parties are "just and true," if they are worthy, a ratifying seal is placed on their temple marriage; if they are unworthy, they are not justified by the Spirit and the ratification of the Holy Ghost is withheld. Subsequent worthiness will put the seal in force, and unrighteousness will break any seal.__* (*Mormon Doctrine*, p.362)

Cree-L Kofford (*Quorum of the Seventy*)

The covenants, commitments, and promises that each of you make (D&C 132:7 calls them "covenants, contracts, bonds, obligations, oaths, vows, performances, connections, associations, or expectations") must be sealed by the Holy Spirit of Promise.

> The Holy Spirit of Promise is another way of saying the Holy Ghost. What the scriptures mean when they say that something must be sealed by the Holy Spirit of Promise is that it must receive the approval of the Holy Ghost. The Holy Ghost can see into the heart of each of us and can consequently discern deceit, half-truths, or misrepresentations. Thus, when a sealing ordinance is "sealed by the Holy Spirit," the Holy Ghost is satisfied that the parties to the sealing ordinance have been obedient in order to enter into the sealing ordinance and afterward obedient to the covenants they have made. ("Marriage in the Lord's Way, Part One," *Ensign*, June 1998, p. 12)

The Holy Ghost is the Holy Spirit of Promise (Acts 2:33). He confirms as acceptable to God the righteous acts, ordinances, and covenants of men. The Holy Spirit of Promise witnesses to the Father that the saving ordinances have been performed properly and that the covenants associated with them have been kept.

They who are sealed by the Holy Spirit of Promise receive all that the Father has: D&C 76:51–60; (Eph. 1:13–14;)

- All covenants and performances must be sealed by the Holy Spirit of Promise to have force after this life: D&C 132:7, 18–19, 26;

Chapter Twenty-Eight
Podcast 028 The Powers of Heaven

I'm going to read a parable to you tonight. This is called:
"The Parable of the Advanced Placement Student."
"There once was a girl who loved to learn. While other kids would be outside playing, she could be found sitting on her porch, eagerly and excitedly reading books on advanced topics. As she progressed from grade school to middle school to high school, her desire to learn more grew as well. Unfortunately, it soon became apparent that school wasn't challenging enough for the young woman. Although she read all the textbooks she was supposed to read in school and got good grades, she still wasn't academically fulfilled. One day, she seized the initiative and approached her high school principal about her situation. After she expressed her feelings and frustrations, he leaned back in his chair, looked outside and felt the warmth of the sun shining through his office's windows. After pausing for what seemed like an eternity for the young woman, the principal spoke. His response was both thrilling and disquieting. He said: 'I've been watching you, and have seen you reading and learning wonderful things that don't interest the other kids. I have to say; I am so proud of you, and for the love of learning you have. I have no doubt you are going to go far in life. Now, we have an accredited program just for kids like you. It's a curriculum that's custom-made for you. That means you'll have to keep attending this school and taking the same classes as all

*the other kids. But after school, you'll be able to log on and
study at your own pace, as fast and as far as you can handle.
This also means that, provided you pass all your personal
curriculum tests, you'll get to graduate early, and with college
credits as well. But I need to warn you of two things: First, I
don't think there are any other kids in our city who are taking
this online course. You just may be the first. So, if you want to
interact with other kids just like you, you'll need to seek them out
and find them. You'll probably succeed at this, but you'll find
they live in other cities far away from ours. So, don't be
surprised if some days you feel alone. Second, about the other
kids here -- they are just as special, and just as wonderful as you
are. But they will have a difficult time relating to you, and
understanding why you've chosen to study a more customized,
accelerated program after school hours. They will think you're
weird, maybe even a freak. It'll be even worse if you start telling
them about other kids, just like you, in far away cities; they'll
likely consider you a member of a group of freaks. You can
forget about assuming significant leadership positions like class
president or student body president, because not only the kids,
but even some of the teachers here in our area will call you
names and will question your motives. On the flip side: First,
you will learn things about people, places, nature, even the
universe that will excite you, maybe even take your breath away.
And although your mom and dad can't take the special
curriculum tests you'll have to take, you'll be able to tell them all
about what you're learning, and they'll be thrilled to see how
their little girl is growing up. I mean, really thrilled. Second,
about the kids you'll eventually meet -- you know, the ones in the
other cities? They'll totally relate to you, and you to them.
They'll tell you the things they're learning, and you'll tell them
the things you're learning, and you'll all be really amazed at all
the cool things you can learn about, and even do. Not today, and
maybe not this year, but over time, a few people here in our city
may see a little gleam in your eye and a smile on your face.
They'll be genuinely curious about why you're so happy and
beaming. Those are the people who will be ready to hear about
your after-hours online school. I can't tell you what to do -- this
is your decision.' As the girl sat in her chair across from the*

*principal, she heard a **song** softly playing on his radio behind his desk... As the song was ending, the girl looked outside...felt the warmth of the sun on her face...and with a little gleam in her eye...she smiled a huge smile."* ["My Wish" by Rascal Flatts; see the lyrics at the end of this chapter]

I give that for you to think about and see if you discern and can relate to what that's all about.

Today in Church, we heard some interesting things. We heard a high counselor get up and say that the Brethren are really concerned about the loss of members in the Church. There are a lot of members leaving the Church. Because of that, the brethren had emphasized the Sabbath Day observance to try and curb this. They feel that if people would keep the Sabbath Day holy, that this flow of people leaving the Church would be lessened and even halted. Certainly, keeping the Sabbath Day holy would be a blessing to all the members of the Church. I'd like you to go with me to Moroni 6, and see what the *Book of Mormon* says about how we can stop this flow. I think the answer is right here in the scriptures for us. I think the cause of the problem is there and the answer to the problem is there. We should be able to go to the *Book of Mormon* and find all the answers to the challenges that we have in today's society. Moroni 6 talks about church members. It also talks about meetings that are conducted by the power of the Holy Ghost. You can look at the first three verses where it talks about them being baptized. Then in verse 4:

> *[4] And after they had been received unto baptism, and were wrought upon and cleansed by the power of the Holy Ghost, they were numbered among the people of the church of Christ;*

We've all been through that up to this point, and it's interesting that we each have an LDS Church identification number:

> *and their names were taken, that they might be remembered*

That's the purpose of record keeping in the Church, so that no one drops between the cracks and that we're remembered. It's from these records and others that home teaching/visiting teaching assignments are made so that those not attending church

handwritten: Isiah Commentary - Gilead,
end time Prophecy - chap 7
Isiah chap 1 - water downed gospel that doesn't nourish

can be remembered by those that are and that we can do something to help them. Now, here's your key:

and nourished by the good word of God,

I think that is the absolute key to activity and success as a member of the Church. I think that if you are not spiritually nourished by the *"good word of God,"* whatever that means, then eventually, you are going to go somewhere else to find that nourishment. I think that in too many places, we as members are being spiritually starved to death. Look what happens in the next lines that follow. Look at the three promises here, after *nourished by the good word of God.* If that happens, look at what the results are:

[#1] to keep them in the right way,

There's your answer to inactivity and apostasy in the Church. People who are leaving the Church are not being *kept in the right way.* Nourishing them will do that. Look at the next one:

[#2] to keep them continually watchful unto prayer,

We've talked at some length about the warfare that takes place in the telestial world. Anciently, what the Lord used to do was build up walls to protect communities, properties, and vineyards, and on these walls were watch towers. They even divided the night into various "watches." They measured the twelve hours from 6 P.M. to 6 A.M. into four 3-hour watches: the first, second, third, and fourth watch. The people who were on the towers were called "watchmen." So, when it says, *"to keep them continually watchful unto prayer,"* that word *watchful* refers to detecting the enemy, understanding what their strategies are, and being able to defeat the enemy and come off conqueror and victorious. So, notice if you're *"nourished by the good word of God,"* not only will you stay in the right way, but you'll be kept *"watchful unto prayer."* You'll realize the importance of prayer in escaping the hands of the enemy, and you'll develop prayer habits that go beyond the primary prayers that we say in the Church. You'll go into something mightier than that. Then the third promise of being *nourished by the good word of God*:

*[#3] relying **alone** upon the merits of Christ, who was the author and the finisher of their faith.*

If you are *"nourished by the good word of God,"* then you will rely **alone** on Christ. I've got that word *alone* circled. In other words, you don't do as Nephi says in 2 Nephi 4:34:

> *Cursed is he that putteth his trust in the arm of flesh. Yea, cursed is he that putteth his trust in man or maketh flesh his arm.*

You won't put your trust in man. You will rely alone on Christ because being nourished by the good word of God, the absolute by-product of that nourishment is *"a mighty change [of] heart;"* you're transformed and develop the characteristics of the Master. Look at the wording. Eventually, you are *"relying alone upon the merits of Christ who is the author **and the finisher** of their faith."* Isn't that an interesting statement? That comes out of Hebrews 12:2 where that exact statement is said, *"the author and finisher of our faith."* What do you think about the *"finisher of our faith?"* It goes from being exposed to the author of our faith, to where our faith is finished. And when faith is finished, what takes the place of *finished faith*? **Perfect knowledge**. So, you go from being behind the veil, to where the veil parts and you see the Son of God, the author of your faith, and you see Him face to face.

Margie and I are fasting often. We feel that once a month fast doesn't fit the criteria that the scriptures talk about to *fast and pray oft*. I understand that the minimal *"praying oft"* is praying three times a day, according to the *Book of Mormon*—morning, mid-day and evening. What does it mean to *fast oft*? Because if you *fast and pray oft*, you end up being endowed with *"the spirit of prophecy, and the spirit of revelation, and when [you teach, you teach] with power and authority of God."* So, Margie and I are *fasting oft*. We did this once in the Philippines for eight months, and the result of this eight months was dreams and visions, inspiration, and marvelous things that the Lord opened up because we were willing to give up those meals on a more often basis. So, my grandson is with us right now and is preparing to go on a mission. Every morning we get together, and we have a scripture study—the three of us. We were mentioning about fasting; we had a little lesson on that. We took Isaiah 58 as our text. We mentioned to him how oft we were fasting and he said he wanted to join us in that. Later on, he said,

"Why are you fasting so oft, Grandpa?" And I said, "Because I want to see the face of God in this life; *the author and finisher of our faith.*" Then in Moroni 6:5 it says:

> *And the church did meet together oft, to fast and*
> *to pray, and to speak one with another concerning*
> *the welfare of their souls.*

So, brothers and sisters, I think the *Book of Mormon* has provided us with the answer to the general apostasy that we see in the Church, and to which the Brethren are rightly concerned, very concerned. I'm also convinced that keeping the Sabbath day holy will be a great way to strengthen the Saints and bring down the blessings of heaven upon their heads. Here's another one you've heard me talk about many times, by Brother Packer:

> *True doctrine, understood, changes attitudes and*
> *behavior.*

In tonight's Priesthood meeting, the overriding theme that went through that was "rescue." If you go on an MLS mission, which is "Member Leadership Support Mission," like Margie and I served in the Philippines, your primary responsibility will be to go out and rescue people who are members of the Church, who are no longer attending church. It seems like we are always developing a new program to help bring them back. In reality, they won't leave if they are *nourished by the good word of God*, and that takes them from faith to "finished faith" with knowledge. But, once they have left, what's a good way to bring them back? Well, it's the same principle that we see in Moroni 6:4. Brother Packer said, *"True doctrine understood changes attitudes and behavior."* So, what do we do to get them back? We go out and find them, and nourish them with the good word of God. We don't tell cutesy little stories, and we don't tell long experiences about where we've been and what we've done. We try as soon as possible to immerse them, one more time, in God's word.

Let's go to Alma 31:5 and let me show you the power of this. Alma understood this. This is one of the great messages of the *Book of Mormon*. How does this apply to us? Do you have children, grandchildren, a spouse, or a loved one who has left activity in the Church for whatever reason? Maybe they've had their feelings offended, or they've had a crisis of faith. How do we get them back? If you're like me, every chance you have to talk to these folks, you talk to them about coming back to church. Come back to church. Come back to church. It seemed that the more I talked to them about coming back to church, the more it seemed to drive them away until we discovered these little things that are in the scriptures, Alma 31:5. Now, the context of this scripture is that Alma was the Chief Judge and also the High Priest over the Church, so he fulfilled a dual calling. Because of the massive apostasy that was taking place among the Nephites in 74 B.C., not unlike 2016 A.D. in the Church today, there was just not enough time to be involved in the ministry and also to manage the affairs of the people politically. So, he gives up the judgment-seat to a righteous man and dedicates himself wholly to preaching the Gospel of Jesus Christ. He puts into practice what Brother Packer said, *"True doctrine, understood, changes attitudes and behavior."* The rest of Brother Packer's quote is that:

> The study of the doctrines of the gospel will improve behavior quicker than a study of behavior will improve behavior. Preoccupation with unworthy behavior can lead to unworthy behavior. That is why we stress so forcefully the study of the doctrines of the gospel.

The more you talk about bad behavior, the more bad behavior you get. So, talking about it creates more. Look what Alma says in 31:5:

> And now, as the preaching of the word had a great tendency to lead the people to do that which was just—yea, it had had more powerful effect upon the minds of the people than the sword, or anything else, which had happened unto them — therefore Alma thought it was expedient that they should try the **virtue** of the word of God.

What's he doing? He's nourishing the people with the good word of God, and the keyword here is *virtue*. Another word in the scriptures for virtue is *power*. Now, since we have the *Book of Mormon*, Joseph said:

> A man would get nearer to God by abiding by its precepts, than by any other book.

And it seems to me that when we want to help people come back, the *Book of Mormon* should be the prime volume that we use in helping them understand true doctrine and be *nourished by the good word of God*. I can testify to you that this works. We practiced it in three missions, and we've never had it fail us. Where we started going off on our own knowledge and our own logic, in our own persuasion, in our experiences, and in our own stories, we had less success than if we went straight to the Word of God and quoted it right off the page or from memory. The effect was dramatic and here's why. God's word is truth and light. His word, whether it's on a written page or whether it's spoken from His own mouth, it doesn't matter; His word is food for the spirit. So, when we talk about being nourished, think about that. Being nourished is literally feeding your spirit with the fruit of the Spirit, which is truth and light. Truth, light, glory, and intelligence are all synonymous, meaning the same thing. Section 93 tells us that any one of those three things describes the four: glory, intelligence, light, and truth are all the same thing. So, just as physical food nourishes the body, those things feed the spirit and transform the man or woman into a man or woman of Christ. That's how it works. Nothing invites the Spirit of the Lord into a discussion quicker than quoting His word from the scriptures or memory. Better than that, having the person read the word out loud, out of their own scriptures—there's something magical that takes place with that. So, I think that in our meetings and in church and various places, we spend a lot of time coming up with the latest program when it appears to me the Lord has already given us the answer, and it's in the *Book of Mormon*. I'm studying the book of Isaiah. I felt impressed to go through all sixty plus chapters, so I've been doing that in my morning studies. The other morning I read this scripture, Isaiah 5:13:

> *My people are gone into captivity, because they*
> *have no knowledge.*

In Proverbs 29:18 it says:

> *Where there is no vision, the people perish.*

Doctrine and Covenants 93:24 gives us the definition of truth:

> *And truth is knowledge of things as they are, and*
> *as they were, and as they are to come.*

So, we need to realign ourselves now and start looking at things a bit more seriously.

I want to share with you a couple of thoughts; just some random things tonight. The problem with the solution of *"True doctrine understood changes...behavior,"* is that if you're going to be an instrument in the hands of the Lord in helping someone's behavior be modified, it's going to require that you know the doctrines. If you don't know the doctrines, you're going to be hard-pressed to help a person understand the truth of any particular doctrine. So, it's going to require you to be a scriptorian. You are going to need to know what's in the scriptures. Hence, you're going to need to be able to read the scriptures every day. If we want to be an instrument in the Lord's hands in helping people come back home, or once they are baptized, stay there, stay in the right way, we're going to have to know the doctrines of the Church. And we're going to have to teach those doctrines and not get caught up in "spiritual twinkies and fried spiritual froth," which we hear too often. We need to get back to the things that change behavior and strengthen the soul. Let me read to you a couple of things from the Prophet Joseph Smith. I love these statements. He says:

If we start right, it's easy for us to go right all the time; but if we start wrong we may go wrong, and it will be a hard matter to get right.

Listen to these statements! These are doctrines that change people's behavior:

If men do not comprehend the character of God, they do not comprehend themselves.

Think about that for just a minute. For you to know who you are, you need to know who your Creator is. The more that you understand God, your Heavenly Father, the more you are going to understand yourself. Joseph said:

I'm going to inquire after God; for I want you all to know Him, and to be familiar with Him.

Why can't we teach these kinds of things? Go with me over to 2 Nephi 25. Here's a pattern I would just love to see us develop more in the Church. Instead of talking about ward councils so much, and different things like that, administrative deals, why don't we do like the Nephites who had obtained an aliveness in

Christ? Look at verse 25. This is talking about the Law of Moses:

> *[25] For, for this end was the law given; wherefore the law hath become dead unto us, and we are made alive in Christ because of our faith; yet we keep the law because of the commandments.*

I feel convinced that we need to do this. Maybe when you're asked to teach, and maybe when you're asked to testify or speak in Church, maybe you can look at verse 26, and it will be a little reminder:

> *[26] And we talk of Christ, we rejoice in Christ, we preach of Christ, we prophesy of Christ,*

Look at that! We talk, rejoice, preach, and prophesy of Christ. Margie and I went to the Assembly of God and attended their meetings a couple of weeks ago. I tell you, when I left there I was edified. I was just flat edified because their whole meeting was centered in Jesus Christ. It didn't matter that they're not Mormons. It didn't matter that they don't have the "gift of the Holy Ghost." It doesn't matter that they don't have the restored priesthood. Everything they said was just simply rejoicing in the Savior. Then verse 26 goes on:

> *and we write according to our prophecies, that our children may know to what source they may look for a remission of their sins.*

Become more Christ-centered! Let's talk about Him! Let's do it more. Then Joseph says:

> *What sort of a being was God in the beginning? ...God himself was once as we are now, and is an exalted man, and sits enthroned in yonder heavens!*

If you ask, "What is the first principle of the gospel?" As members of the Church, we're going to go to Article of Faith #4. The first principle of the gospel is "Faith in the Lord, Jesus Christ." The second is "repentance," and so on through the principles and ordinances of the gospel. That's in Article of Faith #4, but listen to what Joseph Smith says three months before he was murdered in the Carthage Jail. He was before 21,000 people on April 7, 1844. He said:

*It is the first principle of the gospel **to know for a
certainty the character of God,** and to know that
we may converse with Him as one man converses
with another, and that He was once a man like us;
yea, that God Himself, the Father of us all, dwelt
on an earth, the same as Jesus Christ Himself did.*

Now, those are the kinds of doctrines that start to transform.
That's the kind of stuff that changes behavior. When you start to
learn about who God is, then you start to learn about who you
are, and that relationship between the two of you becomes
strengthened. But, we need to learn these kinds of things, and
how are we ever going to learn them if we are not talking about
them and they are not taught?

So, let's go over to *Doctrine and Covenants* 121:34 for a
minute. Let me show you a couple of little things here. Section
121 is the priesthood section that the Lord has restored for men,
on how to honor and magnify their priesthood and have what we
call *power in the priesthood*:

[34] *Behold, there are many called, but few are
chosen. And why are they not chosen?*

Let's put that this way. When we talk about the priesthood, many
are ordained, but few have power. Let's just make a little change
there because that's true and it's going to fit into this in just a
minute, as you'll see. So, Brother Packer, a couple of years ago
when he was physically incapacitated, but still able to speak in
General Conference, lamented in the following way. He said that
we generally had done a good job in the Church ordaining men
to the priesthood. We now have conferred and ordained men
throughout the world, but we have not done a good job in
helping them to be powerful in the priesthood. He stated that. He
didn't give us any specific directions about how to turn that
around. He just stated a fact about the current status of the
Church when it comes to Melchizedek Priesthood. So, now we
look at verse 34 again:

Many are called [ordained, conferred priesthood],
but few are chosen.

They don't have power. *"And why are they not chosen?"* There
are two reasons in verse 35:

> *Because* [1] *their hearts are set so much upon the*
> *things of this world, and* [2] *aspire to the honors*
> *of men, that they do not learn this one lesson—*

Those are the two reasons why the Melchizedek Priesthood in the Church, according to Brother Packer, lack power in the priesthood. *"They do not learn this one lesson,"* and here's the lesson:

> *[36] That the rights of the priesthood are*
> *inseparably connected with the powers of heaven,*
> *and that the powers of heaven cannot be*
> *controlled nor handled only upon the principles*
> *of righteousness.*

tap into

Let's talk about two things for just a minute: the *rights of the priesthood* (rights, not rites) and the *powers of heaven*. Let's look at this *power of heaven*. It is an ambiguous, impersonal thing that's something like electrical, celestial electricity, right? Let's switch this around and look at it a little differently. If one of the *rights of the priesthood* is to heal the sick, where does the power come from to perform that ordinance? If you're going to say, "Well, it comes from God," then you'd be right because you are officiating in something He possesses and He's allowing you to tap into that, so that you can pronounce a blessing. That blessing is acknowledged, and the sick are healed. But, the source of the power to perform that healing comes from behind the veil. No man or woman on this side of the veil can give you the power to perform that healing and have it acknowledged. It doesn't come from man. It has to come from a society of individuals who live on the other side of the veil. In other words, you're tapping into something: a group of men that live in heaven on the other side of the veil. That's the *powers of heaven*. So, instead of thinking of some celestial, electrical conduit, make the *Powers of Heaven*, with a capital P and a capital H and turn it into something personal. God and Jesus Christ live in heaven on the other side of the veil. If you are going to have priesthood power, you're going to have to have a connection with Them because They are the source of all power and miracles that are performed in the telestial world behind the veil—always. So, look at what he's saying, *"The rights of the priesthood are inseparably connected with the powers of heaven."* Let's take a look and see what the *rights of the priesthood* are. Go to Joseph Smith's Translation, at the end of your *Bible* dictionary, to Genesis 14. I think the most powerful scriptures in the Joseph Smith Translation are Genesis 14: 25-40. We're going to look at verse 30-31 to see what the *rights of the priesthood* are. In other words, if you have power in your priesthood, there are certain rights that you have available that you can access and perform. Let's see what some of those rights are. You should read that whole set of verses, but I just want to point out 30-31 right now. We are looking for the *rights of the priesthood.* Verse 30:

> *For God having sworn unto Enoch and unto his*
> *seed with an oath by himself;*

By the way, Enoch had established this connection with the *powers of heaven,* and as a result, look what it says:

> *that every one being ordained after this order and*
> *calling should have power, by faith,*

Here are some priesthood rights:

> *to break mountains, to divide the seas, to dry up*
> *waters, to turn them out of their course;*
> *[31] To put at defiance the armies of nations, to*
> *divide the earth, to break **every** band, to stand in*
> *the presence of God; to **do all things** according to*
> *his will, according to his command, subdue*
> *principalities and powers; and this by the will of*
> *the Son of God which was from before the*
> *foundation of the world.*

Those are the *rights of the priesthood.* So now, go back to section 121: 36:

> *[36]That the rights of the priesthood*

In other words, power comes from something that verse 36 says:

> *are inseparably connected with the **powers of***
> ***heaven,***

Think *people*, don't think *things* or *something* or an *it*. Think PEOPLE.

> *and that the powers of heaven cannot be*
> *controlled nor handled*

You can't control those people who have earned that right to have that power. They're sharing it with you, on conditions. *"The powers of heaven cannot be controlled **nor handled**."* I think that's interesting because when the *powers of heaven* manifest themselves physically to you, you're going to have to know if they are the powers from the dark side or they are the powers from the light side. The only way you can do that is to *handle* them. *They cannot be controlled nor handled:*

> *only upon the principles of righteousness.*
> *[37] That they may be conferred upon us,*

Think about *"conferred,"* as *"many are called."* That's the ordination and conferral that President Packer is talking about:

> *it is true;*

And we've done a good job in that area, but here are the things that break the commitment:

> *but when we undertake to cover our sins, or to gratify our pride, our vain ambition, or to exercise control or dominion or compulsion upon the souls of the children of men, in any degree of unrighteousness,*

That's husbands exercising that control or dominion over wives and children:

> *behold, the heavens withdraw themselves;*

See, what I would do is I would draw a line from the words *"the heavens"* up to verse 36 and connect the heavens with the *"powers of heaven."* We're talking now about *people.* We're talking about individuals. Some**one**, not some**thing**. *The heavens withdraw themselves:*

> *the Spirit of the Lord is grieved; and when it is withdrawn, Amen to the priesthood or the authority of that man.*
> *[38] Behold, ere he is aware, he is left unto himself, to kick against the pricks, to persecute the saints, and to fight against God.*

This is where we need to go. These are the things we need to do.

Now, in the last few minutes, I want to share with you a couple of thoughts that will take us into next week's lesson. All my life I have been a shooter and I've had guns. I started shooting when I was 7 or 8 years old. My dad was a police officer. I had my first 12 gauge shotgun when I was 10 to 12 years old, as soon as I could get a duck hunting license. I'm wearing dual hearing aids now at this point in my life. One of the reasons I'm wearing hearing aids is because my hearing has been impaired by gunfire over a lifetime. I still enjoy shooting. I've been shooting for all of my life. Part of my reasoning for learning how to shoot, at least later in life was because I read the *"signs of the times"* and the *Book of Mormon* and could see what was required of them and what might be required of me. The members of the Church in 3 Nephi 2, were compelled to be armed. The members of the Church were compelled to arm themselves and to take up weaponry in defense of their families, their faith, their religion, their country, and their liberty, which is a theme all through the *Book of Mormon.* You can read it starting in Alma 43 with Moroni, and you can take it right on up through to the end of the *Book of Mormon*, where you see the members of the Church struggling **with weaponry** to stay alive. And, we're commanded to do so by the Lord. So, reading all that, over the years I've become quite proficient with the use of firearms. Not only with handguns, but also rifles, and for many many years I stockpiled battle weapons and literally tens of thousands of rounds of ammunition as a part of my preparedness storage program. This, along with the program of the Church: a year's supply of food, clothing, and where possible, fuel, getting out of debt, and saving a little. Mike Stroud had quite an arsenal because I interpreted what I read in the scriptures as to needing that. However, when we were in the Philippines we had a different feeling that came upon us, and the Lord brought us to something. We were praying to be a part of that *remnant* that we spoke of a few weeks ago: a small group of people that are going to be able to "come up" and claim the priesthood power that we've been talking about a little bit tonight. As I studied the scriptures, it became obvious to me that in the coming day with the establishment of Zion and New Jerusalem, **if you take up a weapon in that day, it will disqualify you from being a part of that** *remnant*, building the New Jerusalem, and helping establish the cause of Zion. That is what I understand from the scriptures. We're in a different time now. In a future day, things are going to be expected of us that are different than it has been in the *Old Testament* and in the early history of the Church, and especially in the *Book of Mormon.* You'll notice that when the Saints were persecuted, even though Joseph Smith raised up a force called Zion's Camp, where the mobbers thought that was a force to come down and use the force of arms to deliver their brethren in Jackson County and to restore stolen property and to make wrongs right, it ends up that no shots were fired by Joseph Smith. The force of arms was not used. The Lord had a different program involved there. We'll talk a little about that.

Let me share with you a little story that took place in the Philippines. We have pictures that we'll put with this that are just marvelous (see back cover). While we were there, there was a non-member woman who was staying in a hotel in downtown Cebu, on the island of Cebu, in central Philippines. She was on vacation, I think, and she was standing on her balcony taking pictures of the Cebu skyline. As she took pictures, she didn't pay any attention to it at the time, but later was looking at the pictures she had taken from her balcony. She noticed a building with a big tall spire on it in her photograph. It had a bubble around it. So, she thought that was a photographic anomaly, maybe a light refraction, maybe it was the glass in the hotel room window, or whatever. She went out and found that same scene and took numerous pictures of this white building with this spire, at night, during the day, in the early morning, in the late evening, and every one of them showed this "bubble." So, she's curious and gets a Filipino taxi cab and shows a picture to the cab driver and asks, "Do you know this building?"

The cab driver says, "Everyone in Cebu knows that building. That's the Mormon Temple."

So, she asks the cab driver to take her to this building. They drive up past the guards and go down into the complex. There's a mission home complex there and the patron housing complex, the mission office, and the temple. So, she finds herself in the mission office talking to Sister Ernstrum, who is President Schmutz's private mission secretary. And she says, "What is this place?" And Sister Schmutz, sensing a mission opportunity, begins to explain to her what this is all about. So the lady says, "What's this?" and she opens up her camera photos and shows the pictures with this bubble around the complex.

Sister Ernstrum says, "Can I have a copy of that?"

So, she was able to make a copy and gave it to the mission president who, in turn, gave it to all the senior missionaries.

Perhaps you've seen it. At one time it made a pretty potent round throughout the internet community. What happened was that I saw something there and the Spirit whispered to me, "This is something that you need to look at and ponder and pray about because it's the key to surviving what's coming." What that boils down to is this, brothers and sisters; in a future day, we're going to need to have that kind of priesthood shielding and protection to make it through what's coming. If necessary, you're going to have to be able to, through the priesthood, make yourself invisible to your enemies, so they cannot see you.

Here's a closing thought. We need to have a shift in our thinking. I'm going to present this to you in scriptures. You do with it what you want. I know what I've done. Once this distilled upon me and I felt that it was true, and I feel even more so now, I asked myself what kind of a sacrifice would be acceptable to the Lord, to access this kind of shielding and protection? What can I give the Lord? What can I do to show Him that I've received this message and I believe that this is verily true? The one thing I had collected, stored and learned how to use pretty proficiently was thousands of rounds of battle ammunition and semi-automatic military weapons. So, here's the thought. Do you really believe what I've given you, this message I sensed from the Lord? Then show how much faith you have in this by sacrificing something that you feel strongly about. When we came home from the Philippines, it was at a time when everybody, because of Obama and his war on guns and the Second Amendment, was buying weapons and you couldn't get ammunition because it was sold out almost everywhere. At that point, I sold all of my battle ammunition and my military weapons. I might mention that I made a tidy little profit, but I sold it all as a sign, as an indicator, that what I believe the Lord has shown me is true. I wanted to put my money where my mouth was. I didn't want to just talk about it, but I wanted to show Him that I believe in what I had been shown. We did that. As a result, the Lord has opened up more to us, and we're even more convinced about what's coming. It's what Brother McConkie referred to when he said:

All of the sorrows and perils of the past
And I interpret that as from Adam up to the present day:
are but a foretaste of what is yet to be.

I was reading in Isaiah today. Go to Isaiah 10. It's also 2 Nephi 20. It's one of the chapters that were included in the plates of Nephi, coming off of the *Brass Plates.* The chapter heading of Isaiah 10 says:

> *The destruction of Assyria is a type of destruction of the wicked at the Second Coming—**Few people will be left after the Lord comes again—The remnant of Jacob will return in that day—***

I think the only way that we can get through this is to put our trust in the Lord and sanctify ourselves. Come up through sacrifice and observe our covenants through sacrifice. Let the Lord teach us how to be shielded and protected by priesthood power.

With that in mind, I'll close with just one statement here. This was given this last General Conference. I'll refer to it just a little bit, and we'll go into more detail next week. It is by Russell M. Nelson, April 2016. Think about what we've been talking about here tonight. He talked about being in a meeting where a guy was playing the organ and all of sudden the power went off. He was playing on the keys, but there was no sound. President Nelson whispered to his wife, Wendy, "He has no power." Then he begins his talk:

> *Well, brethren, in like manner, I fear that there are too many men who have been given the **authority** of the priesthood but who lack priesthood **power** because the flow of power has been blocked by sins such as laziness, dishonesty, pride, immorality, or preoccupation with things of the world* [this is coming right out of section 121]. *I fear that there are too many priesthood bearers who have done little or nothing to develop their ability to **access the powers of heaven**. I worry about all who are impure in their thoughts, feelings, or actions or who demean their wives or children, thereby **cutting off priesthood power**.*

Now, I'll close by just quoting one part of this talk. He says:

> *In a coming day, **only** those men who have taken their priesthood seriously by **diligently** seeking to be taught by the Lord Himself, will be able to*

*bless, guide, protect, strengthen, and heal others.
Only a man who has paid the price for priesthood
power will be able to bring miracles to those he
loves and keep his marriage and family safe now,
and throughout all eternity.*

We'll go into that talk a bit more next week. Now, in tonight's
handouts, I'll put up pictures of the Cebu Temple so that you can
see it. Also, I told this to a friend of mine, who is a former
temple president, and he put it into a little story book form, and
I'll include that for you (see introduction, "Exchanging Bullets
for Bubbles"). That will set the stage for next week's lesson as
we talk about accessing the *powers of heaven*.

Student 6: I just read something recently, I'm not going to say
by whom, but when he talked about learning certain laws when
he was in law school, he was becoming very confused by the
professor's method of teaching. The more they learned, the more
confused they became. Finally, in the end, it all came together.
They recognized that this professor was teaching them, actually
through this mist of confusion, how to get to a place of
understanding. That's where I feel I am. I sometimes feel like I
know nothing. I know less today. All my adult life I have tried to
be a scholar of the Gospel to some degree, but I feel like I know
nothing. I feel like I know less today than I've ever known. Does
that sound right?

Mike: Yeah, I think that's healthy. You've heard people say,
"The more you know, the more you find out you really don't
know." I think what that is, is that you're comparing things
you're learning now with a body of truth that's still in eternity,
that's undiscovered. When you compare what the Lord has
reserved for us, and we get these little feelings for it periodically,
then it truly is astounding that what you know and the
experiences you have in comparison with what's available is
pretty small. The problem is that we end up comparing ourselves
to others all the time. We determine our self-worth and where we
are in our knowledge based on where we perceive others are and
what they know. In reality, the body of truth that is out there,
available from our Heavenly Father, is so massive, so unending,
that once you start to get a grasp for that, it's truly humbling.

You realize and say, "Man, I thought I knew quite a bit, but I don't know anything at all!"

Student 6: Absolutely!

Mike: A friend of mine who has stood in the presence of Christ and had his *Second Comforter* experience, said that the feeling that you have is that the distance between where you see that the Savior is and where you observe yourself, is so vast that you'll say things like Isaiah said, *"Woe is me! I am undone; because I am a man of unclean lips."* So, all of a sudden, everything is put into perspective. And yet, even with that vast difference between where the Son of God is, and at this point, where you are, you stand in His presence and He embraces you, and it's like my friend said, "All of that disappeared when He took me in his arms and blessed me. Then there was no more feeling of 'I am nothing.' All there was, was the love of Christ." You know what he said about that love? I've never forgotten his words. He said, "His love will **crush** you." I thought that was so interesting. But, the first response, as you stand in His presence and you see where He is and who he is, and where you are, is that it is intimidating and hopeless. [Mike laughs] I think, [student], that's the same feeling you're talking about, maybe in a little different vein. Maybe that will give you a little better feeling. But, quickly, in His presence, that disappears because He doesn't want you to feel alienated. He wants you to feel included. He doesn't want you to feel hopeless. He wants to fill you with hope. He doesn't want you to be afraid. He wants you to *"be of good cheer."*

So, I read about these experiences, the *chosen vessels* that Moroni 7 talks about, and they share them at times, when the time is right, to *the residue*—those of us who haven't had that experience. Those who have had these experiences testify of them, so *the residue* may have faith in Christ and come up and claim the same blessings and become a *chosen vessel*. That's how it works. Thanks for sharing that with us. It's time for us to end. Next week we'll talk about the establishment of Zion.

References:
The Parable of the Advanced Placement Student: ldsperfectday.blogspot.com
April 1979 General Conference, "Stand Independent above All Other Creatures" by Bruce R. McConkie
Moroni 6:4
2 Nephi 4:34
Alma 5:9 "...a mighty change [of] heart..."
Hebrews 12:2 "...the author and finisher of our faith..."
Helaman 3:35 "...fast and pray oft..."
Alma 34:21 praying "...morning, mid-day, and evening."
Alma 17:3 "the spirit of prophecy, and the spirit of revelation, and when [you teach, you teach] with great power and authority of God."
Isaiah 58- true law of the fast
Moroni 6:5Oct 1986 General Conference, Boyd K. Packer
Alma 31:5
Joseph Smith; History of the Church, 4:461
D&C 93:36 "...glory...intelligence...light and truth."
Isaiah 5:13
Proverbs 29:18
D&C 93:24
2 Nephi 25:25-26
Joseph Smith, King Follett Sermon
History of the Church, 6:305; from a discourse given by Joseph Smith on Apr. 7, 1844, in Nauvoo, Illinois; reported by Wilford Woodruff, Willard Richards, Thomas Bullock, and William Clayton
D&C 121:34-36
April 2010, General Conference, "The Power of the Priesthood" by Boyd K. Packer
Joseph Smith Translation, Genesis 14: 25-40. (Verses 30-31)
D&C 121: 36-38
General Conference April 1979 "Stand Independent above All Other Creatures" by Bruce R. McConkie
Isaiah 10 / 2 Nephi 20 Chapter heading
April 2016 General Conference, "The Price of Priesthood Power" by Russell M. Nelson
Isaiah 6:5
Moroni 7:31-32 *chosen vessels; residue of men*

My Wish
by Rascal Flatts
I hope the days come easy and the moments pass slow
And each road leads you where you want to go
And if you're faced with the choice and you have to choose
I hope you choose the one that means the most to you
And if one door opens to another door closed
I hope you keep on walkin' 'til you find the window
If it's cold outside, show the world the warmth of your smile
But more than anything, more than anything

[Chorus:]
My wish for you
Is that this life becomes all that you want it to
Your dreams stay big, your worries stay small
You never need to carry more than you can hold
And while you're out there gettin' where you're gettin' to
I hope you know somebody loves you
And wants the same things too
Yeah, this is my wish

I hope you never look back but you never forget
All the ones who love you
And the place you left
I hope you always forgive and you never regret
And you help somebody every chance you get
Oh, you find God's grace in every mistake
And always give more than you take
But more than anything, yeah more than anything

[Chorus:]
My wish for you
Is that this life becomes all that you want it to
Your dreams stay big, your worries stay small
You never need to carry more than you can hold
And while you're out there gettin' where you're gettin' to
I hope you know somebody loves you
And wants the same things too
Yeah, this is my wish

This is my wish
I hope you know somebody loves you
May all your dreams stay big

111

Chapter Twenty-Nine
Podcast 029 Power in the Priesthood

Did you look at the pictures of the Cebu Temple (see back cover) that showed the interesting bubble over the temple complex? I'd like to continue that discussion tonight. It somewhat centers on that kind of a principle. Let's go to *Doctrine and Covenants* 45 real quick. This, to me, is the main take-off scripture of how to successfully and safely get through what's coming at us. First of all, everyone should know that I'm not a "pickle-sucker." I don't find any joy in doom and gloom type things. However, the Lord has given us information, specifically concerning the events that are coming in our future, for a purpose. I choose to study those things and discuss them only to the degree that we can glean information about how to successfully maneuver through these events because the truth of the matter is that on the other side of these events there is something glorious. As a matter of fact, it's these very events that are going to prepare a people for that glorious thing on the other side of these great tribulations and travails. In a talk back in the 1970's, Elder McConkie said this:

All of the sorrows and perils of the past

Now, just stop and think about that for a minute. In other words, from Adam up to when Elder McConkie made this statement, and that includes all the wars, plagues, destruction, and the adversity—all the tribulations of the past:

are but a foretaste of what is yet to be.

Now, if you dwell on that, it can be a little bit discouraging and depressing, especially if you are a student of history, and you've studied the rise and fall of nations and warfare. I'm just fascinated by, and a great student of World War II. I have studied it for a good portion of my life and served a mission in Germany just sixteen years after the fall of the Third Reich. When I think of that comment by Brother McConkie that was given in a general conference, my question is, how can we ever hope to survive that kind of a situation that will refine, through fire, a people that will be prepared to stand in the presence of the resurrected Christ and survive that encounter? Here's the point: None of us in this telestial world, the way we are right now, are prepared for that encounter. There has to be something that happens in order for us to physically, psychologically, sociologically, and in every way be prepared to survive the encounter of standing in the presence of the resurrected Christ when He appears in glory. That encounter with a glorified Christ will destroy you. Forget about wars and everything that precedes it. That encounter with glory will destroy men and women unless they have been changed through the gospel of Jesus Christ and the power of the Holy Ghost. Without going into detail on all the signs in the scriptures, how are we going to get through what's coming? And there are plenty of scriptures on that, especially in the *New Testament* in Matthew 24. The *Doctrine and Covenants* is loaded with signs that are on us right now and are going to intensify, along with other signs that we haven't seen yet but are certainly coming. How are we going to get through that? The key is in *Doctrine and Covenants* section 45. Verse 55 is talking about the millennial world:

> *And Satan shall be bound, that he shall have no*
> *place in the hearts of the children of men.*

Now, that's the Millennium, and the Millennium begins with the Second Coming of Christ. That's the official starting point of the thousand-year Millennial Kingdom. This is the key or the take-off for tonight's discussion. Look at verse 56:

> *And at that day, when I shall come in my glory,*

This means, the day of the Second Coming that ushers in the Millennium:

*shall the parable be fulfilled which I spake
concerning the ten virgins.*

You can read about that in Matthew 25. I find it interesting that the parable of the Ten Virgins is in the chapter just following Matthew 24, where it talks about the destruction of the world and all of the signs leading up to the Second Coming. Then, the chapter right after that talks about the parable of the Ten Virgins. Now, back to verse 57. It's just a little short verse, but here's the key to survival of what's coming:

*For they that are wise and have received the
truth, and have taken the Holy Spirit for their
guide, and have not been deceived—verily I say
unto you, they shall not be hewn down and cast
into the fire, but **shall abide the day**.*

The day is the day of burning and the day of transformation; the day when the earth is renewed and receives is paradisiacal glory, when this planet moves out of its present solar system, moves closer to the center of the Milky Way Galaxy, and takes up its position in a terrestrial realm. Now, notice the keys. There are certain keys. The wise virgins have done certain things. They *received the truth.* That sounds simple, but in the telestial world, it is not a simple proposition to recognize truth. It's that same discussion where Jesus is talking to Pilate, as he is brought before him, and Pilate is talking to Him, and Christ says:

*For this cause came I into the world, that I should
bear witness of the truth.*

And Pilate says:

What is truth?

And that's a great question! We don't want the philosophies of men, mingled with scripture. We don't want what the *Book of Mormon* calls *the precepts of men.* We don't want what section 123 says is the *mainspring of all corruption* in the telestial world, which are the traditions of the fathers that are passed on to the children, and the children inherit lies from their parents, from the fathers. We don't want that. The world is full of that. So, what we are looking for is *the truth.* Section 93 defines it:

*[24] And truth is knowledge of things as they are,
and as they were, and as they are to come;*

That's what we're looking for. So, go back to section 45, verse 57:

> For they that are wise and have received the
> truth, and **have taken the Holy Spirit for their
> guide,**

Remember, we talked in some detail about that. The Holy Spirit is not the same thing as the Holy Ghost. The Holy Spirit is that channel, that conduit that comes from the Father and the Son. It is the channel of all truth. It's also called the Light of Christ, the Spirit of Christ, etc. We talked about that. Then it comes out in verse 57 and says that because they have received the truth and taken the Holy Spirit for their guide:

> [they] have not been deceived—

So, you see that formula right there? How are we going to get through, how are we going to maneuver safely and successfully, and be here on this earth through all this turmoil and greet the risen Lord, the King of Kings? How are we going to do that? There is your key. That little verse, in my mind, is the most important verse in all of scripture on how to get through the tribulation of the latter-days and meet the Lord. Verse 57 continues:

> verily I say unto you, they shall not be hewn down
> and cast into the fire, but shall abide the day.

Abide means *to live.* It means *to dwell in.* It means *to take a habitation in* that day. And *that day* is the day of the Second Coming, followed immediately by the beginning of the Millennial Kingdom. That's the key on how to get through it. So, here's the trick. We have to become better at recognizing this message that comes through this channel. The Lord is speaking to us all the time. The problem is, in this world, it's difficult to hear that message because it's still and small and in a whisper, and the world we are in is loud, boisterous, and fast-moving. Mother Teresa made a great statement. I love this statement. She said, *"God is the friend of silence."* I love that. I think that is so true. If you want to find Him, you're going to have to slow down, quiet down, and look inside, because He's inside; He's not outside. This is why one of His names is *"The Great I Am,"* which is a present-tense, not a past-tense or future-tense. It's not "The I Was" or "The Great I Will Be." It's *"The Great I Am."*

That shows us that if you want to find God, you find Him in the stillness of the present. He's right in the present. Isn't it interesting, if you're like me, you spend most of your life in the past or the future? It's very difficult, in the telestial world, to remain in the present and that's where God is. So, the great formula in section 101 for finding God is, *"Be still and know that I am God."* The scriptures teach us bountifully that He's inside. You have to look inside. You have to quiet down, you have to slow down, you have to be in the present, and you have to look inside to find Him. We gave a lesson on being perfected **in** Christ, not by Christ. The key word is *indwelling*. It's an *indwelling* type thing.

With that in mind, we come up to this point. I was talking with a man today about the food storage and preparedness programs of the Church. It's my son-in-law, who has just been asked to be the Ward Preparedness Specialist. He's very talented. He's a Special Forces Austrian Ranger, has great military experience, and is very talented in organizing and developing programs. Within a short period of time, after he'd been called to this position, he had put together an 110-page program for emergency preparedness for his ward. We talked about that at some length. This then, will kind of flow over from where we left off last week. I've been involved in preparedness all my life, and Margie has been involved in it also. We've worked hard to have our home and our property be independent so that in a day of isolation, we could successfully survive that time when everyone might be cut off from everything they need to stay alive in our day. The Church has counseled us for eighty to a hundred years that we should have a program of food storage. The program of the Church is to have a year's supply of food, clothing, get out of debt, have an emergency supply, and where possible, some kind of fuel. Some places in the world don't allow storage of some of those things. That's been the program of the Church for years and years. With that said, it's estimated that roughly about 5%, and I'll give it the benefit of the doubt and say 10%, of the membership of the Church, have followed a program where they could rely on what they have in their home for more than a 2-week period. So, after all this time, even that counsel has not been followed very well by the membership of the Church.

What I'd like to say tonight is that food storage is not going to get you through what's coming. You need to do it because following that program qualifies you to call upon the Lord in an extreme, and have Him answer and say, "Here I am." So, I don't look at food storage and the welfare program of the Church as the vehicle to get us through what's coming. But, I do look at it as a necessary act of faith and obedience to qualify you to tap into the power that will get you through what's coming.

Last week, I ended by talking about guns and weaponry. Let's go over to 3 Nephi 2 and let me show you something that's interesting. There's a lot of discussion going on in the United States about the Second Amendment. The Second Amendment is inspired and it came from Godly men. But, it's my feeling that we're moving into a different day than ever has been seen before. Let me just show you that in 3 Nephi 2:11-12:

> *[11] And it came to pass in the thirteenth year there began to be wars and contentions throughout all the land; for the Gadianton robbers had become so numerous, and did slay so many of the people, and did lay waste so many cities, and did spread so much death and carnage throughout the land, that it became expedient that all the people, both the Nephites and the Lamanites, **should take up arms against them**.*
>
> *[12] Therefore, all the Lamanites who had become converted unto the Lord* [see, these are members of the Church] *did unite with their brethren, the Nephites,* [we are talking about baptized members of the Church] *and **were compelled, for the safety of their lives** and their women and their children, **to take up arms** against those Gadianton robbers, yea, and also to maintain their rights, and the privileges of their church and of their worship, and their freedom and their liberty.*

That's good *Book of Mormon* doctrine. They were commanded and compelled to become weaponized in order to protect their liberties and their privileges. So, you have 3 Nephi 2:11-12, and then the Second Amendment was given in the United States Constitution, according to the Founding Fathers, for American citizens to protect themselves against a government gone amuck! So, it wasn't to protect ourselves from foreign invaders; it was to protect ourselves from our own government. That's in the *Federalist Papers* by James Madison. That's the purpose of the Second Amendment. All of those things I have used in the past to justify buying and learning how to use weapons. So, over the years, as I mentioned last week, I had developed quite an arsenal. If you read that article (*Exchanging Bullets for Bubbles*, see introduction) that was written by my friend Wayne Shute, you know that he's seen that arsenal. When we went to the Philippines, the Lord showed us something different. He showed us that in our day, we're going to be doing something that the Founding Fathers did not look at and that the Nephites were not doing. That is, to establish a Zion society, preparatory to the Second Coming of the Lord. **In a Zion society, you cannot use weapons.** Go with me to 2 Nephi 4 and let me show you the take-off scripture for that thought. I know that this is going to raise a lot of questions and maybe will upset some people who listen to this. Just bear with me, and you're not compelled to believe, but let me lay out my case for what I'm thinking. I felt that I was taught by the Spirit that if I want to be a part of what's coming, in other words, not only to survive the day of the tribulation prior to the Second Coming, but also be a part of a group that the Lord will use to build the New Jerusalem, that it's not going to be done with weaponry. So, in 2 Nephi 4:34 Nephi comes out and gives us a little take-off here. This ties in with our scripture in section 45, and I'll show you how in just a second:

> *[34] O Lord, I have trusted in thee, and I will trust in thee forever. I will not put my trust in the arm of flesh; for I know that cursed is he that putteth his trust in the arm of flesh. Yea, cursed is he that putteth his trust in man or maketh flesh his arm.*

I've learned that when the Lord repeats a statement twice in the same verse, we probably ought to pay attention. Here, He is telling us, in this place and in other places, "You need to learn to put your trust in ME, and let ME fight your battles, unless I tell you otherwise," which He did in the *Book of Mormon*. "You need to put your trust in ME and not man, or in your own strength, or in your own ingenuity, or in your own weapons of warfare." That verse (and several others that we'll refer to tonight) led me to believe that if you want to be a part of what's coming, it will not be by force of arms, by weaponry. People will come out and say, "But Brother Stroud, they did in the *Book of Mormon*." Yeah, that's right, but nowhere in the *Book of Mormon* were they seeking to establish a Zion society. In our day, we're commanded to do that.

Let's go back to section 45 again for just a minute. That little article that Brother Shute wrote (see introduction) has all of these scriptures laid out in it. That article will go into more detail about this. Section 45:66 is talking about the establishment of Zion, the New Jerusalem. The New Jerusalem will be built and be functioning **before** Christ comes. It will be built and inhabited by a group of people who have been transformed and refined by the things that are going to take place in our near future so that they can qualify to build this place and to be involved in that:

> *[66]And it shall be called the New Jerusalem, a*
> *land of peace, a city of refuge, a place of safety*
> *for the saints of the Most High God;*

Notice the three words *peace*, *refuge*, and *safety*. You are not going to enter into the boundaries of the New Jerusalem unless you have made and entered into a covenant offered to you. That entrance covenant is baptism. There is no place within the boundaries, within the city itself, within its walls, for people who have not made covenants with the Lord and kept those covenants. Now, you'll have millions of people, who are not members, who will make their way to this place but will have to be taught and instructed by messengers sent from the city, out to those camps and villages and towns outside of the general city limits of the New Jerusalem. Those people that come that far will have gotten there because they, at minimum, are the honorable and just men and women of the earth and have kept the law of chastity and are morally clean. To get to that place does not require a covenant. To get **into** the city and to participate in what goes on there, does. Now, I don't know all of the details, but the

New Jerusalem will be the place where the 144,000 that we read about in the scriptures, will leave from. These are translated beings that are ordained by the angels and given priesthood power over the elements. The world will be in a societal collapse, with economic collapse and war and turmoil. Pockets of righteous people, members and non-members, will be trapped and will not escape where they are without divine help. These ordained people will rescue those who are trapped and bring them to the confines and perimeters of the New Jerusalem so that they can experience *"a land of peace, a city of refuge, [and] a place of safety."* There, they will be taught. If they accept the gospel from the messengers that come from the city out to the surrounding areas, then they'll be allowed to participate and enter into the city and have the blessings that are available from citizenship of that city.

Student 1: Now, the enemy does not have power over these translated beings, right?

Mike: No, they are beyond that situation. These are men **and women** that now have power over all the earthly elements. A mixture of these are people who are on the earth right now, that are within the membership of the Church, a remnant that is being prepared, and then with that, you'll also have a group that returns with the City of Enoch that will join them. These are the people that are going to be the messengers, the rescuers, to catch people who are trapped in pockets of the world when the world collapses in a general collapse.

Student 6: Brother Stroud, are these the 144,000?

Mike: These are the 144,000, and it's my personal opinion, and I can't prove this, but it's not an exact number. It represents a group of people. I personally believe that it could be a bunch more than 144,000. I believe that it will be men and women and it can even be husband and wife pairs that go out. The important part is that they have their Father's name written in their forehead. That means that they have received the *fullness of the Melchizedek Priesthood,* they've been *called, elected, and made sure,* and their names are written in *the Lamb's Book of Life.* Then they've had hands laid upon their heads by angels or by Gods, and received a higher priesthood order, in order to go out into the telestial world, have power over the elements, and literally not be restrained by time or space.

Student 6: And they are led by a Davidic King?

Mike: The Davidic King is going to have a role in Judah. As I understand it, the Davidic King will be over in the Jerusalem area. This is my opinion now; this is Mike Stroud. The leader on this side, the New Jerusalem, will be Joseph Smith. That's just my opinion. I can't prove it. It's kind of based on what some of the early brethren said.

Go to verse 67:

> *[67] And the glory of the Lord shall be there, and the terror of the Lord also shall be there, insomuch that the wicked will not come unto it, and it shall be called Zion.*

I don't read anywhere in here that there are telestial men and women that hold back the wicked by machine gunfire, or grenades, or tanks, or whatever. I don't see that at all. Look at verse 68:

> *[68] And it shall come to pass among the wicked, that every man that will not take his sword against his neighbor must needs flee unto Zion for safety.*

In other words, if you want to escape and don't want to be out among the wicked, involved in the warfare, in turmoil, and you don't want to be involved in taking the life of another human being, you'll need to be in Zion. Next verse:

> *[69] And there shall be gathered unto it* [the New Jerusalem] *out of every nation under heaven; and it shall be the only people that shall not be at war one with another.*

Can you picture that? The whole world is in a meltdown mode, and we have good people, we have God's people, who are trapped. They can't fly, they can't take ships, and they can't drive cars. I think of my friends in Mongolia. Mongolia is a nation that sits between two superpowers: China and Russia. Mongolia's history has been one of occupation all the way back to the days of Genghis Khan. We went on a mission there in 2006. They had only been released from Russian occupation for a number of years. Before the Russians came in, the Chinese Manchu controlled Mongolia. Now, some of the strongest Latter-day Saints and two stakes of Zion are found in Ulaanbaatar, Mongolia. I was talking to the stake president the other night; we talk weekly on Skype, and we have gospel discussions. I was talking to him, and I said, "Mongolia is like a bone between two junkyard dogs."

He just laughed and said, "That is so true, Elder Stroud."

And, it's not over yet. There are already political things going on that are portending occupation of Mongolia one more time by one or both of these nations. So, here are my beloved friends that I know and love over there, that stand an excellent chance of being trapped, cut off from church, and isolated like nobody you've ever seen. How would they, so many thousands of miles away from where the New Jerusalem will be, ever escape that kind of a thing and come to Zion with praising and singing to a place of refuge, peace, and safety? How can they make it? There's no earthly way that that can happen if you have World War III and thermo-nuclear explosions going off. It will require divine assistance, and that's what we're talking about here. If you're not in the New Jerusalem as in verse 69, you will be in a place of war. It's the only place where there won't be war. Let's read verse 70 and think about bearing arms to protect yourself now:

> *[70] And it shall be said among the wicked: Let us not go up to battle against Zion, for the inhabitants of Zion are terrible; wherefore we cannot stand.*

Ask yourself the question: Do you think Zion's inhabitants are terrible because they are weaponized and fully armed? Look at verse 71:

> *[71] And it shall come to pass that the righteous shall be gathered out from among all nations* [because they are trapped], *and shall come to Zion, singing with songs of everlasting joy.*

Do you know why they're going to be singing those songs when they come? Because they are rescued, and there was no hope for them to get out of the situation they were in without divine intervention. I believe this principle. It's a principle of being able to have *power in the priesthood* by calling down the *powers of heaven* to put a shield of protection over you, your family and loved ones, your property, your possessions, and anything else that you feel inspired to be protected and shielded. I believe that the Lord showed us this at the same time that we were contemplating this whole idea. This all started with my wife because I was going to buy some more ammunition. My wife said, "No matter how much you buy, there is always someone who will have bigger and more."

Yesterday I had a conversation with a man who is a preparedness instructor in his ward. He said, "Mike, I have no doubt that if two people were standing on your doorstep in a hostile situation, you could probably take care of two. What are you going to do if you have two hundred of them standing in the street?"

I said, "Exactly! That's not the answer." So, if you're going to rely on your own wisdom, your own strength, the arm of flesh, you're not going to make it. For that very reason, weapons are not the answer. The answer is the priesthood. I will tell you this. It's a lot easier to go to the store and buy weapons and store up ammunition than it is to come to a point of spirituality where you have ***power in the priesthood***. That's why most people won't make it. It requires more of you in a different direction, to come up and have power to do what we're talking about. The Lord showed us those pictures of the Cebu Temple at the exact time when we were contemplating and pondering this conundrum. I don't know for what other purposes those pictures of the Cebu Temple were given, but I know that they had a profound and lasting effect on Mike and Margie Stroud, and changed our whole direction of thinking about preparedness and how to get through the day that's coming.

I was talking to my son-in-law last night, and he asked, "What are you going to do when you have two hundred people out there that are in a hostile situation, they know you have things that they need, and they're going to come? What are you going to do?"

I said, "Exactly! So, what we need to do is to become invisible." And he said, "What?"

And I said, "You need to become invisible. You need to be able to be in a position, through priesthood power, that these people don't even know you are there. Now, is it possible for the Lord to do such a thing?"

And then my brother-in-law said, "You mean like Jesus in the synagogue at Nazareth when they tried to take Him and throw Him over the brow of a hill, and the scriptures say He disappeared out of their midst?"

And I said, "Exactly." Or, how about the two disciples on the road to Emmaus where the resurrected Christ appears to them? These two men had known Christ before He died. These are two disciples. And yet, they could not recognize Him because it says *"their eyes were holden."* Something happened, and these two men could not recognize the Master until they sat down and He blessed the food. Then it says, *"their eyes were opened...and he vanished out of their sight."* That's the kind of power we need to have. And not only to navigate for ourselves and our family and to help others, but that's also the kind of power you're going to need to have in order to be an instrument in the hands of the Lord, to be used in the days that are coming.

Go with me to *Doctrine and Covenants* 105:9. There are so many of these, and once you start thinking along this line, then the scriptures take on a whole new direction for you:

[9] Therefore, in consequence of the transgressions of my people, it is expedient in me that mine elders should wait for a little season for the redemption of Zion—

The Lord is telling the members of the Church that they need to wait a little season for the redemption of Zion. They tried to do it, but because of jarrings, bickerings, and the general unrighteousness of the early members of the Church, Zion was postponed. Verse 10:

[10] That they themselves may be prepared, and that my people may be taught more perfectly, and have experience, and know more perfectly concerning their duty, and the things which I require at their hands.

*[11] And this cannot be brought to pass until mine elders are **endowed with power from on high*** [that's your temple endowment].

> *[12] For behold, I have prepared a great endowment and blessing to be poured out upon them, inasmuch as they are faithful and continue in humility before me.*
>
> *[13] Therefore it is expedient in me that mine elders should wait for a little season, for the redemption of Zion.*
>
> *[14] For behold, **I do not require at their hands to fight the battles of Zion**; for, as I said in a former commandment, even so will I fulfil—**I will fight your battles.***

Now, you start to put this together. One reason that Zion is terrible is that it can't be defeated. And, anytime anyone makes an attack or attempt against the New Jerusalem, or against translated beings (the 144,000), they end up dead. Not because the people they're attacking have weaponry and arms, but because God fights their battles, or they have *power in the priesthood* where they can call down fire and consume their enemies. That's the place we need to go.

Go to section 103 and let me show you another one. Get a feel for this and start thinking along this line. Don't think about having weaponry. There was a time for that. The Second Amendment was there to protect, and we may, even yet, use Second Amendment rights. But, I'm talking about a *remnant* of people here, brothers and sisters, who are going to have a specific mission to prepare people for Zion and to build up that city. Now, section 103:15 is really an interesting verse:

> *[15] Behold, I say unto you, the redemption of Zion must needs come **by power**;*

In other words, what we're going to do here is not going to happen by political wranglings or by societal manipulations or meanderings. It's going to happen because God is going to endow a *remnant* of men and women **with power** to redeem Zion. This is called *power **in** the priesthood*:

> *[16] Therefore, I will raise up unto my people a man, who shall lead them like as Moses led the children of Israel.*

We're talking about "over here" now because when we're talking about Zion, we're talking about the American Continent, specifically the United States of America, which is the *Book of Mormon* latter-day Promised Land. We're not talking about Judah here. Judah has their own struggle. They're going through their own program over in the Middle East while all this is happening in America. Now watch:

> *[17] For ye are the children of Israel, and of the seed of Abraham, and ye must needs be led out of bondage **by power, and with a stretched-out arm**.*

I want you to look at the word *bondage,* and you'll see footnote 17c. Go down and see what kind of bondage we're talking about here. It's physical bondage, not spiritual. So, what the Lord is doing here, through Joseph Smith in section 103, is making a comparison with what took place with our ancient fathers in Egypt and saying that the exact thing is going to take place in our day. But, now we're talking about the redemption of Zion:

> *[18] And as your fathers were led at the first,* [think Egypt and Moses after 400 years of bondage] *even so shall the redemption of Zion be.*

So, look at the story that took place with Moses there, and the Passover. Look at Egypt. Look at the ten plagues. Look at the things that caused Egypt to be the superpower in the world in its day, and also look at the things that caused it to decline. You can see the same thing in our day. Now, brothers and sisters, when Isaiah sees Egypt, he is seeing a latter-day superpower, the largest superpower on the face of the earth, as was ancient Egypt in his day. When you read Isaiah 19, put the United States of America in place of Egypt because, in Isaiah's writing, Egypt is the USA. When you look at Isaiah chapter 18, you'll see a *"land shadowing with wings."* That is North and South America with the isthmus in between. It looks like a giant bird, with the body and the head of the bird in the center and two outstretched wings as North and South America. You can google that and see that it's very interesting. Chapter 17 is talking about Damascus and the doom of Damascus. Damascus is the capital city of what nation today? Syria. You can go into chapter 17, and it's like reading the headline of the news today on what's happening with Syria and with the refugees and with Damascus in ruins. It says, *"Damascus is...a ruinous heap."* Just google and go to Damascus and ask for images and look what's going on. Think what's happening with the Syrian refugee situation. You read chapter 17, and it's like reading today's headlines. Then in chapter 20, Egypt is attacked and overcome by Assyria. And, like today, Syria is Iraq, Iran, all of the Islamic States, and they form an allegiance with other countries, which I believe are China, Russia, North Korea, and all the Islamic States. The bottom line is, the United States is invaded and overcome for awhile. Now, go back to section 103:17:

> [17] For ye are the children of Israel, and of the seed of Abraham, and ye must needs be led out of bondage [physical bondage] by power, and with a stretched-out arm.
> [18] And as your fathers were led at the first, even so shall the redemption of Zion be.

Now, go back to Exodus and read what happened there, and we're going to see a replay of that in our day. The interesting thing is that if you'll look and find out what the modern-day name is for the nations that participated in Exodus, you'll see that it's happening today, just like it did in Isaiah's day. It's so fascinating! Now, we're not through yet. The United States is going to suffer a period of occupation. It's my opinion, this is Mike Stroud, that the Russians will attack the East coast, the Chinese will attack the West coast, and they'll move inward from there. Their invasion will be successful. They'll put all of those cities and states into bondage until they reach about eleven states that go from the Canadian border to the Mexican border, right on through the heart of this country, called the Rocky Mountain States; and there the invasion will stall. We'll talk about that. There's a prophecy by Joseph Smith on that. Now, come back with me now to verse 19. Daniel and Revelation both talk about the saints being attacked by a foreign power and taken into bondage, but it will be for only a short time. Therefore, we'll have to learn how to submit and wait patiently on the Lord:

> [19] Therefore, let not your hearts faint, for I say not unto you as I said unto your fathers: [think about the Israelites in Egypt under Moses] Mine angel shall go up before you, but not my presence.

See, anciently, Christ did not lead the Children of Israel out of bondage because they couldn't come up to that level of spirituality. They had an angel that brought them out, an angel of death. And then Christ wanted to be their God, but they rejected Him, so that angel continued to guide them in the wilderness for forty years. They did not have the presence of Christ as their guide for forty years while wandering in the wilderness. But, now watch:

> *[20] But I say unto you: Mine angels shall go up before you, **and also my presence**, and in time ye shall possess the goodly land.*

And, *"the goodly land"* is the New Jerusalem. It's the Heavenly City.

We've got some real exciting times ahead of us. Joseph Smith said this, *"Noah came before the flood. I have come before the fire."* Now, with that in mind, I'd like to turn again, in ending tonight's lesson, with President Russell M. Nelson's priesthood talk, given in April 2016. He opened the Priesthood Session with this talk, and President Monson closed it with a little five-minute talk. This is my opinion: I think those opening and closing addresses give the most important message we've received in general conference in fifty years. I think what President Nelson was inspired by the Lord to do, was to lay out a program where we can now start to seek for something beyond putting our trust in our **own** strength and our **own** wisdom and seek for something that he calls *"power in the priesthood."* He has four fears. You can look at this. I've done this a little bit, but I'm going to go over it again and end tonight with these four fears because I think this is a clarion call for Melchizedek Priesthood men to "come up" and obtain what we've been talking about tonight: power to call down the *powers of heaven*, power to put a shield over your property and over your family, power to pray differently than you've ever done before, and power over the elements to bless your animals, your land, your trees, your family, your wife and your children. And you need the power to put a shield of protection over them because, as I read the scriptures, that's the only way that you're going to get through what's coming, and the only way the Lord can have a people prepared to use as instruments to fulfill these end-time purposes.

Fear #1:

> *I fear that there are too many men who have been given the **authority** of the priesthood but who lack priesthood **power.***

And then he talks about why. We won't go into that. You can look at this talk. Fear #2:

> *I fear that there are too many priesthood bearers who have done little or nothing to develop their ability to access the powers of heaven.*

That's what we talked about last week. Fear #3:

> *I fear that too many have sadly surrendered their agency to the adversary and are saying by their conduct, 'I care more about satisfying my own desires than I do about bearing the Savior's power to bless others.'*

Fear #4:

> *I fear, brethren, that some among us may one day wake up and realize what power in the priesthood really is and face the deep regret that they spent far more time seeking power over others or power at work than learning to exercise fully the power of God.*

I want you to notice that he uses a term here, when he says, *"[we'll] one day wake up and realize what power **in** the priesthood really is..."* Not power **of** the priesthood. He uses this term in this general conference talk that is not found in the scriptures anywhere. That term, *power **in** the priesthood* is not found anywhere in God's written word. It's only found at the veil when you converse with God on the other side. And President Nelson used that term here, and it is a direct reference to the temple. It's subtle, but it's referencing the temple. And then he says:

> *I urgently plead with each one of us to live up to our privileges.*

What are our privileges? Go with me to Jacob 4 in the *Book of Mormon.* Let me show you what our privileges are. These Nephites got to this place. There's a reason we have a record of the Nephites. There are lots of hidden civilizations that have had God minister to them. They have kept records, and those records are hidden in the earth. They are there still, and we'll have them one day. But, He's given us the Nephite record. The reason He's given us the Nephite record is that **these** people came up and obtained what's necessary for us to obtain, in order for us to build the New Jerusalem and be there when Christ comes. Jacob 4:6:

> *[6] Wherefore, we search the prophets, and we have many revelations and the spirit of prophecy; and having all these witnesses we obtain a hope,* [we gave a whole lesson on that hope] *and our faith becometh unshaken, insomuch that we truly can command in the name of Jesus and the very trees obey us, or the mountains, or the waves of the sea.*

Now, this was early in the history of the Nephite people. You see, when Jacob was writing that down, it was five hundred years before the birth of Christ. Here is a group of people who obtained *power **in** the priesthood.* And, they used it. That's why we have this record and not some record of another lost civilization which was ministered to by God. This group obtained the fullness of the priesthood. That's one reason why they became extinct. That's why they were wiped out in genocidal war because where *"much is given much is required; and he who sins against the greater light shall receive the greater condemnation."* These people had *the perfect day*-light. Back to President Nelson's talk:

> *I urgently plead with each one of us to live up to our privileges as bearers of the priesthood.*

Here's your promise in this statement:

> *In a coming day **only** those men who have taken their priesthood seriously, by **diligently** seeking to be **taught by the Lord Himself.***

Take that literally now. Don't try to wrest that. Don't try to manipulate that around. Take that literally. That means you have communion with, an encounter with Jesus Christ, first speaking to you behind the veil and then appearing to you face to face:

> *only those...who...[seek] to be taught by the Lord Himself, will be able to bless, guide* [think about all this]*, protect, strengthen, and heal others.*
> *Only a man who has paid the price for priesthood power will be able to bring miracles to those he*

*loves and keep his marriage and family safe, now
and throughout eternity.*

In the rest of the talk, he lays out three things on how we get this priesthood power. He says:

[#1] *Are you willing to pray **to know how to pray**
for more power? The Lord will teach you.*

Think of 2 Nephi 4. Don't put your trust in man. We've got to come to a point where we're so adept at receiving personal revelation that you drop the training wheels of counsel and teaching and instruction from mortal man. It has its place, but you've got to come up to where you go to heaven yourself and receive light.

[#2] *The Lord loves to do His own teaching in His
holy house. Imagine how pleased He would be if
you asked Him to teach you about priesthood
keys, authority, and power as you experience the
ordinances.*

You aren't going to priesthood manuals, folks. Did you catch what President Nelson was telling us? You aren't going to manuals and classes for this. That's not to say that manuals and classes aren't important, but they're training wheels. They are to get you to a point where you go to Him. Catch this one:

[#3] *And if you truly want more priesthood power,
you will cherish and care for your wife,
embracing both her **and** her counsel.*

Last one:

[#4] *Priesthood power can calm the seas and heal
fractures in the earth. Priesthood power can also
calm the minds and heal fractures in the hearts of
those we love.*

Then he ends by saying:

*May each one of us rise up as the man God
foreordained us to be—ready to bear the
priesthood of God bravely, **eager to pay whatever
price is required** to increase his power **in** the
priesthood.*

There it is again!

Student 1: We are relying on you so heavily to teach us, but I guess in a few years I should be to where I don't need to rely on others, right? Is that what you're saying?

Mike: Yes, that's one thing. You may find that one day we are cut off from Salt Lake City. It may be that you'll have to have an open conduit to come just to you, directly through the Holy Spirit, where you can receive guidance and instruction in everything you do—where you go, what you say, what you do—in a coming day.

I think it's no coincidence that this conference was ended by President Monson who tells a story, and I'll close with this. He said:

> *During World War II, a friend of mine was serving in the South Pacific when his plane was shot down over the ocean. He and the other crew members successfully parachuted from the burning plane, inflated their life rafts, and clung to those rafts for three days.*
>
> *On the third day they spotted what they knew to be a rescue vessel. It passed them by. The next morning it passed them by again. They began to despair as they realized that this was the last day the rescue vessel would be in the area.*
>
> **Then the Holy Spirit spoke to my friend:** *"You have the priesthood. Command the rescuers to pick you up."*
>
> *He did as prompted: "In the name of Jesus Christ and by the power of the priesthood, turn about and pick us up."*
>
> *Within a few minutes, the vessel was beside them, helping them on deck.*
>
> *A faithful and worthy bearer of the priesthood, in his extremity,* [there's your key, that's the key to the whole story] *had exercised that priesthood, blessing his life and the lives of others.*

Well, brothers and sisters, I hope we can get a different view. In a priesthood meeting today, I taught about the Sacrament. We usually teach that we partake of the Sacrament to renew our baptismal and other covenants, on a weekly basis, so that we can have the Holy Spirit to be with us throughout that week. Today, I taught that the Sacrament has another purpose. The Sacrament has the purpose that by partaking of that Sacrament, it puts you in a place to protect you and shield you, and provide safety in a day of enormous travail. The Sacrament is another ordinance, an ordinance designed to protect you and to shield you in the days that are coming. Well, thank you very much. God bless you and have a great week this week. Be safe, and we'll catch you again next week!

References:
April 1979 General Conference, "Stand Independent above All Other Creatures" by Bruce R McConkie
D&C 45: 55-57
Matthew 24 destruction at the Second Coming
Matthew 25 parable of the Ten Virgins
John 18:37-38 Jesus and Pilate
2 Nephi 28:14 "...the precepts of men."
D&C 123:7 "...mainspring of all corruption..."
D&C 93:24
D&C 45: 57
Exodus 3; D&C 29:1; 38:1; 39:1 "The Great I Am"
Doctrine and Covenants 101:16 "...be still and know that I am God."
3 Nephi 2:11-12
The Federalist Papers #46 by James Madison
2 Nephi 4:34
D&C 45:66-71
Revelation 7; D&C 77:11; 144,000
Luke 4:28-30 Jesus disappearing from amid those who would cast him off the brow of the hill.
Luke 24 Road to Emmaus
Luke 24:31 *"their eyes were opened...and he vanished out of their sight."*
D&C 105:9-14
D&C 103:15-20
Isaiah 17-20
April 2016 General Conference, "The Price of Priesthood Power" by Russell M. Nelson
Jacob 4:6
D&C 82:3 "...much is required much is given..."
April 2016 General Conference, "A Sacred Trust" by Thomas S. Monson

Mother Teresa: "We need to find God, and he cannot be found in the noise and restlessness. **God is the friend of silence**. See how nature—trees, flowers, grass—grows in silence; see the stars, the moon, and the sun, how they move in silence...We need silence to be able to touch souls."

Chapter Thirty
Podcast 030 Temple Thoughts

As I thought yesterday and today about what we could talk about tonight, I kept having the thought to talk a little bit about the temple. I've really prayed to be directed by the Spirit here. Margie asked, "So, what is the purpose of you wanting to do that?" And the purpose is that maybe some of the things we chat about here will inspire people to want to look at the temple endowment and the things that go on in the temple in a little different view, and elevate their temple worship to a different place. So, what I want to do is share scriptures, the words of the prophets, Church History, and some of my own experiences. I hope the Holy Ghost, gives us utterance and the Holy Spirit guides us here, as we talk about this because it's a very important, and yet, sacred subject. So, first of all, I don't want to do anything that would offend the Spirit of the Lord; and second, I don't want to offend anyone who might be listening to this. And yet, I feel that I need to talk about it. Let's go to section 93 in the *Doctrine and Covenants* for just a minute. It's a take-off scripture. I want you to think about everything that goes on in the temple with the allegory. In a broad spectrum, think about the instruction that we receive. Think about the promises we receive. Think about the doctrine that's taught. Put all of those things together, and let's look at 93:19. The Lord is talking to the Prophet Joseph Smith:

> *[19] I give unto you these sayings* [think about everything that goes on when we enter the

temple] *that you may* **understand** *and* **know** [#1]
how to worship, and [#2] *know what you worship,*

So. this verse is telling us that all of the sayings of the Lord are for a purpose. Specifically tonight, our purpose is talking about the temple, which contains the *mysteries of godliness.* The Lord gives us those things for two reasons: so that we can know **how** to worship Him and know **what** we worship. Now, look at the rest of it. When you know how and what to worship:

that you may come unto the Father in my name, and in due time receive of his [the Father's] *fulness.*

I think that's a significant verse, especially when we're seeking to understand the *mysteries of godliness.* In the temple, there used to be a lecture at the veil. Perhaps you can remember that. I remember sitting in the Salt Lake Temple. When I first got married, I used to go there with my father weekly. I remember that they had the lecture given at the veil after every session. Then it was given only to living endowment sessions. The last time I remember hearing the lecture given at the veil was in the Mesa Temple. At that point, that lecture was only given during living endowments, for somebody going through the temple to receive their own endowment blessings. Between when the prayers were offered in the temple, and when a person passed through the veil is when they gave that lecture. What it was, was a very quick summary of everything that had taken place from the minute you entered into the first room of the endowment ceremony, up to that point, where you were presented at the veil. They gave everything in quick summary. They went over all the names, signs, tokens, and everything that had to do with the endowment. Then they made this statement: "Brothers and sisters, this (meaning all of the signs, tokens, and everything you've received in the temple) is what is called the *mysteries of godliness.*" They summarized that whole veil lecture with that one thing, *the mysteries of godliness.*

So, here are just some thoughts tonight and a couple of little things. Nowhere in the temple allegory is physical death portrayed; the separation of the body and the spirit. In fact, the only time that death is mentioned is when they say *"if you eat of this fruit, thou shalt surely die."* That's the only time that death is mentioned in the temple endowment ceremony. And yet, if you're like me, you've believed that the veil that you pass through in the temple is the veil of death. I always thought that when I pass through that veil, that it represented my death and that I left this world on this side of the veil, and if I was faithful, I entered into the Celestial Kingdom. I have since found that that isn't what is being talked about because death isn not mentioned at all. I've since found that there are many different meanings for the various doctrines in the temple. There are layers of meanings. For a person to come out and say "this particular thing means this, and only this" is not wise because at that point, you put a cap on what God can teach you and that may go many layers deeper and be more significant and more profound than what you knew at that present time. So, I guess you could take going into the Celestial Room as meaning that you're passing through death and entering into the Celestial Kingdom. I suppose that's okay, but it really doesn't fit with what we're learning in the temple.

Let me take you over to another scripture. Go to Hebrews 10. We have little hints and keys that if we're **prayerfully** studying the scriptures, not just reading the words, but prayerfully studying the scriptures, we can pick up bits and pieces of temple truth all through the scriptures that will help us gain a better understanding of them. Hebrews 10:19-21, you'll see some temple things in these three verses:

> *[19] Having therefore, brethren, boldness to enter*
> *into the holiest by the blood of Jesus,*

Notice that the phrase *"enter into the holiest"* has some definite temple references through there. Now, in the temple, you pass through something to enter into a place that is holier than where you are currently standing. In the next verse look at what it says:

> *[20] By a new and living way, which he hath*
> *consecrated for us, through the veil, that is to say,*
> ***his flesh;***

The person we are talking about here is Jesus. So, here's Paul teaching us that we pass through a veil in order to enter into something holy, and that veil is the flesh of Jesus Christ. That's a really interesting statement. So, now we take a look at the veil in the temple. You'll notice that when Jesus was crucified and *"gave up the ghost,"* (in other words, He suffered that physical death) the veil of Herod's Temple, which separated the *Holy Place* from the *Holy of Holies,* was ripped from the top to the bottom. Notice also, that the veil was torn at the same time that the torn and bruised and bloody body of Christ hung on the cross. So, here's the question. Does the veil represent Christ's body? And if so, if we pass through the veil and enter into the presence of another person, and if the veil is the body of Christ, who is the other person on the other side? Whose presence are we entering into when we pass through the veil? Notice what Jesus said:

> I am the way, the truth, and the life: no man
> cometh to the Father, but by me.

So, when you look at the veil, one of the things you can look at is, how many marks are in the body of Christ? If you count up the crucifixion marks in the resurrected body of Christ, you will see that there are two in his feet, two in his hands, two in his wrists, and one in his side, for a total of seven wounds in the body of the Savior. The next time you go to the temple, I want you to take a look at the veil and think about that. If you listen closely to the films and you try to identify the voices, the voice on the other side of the veil is the voice of the person playing The Father. So, what you're doing is, you're passing through Christ, in order to come into the presence of the Father. So, there are some interesting things to talk about there.

Brigham Young said that all of the ordinances of the temple are ordinances of the *Church of the Firstborn.* So, when you enter the temple, you're being introduced to a whole new level, a whole new doctrinal feast of things that pertain to a heavenly church. One of the first ordinances that you participate in is called the initiatory. I remember how thrilled I was when the thought dawned on me that the initiatory ordinance is an *initiation*, hence the word initiatory. You're being initiated from something lower into something higher. The thing you're being initiated into, through the initiatory ordinance, is the *Church of the Firstborn.* So, all along the way, the gospel of Jesus Christ is set up in such a way so that we go from lower to higher, by steps, by increments, and by degrees. The Lord calls it line upon line, here a little, there a little, precept upon precept, until you come to a place where there is exaltation upon exaltation. There isn't just one exaltation. I think that we are used to thinking that once you obtain exaltation, you've obtained all there is. In reality, exaltation is just the beginning of a whole new paradigm of progression. In the scriptures you'll hear terms like *"from eternity to eternity,"* and *"from exaltation to exaltation."* So, when you obtain the celestial world, and you enter in there with your spouse, you've obtained **an** exaltation, not **the** exaltation. That opens up some other things. The next time you go to a sealing ceremony, listen carefully to the words of the sealing prayer. The blessings that the sealer pronounces are not singular; they're all plural. One of the words used in the sealing blessing, sealing ceremony, whether for the living or the dead, is **exaltations**. Another word used is thrones. So, we need to go slower when we go into the temple and listen carefully because single words in the temple can have profound, deep significance on what they are trying to teach us.

I like to make a statement, and it's that the temple ceremony is designed to bring us into the presence of God while in this life, and redeem us from our lost and fallen state. It's not talking about something in some future realm or kingdom, i.e., the Millennium, the spirit world, or the Celestial Kingdom after the resurrection. That's why I mentioned at the beginning that nowhere in the temple allegory is physical death—the separation of the body from the spirit—mentioned. That's our first indicator that what this is trying to teach us is to come up and obtain something in this life, and the temple ceremony is trying to teach us what that is and how to accomplish it. If we grab hold of that idea, then what we see in the temple takes on a whole new appearance, a whole new deeper meaning. So, even though we progress from small to large, from portion to fullnesses, from lower to higher, there is nothing in there that says what the temple is trying to teach us cannot be done in this life. In fact, it's desirable for us to reach out and obtain these fullnesses while we're still a mortal in the telestial world. If we don't do that, does that mean that we're dinged or that we cannot do it sometime after this world? I'm not saying that at all. I'm simply saying that there are advantages to obtaining certain things that most people think are not available until after life in this world. But, what we're talking about here, what the temple is teaching, at least at a deeper meaning, is that we can obtain those things now! It's desirable and advantageous to do so. And, here's the better part. There are people around us, in our wards and stakes, who don't hold significant priesthood positions or leadership positions, either in the ward, stake, branch, or General Authority level who are doing this. That's the important thing. It's being done! The advantages of that are many, but I don't want to go into that tonight. If we were to attain in this life what the temple endowment is trying to teach us is possible to attain, it would change us and how we live our lives from that point forward. It would put us in a position where we would be powerful instruments in the hands of God to bless His other children. There are advantages. Now, I want to talk about one of the things that would happen if this were to happen to you. Again, what we're talking about is to be redeemed from the Fall. Go with me over in the *Book of Mormon* to Ether 3:12, where there is a definition of what it means to be redeemed from the Fall. The *Book of Mormon* gives us that definition. This is the brother of Jared speaking to God. First, in verse 11 the Lord asks:

> *Believest thou the words which I shall speak?*
> *[12] And he answered: Yea, Lord, I know that thou speakest the truth, for thou art a God of truth, and canst not lie.*

Now, verse 13 is a scriptural definition of what it means to be redeemed from the Fall:

> *[13] And when he had said these words, behold, the Lord **showed himself** unto him, and said: Because thou knowest these things ye are redeemed from the fall; therefore [here it is] **ye are brought back into my presence**; therefore I show myself unto you.*

That is redemption from the Fall. Brothers and sisters, it's my testimony to you that the temple ceremony is teaching every man and woman exactly how to achieve that. Let's go back to section 93:19:

> *I give unto you these sayings that you may understand and know how to worship, and know what you worship, that you may come unto the*

Father in my name, and in due time receive of his fulness.

You come back into the presence of Christ first. We've talked at length about that. This is what happened here because this is God that introduces himself, face-to-face, to the brother of Jared. Look at verse 14, back in Ether 3:

Behold, I am he who was prepared from the foundation of the world to redeem my people.
*Behold, **I am Jesus Christ**.*

That's a Second Comforter experience, and that constitutes being redeemed from the Fall. My message tonight is, that **can** happen if we want it to. THAT CAN HAPPEN to every man or woman who has made covenants with the Lord in the temple. The temple is teaching us how to do that. Everything in the temple is geared toward that. When you are brought to the veil, you're brought up there twice. The first time you go there represents your *calling and election* and having it *made sure*. That's the first time. The second time is the *Second Comforter*. So, when we go there, we need to go there looking and asking questions, i.e. "What does this mean? Why do they do that?" Your questions need to get down into minute detail because the endowment ceremony was formulated in the mind of God. And what you're doing when you participate in that ceremony is you are seeking to plumb the depth of the mind of God. You are seeking to understand what He is showing you in symbolism and, in some cases, what He's trying to show you, literally. I used to think that the whole temple allegory was symbolic and that I had to look at everything that was going on in that hour and a half ceremony as symbolic in nature. I come to find out that much of what we see there is to be taken literally. In both cases, the Lord hides His *mysteries* in literalness and in symbolism. All we need to do is discern what's going on there, whether it's to be taken literally, or whether I'm to regard it symbolically.

Another key in there is that you're told to consider yourself Adam or Eve. That's a great key. I remember how I felt when it dawned on me. I watched this allegory unfold and watched the person who is Adam, and I remember what a great revelation that was when it dawned on me that that's Mike Stroud. Adam represents the example of a saved, exalted being and I think we would all agree that he is. It's like Lecture 7 says in *The Lectures on Faith*, that Christ is the prototype of a saved being and that Adam and Eve looked at Christ as their prototype. In other words, if you want to be like him, and be where he is, enjoying the privileges and powers that he enjoys, you do as he does. That's what prototype means. He is what you can be. That's a prototype. Another interesting thing is that his life is a template for ours. A template. It's an interesting word; look it up in the dictionary and see what that means. The root word of template is temple. So, if Adam is a saved being, he's a prototype. In other words, he has done what Christ has done. And if I am to consider myself Adam, and my wife Eve, we look at our ancient mother and father as prototypes of saved exalted beings, and we do what they did, in order to become who they are. That's another great key to the question of "What's going on here?"

It's been fifty-three years since I went through the temple and received my own temple blessings. For thirty-nine to forty years of those fifty-three years, I went through the temple always monthly and sometimes weekly. I went through in September of 1963 for Mike Stroud, and I thought that once I went through that first time, it was finished for me, and every time I went through there for the next forty plus years, it was for the deceased. I had no idea what had happened to me in September of 1963. I had no idea. All I knew was that I could tell that I felt differently in the temple than when I came out of the temple. It was a stark comparison, leaving the world going in, and then leaving the temple and coming back out. I could tell, easily, the difference between the two places, the atmosphere, and the spirit, and because it was so desirable to be there, it kept me coming back. For decades, the only reason I went to the temple, was to provide a service for those who were deceased, and because I felt so good while I was there. I had no idea of, "What does this mean for me?" It wasn't until about fifteen years ago that things started to change. I don't want this misunderstood because I'm not taking anything away from the work that we do for our deceased ancestors. It is necessary, it is essential, it's Godly, and it's heavenly, but I had it first as my purpose for attending the temple. I've changed that in the last fifteen years. I go through the temple now, first and foremost, to help **me** understand how I can come into the presence of God in this life, and be redeemed from the Fall. Even though that slip of paper has information on it for a deceased brother and isn't my own—and I do that work, and I love to do that work, and I know that it's Godly—my first and foremost purpose for going through the temple is primarily for seeking, searching, asking, and knocking for the welfare of my own soul. After three decades of missing that, I switched it around and realized it took on a whole different meaning for me. Does that make sense? I hope that that right there helps the people who listen to this podcast to maybe re-evaluate how you view your temple attendance and the purpose for it. It's easy to know that we go through for the dead, and we should continue to do that, and I don't want to take anything away from that. But, if that is primarily your purpose, I think you're missing out on something so sublime and so poignant. Just by twisting that around and looking back, and saying, "What am **I** to learn from this? What is this teaching **me**?" Our emphasis is pretty heavy on unlocking doors and making opportunities available for people who are restricted in the spirit world and allowing them to accomplish something they can't do without you performing that ordinance, and that is all true. So, let me give you a couple of other things to think about here. These are just thoughts and random things.

Student 6: You made the statement that when we come to the veil, we come twice.

Mike: Yes.

Student 6: So, the first time we come seeking to have our *calling and election made sure*, and the second time we mainly want to pierce the veil?

Mike: And the second time you do. So, if you'll think about the words that are spoken the first time you are brought up to the veil, and the person presents you there. If you'll think of those words, it has to do with what you've accomplished and how faithful you have been up to that point that enables you to even be at the veil. It's because of your faithfulness and your diligence, your unwavering faith. See, that's the only purpose that comes there. Joseph Smith makes a great comment about *calling and election.* He says that it comes after the Lord has thoroughly tried you in all things. Now, think of that statement by the Prophet Joseph and think about what the presenter says when you come to the veil the first time. It's almost a template, one statement to the other. The Lord is going to test you and see what you have done with what you have been given. So, it's a testing place. This is also where you converse with the Lord through the veil. The scriptures call that *the more sure word of prophecy.* That's where you don't see Him, but what you do is converse with Him, He calls you by name, and a conversation proceeds. Your time at the veil right there can give you an idea of what this conversation entails; He's going to see what you've done with what you've gotten. He's going to see if you've been faithful in keeping certain covenants that pertain to your progression up to that point. In other words, you're not going to get any more until you've been proven and judged that you've been faithful with what you've had. Then He can give you more, which is what has happened all along the way. After that, you are presented the second time and invited into His presence. The second time it's the *Second Comforter.* The first time is *the more sure word of prophecy,* and you make your *calling and election sure* by hearing the voice of God call you by name and extend promises to you.

Let's see one of those examples. Go to *Doctrine and Covenants* 132:49. This is Joseph Smith obtaining his *calling and election* and having it *made sure.* He does that by conversing with the Lord through the veil. Now, the experience that Joseph had in the Sacred Grove was not a *calling and election made sure.* It was the opening of a dispensation. There had to be something that opened up the heavens and gave us a dispensation after a long night of apostasy. After that first vision when Joseph is a fourteen-year-old boy, he still, like all of us, has to press forward and learn certain things. He has to learn some doctrine; he has to learn some principles; he has to learn revelation, and he did. So, by the time we get to this point, this is in 1831, the Lord says this:

> [49] For I am the Lord thy God, and will be with thee even unto the end of the world, and through all eternity; for verily **I seal upon you your exaltation,** and prepare a throne for you in the kingdom of my Father, with Abraham your father.

[50] Behold, I have seen your sacrifices,
Do you see what it's going to take to get to that point? The first time up to the veil the Lord is going to want to know if you've been true and faithful with everything you've received. He will ask and find out before you obtain the promise:

I have seen your sacrifices, and will forgive all your sins; I have seen your sacrifices in obedience to that which I have told you. Go, therefore, and I make a way for your escape, as I accepted the offering of Abraham of his son Isaac.

That's Joseph's *calling and election made sure.* That's what it's teaching us, and I'm not going to say that's the only thing it's teaching us when we approach the veil the first time, but that's definitely a part of it—to have your *calling and election made sure.* You need to have that before you can obtain the experience that the brother of Jared had. The *Second Comforter* experience follows the experience of conversing with the Lord through the veil and obtaining the promise of what? What's the promise that Joseph obtained in verse 49? *"I seal upon you your exaltation, and prepare a throne for you in the kingdom of my Father, with Abraham your father."* See the promise you obtain with having your *calling and election made sure*? There's your key, *made sure.* You can have your calling and have your election, but until it's *made sure,* you don't have that promise of eternal life. So, your *calling and election made sure* is to obtain the word of the Lord when He promises you eternal life and exaltation in the presence of the Father and the Son. He does that **by His voice**. You don't see Him. He does that by His voice. And then, at some future time, the key is now turned for you to enter into His presence. That's the second time to the veil. Now, the Salt Lake Temple and the Manti Temple are, to my knowledge, the only two temples that still have a live endowment ceremony. I can remember when it used to be done in the Mesa Temple. Geez, I'm getting old! If you were to go to the Salt Lake Temple, you would pass through four rooms. You would start out in one room, called the Creation Room. Then you would get up and physically move to into the World Room, the second room. These two rooms are on the same floor. They're on the street level floor of the Salt Lake Temple. The Baptistry is always in the basement, or below where the endowment ceremony takes place.

Student 1: Except Hawaii.

Mike: Right. In these temples—the Nauvoo Temple, the St. George Temple, all of these temples where you move from room to room—the baptistery is always down below. In the Salt Lake Temple, from the World Room, you actually go up a flight of stairs. You go up a level and enter into the Terrestrial Room. This room is where the veil is. And then you pass from that room, through the veil, into the Celestial Room. So, there are four rooms there. It's hard for you to see that in the modern temples. It's important that those four rooms be recognized because those four rooms represent four estates of movement; four estates that you are moving through in order for you to obtain the presence of the Lord. The Terrestrial Room in all temples is always representing the third estate. Now, there are four estates. Estate just means a place where you abide, a place where you live, a place where you accomplish things, a place where you take up residence. Abraham chapter 3 talks about two of these estates. The problem is the way our mind works. You see, because there are only two estates mentioned in Abraham, we assume there **are** only two. But, the temple is teaching us there are four. The Terrestrial, third room, represents the millennial world that's coming. That's a great key. That was lost on me for forty years. I never saw that. I'm hoping that will open up a whole new avenue for people listening to this podcast.

In the scriptures, in section 130 it talks about having an *"advantage in the world to come."* The world to come is the third room. It is the third estate, and it is the great, millennial, one thousand year period that we're on the edge of. It is so important to understand that in your temple endowment experience. We have talked about how, as members of the Church, we have a tendency to want to move from where we are, right into the celestial world. In fact, as I mentioned in an earlier class, if you were to ask a hundred Latter-day Saints, doctrinally, in Latter-day Saint theology, "What is the world to come?" they would either say, the spirit world or the Celestial Kingdom. Very few, if any, would say the Millennium. And yet, catch this: every person who is faithful in their second estate, which we're in now, if you're judged worthy to qualify, you have to have a millennial, third estate experience. You don't bypass that. Now, if you don't pass the second estate, then it's a moot point. But, it's in the Millennium where you will learn how to begin ruling and reigning as a king and a queen, a priest and a priestess. That's where that begins. There's no ruling or reigning in the telestial world. As a matter of fact, if you want to be a king in the next world, you must practice being a servant in this world. Those who want kingdoms and thrones in this world will end up as servants in the next world. That's the great paradox of the gospel in these two worlds. Kings and queens in the millennial, third estate are so because they were successful, meek, humble, and lowly in heart; servants in the telestial world. As a matter of fact, the covenant that you make in the telestial world in the temple is called the *law of the gospel*. That whole covenant is designed to put you in a position where you have *interpersonal human relationship interactions* with others. **You have to learn how to get along with people.** That's the whole purpose of the *law of the gospel* covenant that we make in the telestial world. If you remember, that covenant is made in the telestial world. You can read about the *law of the gospel* in Matthew in the Sermon on the Mount, and in 3 Nephi in the Sermon at the Temple. It begins with *"Blessed are they..."* Then there are three chapters in Matthew (5,6,7) and there are three chapters in 3 Nephi (12,13,14) that lay out for you, *the law of the gospel*. That's the covenant you make in the temple, along with a charge to avoid certain things. All of that is setting you up, preparing you, teaching you how to serve others, how to successfully have *human interpersonal relationships*, and learn from that experience. You learn patience, you learn to turn the other cheek, you learn to go the second mile, you learn to not revile when reviled upon, you learn not to accuse, not to judge, not to condemn, and you learn to forgive. That's all part of *the law of the gospel*. And, it's all preparatory, brothers and sisters, to be able to rule and reign in the House of Israel, in the millennial world. That's where it begins. How do we know that's where it begins? The temple teaches us. If you're looking closely, you can find in the steps in the endowment ceremony, the answers to: What is it that I'm supposed to learn while I'm in the telestial world? What is it I was supposed to learn and covenanted to do in the premortal world? What is the purpose of the millennial world, if I am worthy enough to enter in? What can I expect there? What will I be doing? What is the primary purpose of the great third estate, terrestrial, millennial world? We talked about that when we had a discussion on the terrestrial world. Do you think that you're going to rule and reign as a king and queen in eternity without having some practice at it? Do you think you're automatically just going to climb in and have this huge multiple star-stellared kingdom with billions of people who worship you, and you'll know how to rule and reign properly as a priest and a queen without having some practice, and without learning, like everything else in the gospel, precept upon precept, line upon line, here a little and there a little? Don't you think that also applies to you ruling and reigning as a king and a queen? If you say, "yes," then there must be some practice, there must be some beginning, and there must be some foundation or elementary instruction. You're going to begin learning how to do that in the Millennium. Who comprises your little kingdom? Your kingdom in the Millennium won't be as large a kingdom, or as big a dominion as that of the Elohim. The Elohim rule and reign over galaxies. Their children have to begin learning that somewhere. That's one of the purposes of millennial, third estates. Who are those that you rule and reign over in your little kingdom, your little practice place, your little beginning? Why, it's your own family. It's the seed of your body. If your children, grandchildren, great-grandchildren, and all your posterity also qualify to be in the millennial world, those are they over whom you will govern and rule. There's another group, and that's those who, through your instrumentality, have obtained eternal life because of what you did. You put them on the path. You taught them the gospel. You brought them up to a certain point. And, even though they'll have blood mothers and fathers, they can and will call you Mother and Father in your kingdom. Go with me over to Abraham 2:8-10 and let me show you a remarkable thing. This is what the temple endowment is teaching us. This is the Abrahamic Covenant:

[8] My name is Jehovah, and I know the end from the beginning; therefore my hand shall be over thee. [speaking to Abraham]

[9] And I will make of thee a great nation,

Think about ruling and reigning as a king over a nation. That's what kings do. They rule nations.

and I will bless thee above measure, and make thy name great among all nations, and thou shalt be a blessing unto thy seed after thee, that in their hands they shall bear this ministry and Priesthood unto all nations;

[10] And I will bless them [your seed] *through thy name; for as many as receive this Gospel* [catch that?] *shall be called after thy name, and shall be accounted thy seed,*

That's not only the literal seed of your body, but that's those who come unto Christ because of your instrumentality. You bring people to the Savior and they come up through his gospel and are redeemed. Look at the rest of verse 10:

*and shall rise up and bless thee, **as their father**;*

That's called the *law of adoption.* In the early days of the history of the Church, men were sealed to men through something called the *law of adoption.* It was discontinued about 1894, but was practiced from the time of Joseph Smith. He started it, and I think he was killed before we had more information on it. It has to do with building up a kingdom, a nation, which you would then preside over as a priest and a king. Without going into that further, what I want to tell you is, that's one of the purposes of the third, millennial, terrestrial estate. And the Millennium, by the way, is a probationary place because it's possible for you to fail in the Millennium. The temple endowment teaches us the sin that will cause people to fail the millennial estate. You know that because you know that at the end of the Millennium there is a war and Satan is loosed again. It's called the Battle of Gog and Magog—there are two of those; one before the Millennium and one at the end of the Millennium, where Satan is loosed to gather his hosts together for one final struggle. I believe the temple teaches you what the sin is that causes that struggle where so many fall, and it's sexual immorality. We talked about that once before. This is why it's so important to understand that the terrestrial room represents the next world. If you're looking at the temple ceremony, you'll see that as you go into the terrestrial, millennial world, the covenant that you make at the beginning of that is a covenant to be chaste and sexually pure. I believe the violation of that covenant that belongs to that world is what causes the war and the fall of many at the end of the millennial world. I find it so significant that the thing that's causing people to fail the telestial world is sexual immorality. If you are not sexually clean you cannot enter into the millennial world. It's the same sin at the end of that world that disqualifies many from entering into the celestial world. Isn't it interesting that sexuality is the number one thing that disqualifies people from the telestial, second estate and terrestrial, third estate? The temple endowment teaches us that. Why are you entering into a covenant of chastity in the millennial world? That's what you need to ask yourself.

Well, in summarizing: four rooms in the endowment, and in the initiatory there are four booths; and the four booths in initiatory represent the four rooms in the endowment. And one gives added information over the other. It's the same four progressionary, probationary estates: premortal life—booth one, room one; telestial/mortality—booth two, room two; terrestrial/millennial—booth three, room three; and celestial/exalted—booth four, room four. One other little thing to think about: the human hand has four fingers. There's that number four. There are four covenants. You're told that we make five covenants in the temple, but there are really four. The first covenant has two names. It's called *obedience and sacrifice*. That's one covenant, it's not two, and it's made in the premortal world—booth one, room one. You've got to ask yourself that question. The names and tokens and signs that you're given, all correspond to the places of these rooms and places in the temple. There are reasons for all that, and you need to be asking yourself questions: "Why is this happening here? Why do I do this? Why do I say that?" When you start looking at it this way, then the temple ceremony opens way up, and you have an advantage. Rather than just going through an hour and a half allegory and coming out and saying, "Boy, I sure felt the Spirit." That's good.

But, I think we're missing out on so much. The Lord will open this up. There's nothing written on this. The Lord will open it up. If you will go in asking, seeking, and knocking, He is so eager to give and to open. He is so eager, but you have to be asking. If you are not asking, He's not going to answer. Well, I hope that gives a little insight into some things there. I think we're okay without going any further.

There's a reason why you have four fingers and one thumb on your hand. And, I'll just tell you this for something to think about. The thumb is referred to as *the opposer*. If you've lost your thumb (you got it cut off with a saw or something), so that you have four fingers and no thumb, you know that you have nothing to really grasp a hold of, to hold on to. You're told all through the scriptures to be steadfast, to hold onto the iron rod, to cling to it, etc. Well, without a thumb, you can't do it, and the thumb is called *the opposer*. Symbolically you have four fingers, and an opposing thumb and that *opposer* allows you to do things with your hand that you otherwise couldn't do. I want you to just think about that. Think about what we've talked about, the fingers and the thumb on the hand, and it opens up a whole new dimension of temple information. I remember when the Lord showed that to me. The thumb is called *the opposer*. If you look it up on the internet, you'll see that it is exactly right. You should ask yourself questions when you go to the temple, about your fingers and your thumb. You should be asking questions, and the Lord will reveal answers. Right hand, left hand; left shoulder, right shoulder. Colors: green and black. Follow what I'm saying? Things to think about. Well, going around full circle to section 93, the Lord gives us these sayings:

> *[19] that you may understand and know how to worship, and know what you worship, that you may come unto the Father in my name, and in due time receive of his fulness.*

We're done. I was talking to Margie, and we both feel that the majority of the people that listen to these podcasts are endowed members. I think that the nature of the material that we talk about usually lends itself to folks who have received their temple blessings, their endowment blessings. So, being careful, and yet at the same time, doing what my thoughts were to do. I hope that's a blessing to all of you, as it has been to us.

Student 6: I have a question about the thumb. That opposer is opposition.

Mike: It is. You're thinking! Keep going! I can't go into that more because those are areas we can't discuss. But, I will tell you to think about it, ponder and pray about that, meditate. Let the Lord teach you some things. Remember we said that the endowment plumbs God's mind. This is something that is in His mind. In Isaiah 55, when the Lord says:

[8] My thoughts are not your thoughts, neither are your ways my ways...

[9] For as the heavens are higher than the earth, so are my ways higher than your ways, and my thoughts than your thoughts.

And that's true, but He didn't say you can't discern His thoughts, nor are you never invited to find out what they are. He just said that in our natural condition they are so far apart, it's as the heaven is from the earth. And then guess what the Lord does: He invites you to come within.

References:
D&C 93:19
Hebrews 10:19-21
John 14:6 "I am the way, the truth, and the life…"
Ether 3:11-13
D&C 132:49-50
Abraham 3:26
D&C 130:19 "…advantage in the world to come."
Matthew 5,6,7
3 Nephi 12,13,14
Abraham 2:8-10
Isaiah 55:8-9

Chapter Thirty-One
Podcast 031 Progression in Eternity

We had a couple of questions from last week's lesson, *Temple Thoughts*. I had one brother call up and was really concerned about one of the things we said, so I went back and listened to the podcast. What I said was that in order to qualify to enter into the millennial, third estate, terrestrial world, a person needs to be morally clean and that if you are not morally clean, you cannot enter into that world. Which is true, but he took that to mean that if you've ever been morally unclean, it disqualifies you out of hand. And I said, "No, that is what repentance is all about. So, if you have repented of that moral transgression, through the atonement, and been forgiven and are justified by the Lord, you are qualified to enter into the terrestrial world." He was set at ease as soon as I said that. He just figured that if you've ever committed that sin, period, you just don't have a chance. I reassured him that repentance is the key to qualifying to come into that great millennial world.

Another person asked me about the covenants that were mentioned in the four areas of the temple. If you listen closely, there are four covenants in the temple. It sounds like maybe there are five, but if you listen closely, there are really four. The first covenant is made in the premortal world, which is the Garden of Eden state in the temple allegory. That covenant is *obedience and sacrifice*, and it's one covenant, not two. It's important to remember where that is made. It is made before Adam and Eve enter into the second estate where they are cast out into the lone and dreary world. So, that covenant and all covenants have associated tokens and names. If you want to open up the door to personal revelation, then you need to start pondering these things. Look at what happens in each estate, and there are four estates as the temple points out. There are four booths in the initiatory. Each one of those booths corresponds to a room in the temple that you pass through in the endowment allegory. Like we mentioned last week, booth one is the premortal life and it corresponds to the room in the endowment ceremony where you see Adam and Eve before they are cast into the lone and dreary world. Now, the thing that will be interesting is that after you identify them, separate these four areas of progression. If you separate them, you'll notice that in each one of these four rooms or areas, there are associated with that area, laws, covenants, tokens, names, and signs. And it's really important to understand that the token and the sign are directly related to the name and the covenant that's made in that particular place. It really starts to open up for you, and you can have a flow of personal revelation if you'll just start asking yourself questions. Why am I making this sign here? Why is this sign made this way? Why is this name associated with this particular covenant? And why is it made in this estate? When you start asking yourself those questions, things will come alive. Then the endowment allegory becomes a living thing and not just something you go through whenever you attend the temple, so you can feel the Spirit and come out feeling good. That's wonderful in and of itself, but there's so much more.

Booth two is the second estate that we're in right now, and that's why it is associated with water. So, the second and mortal estate is a water-based world. If you go into booth two, you are going to see that there is water associated with what goes on in there. It's in booth two that a cleansing needs to take place and that cleansing takes place with water. So, this world is a water-based world, and of course, we fit into that with baptism and washings and different things like that. The God of this world is the Holy Ghost, the First Comforter. The purpose of the Holy Ghost is to cleanse you, to sanctify you, to purify, and to perfect. His job is to do everything that He's assigned in order for you to be qualified to enter into the presence of the Lord Jesus Christ. That's His job. His main purpose is to prepare you so that you can come into the presence of the Savior. Now, the sequences in the temple, the booths in the initiatory and in the rooms in the temple, are preparing you to enter the third room, which is the Terrestrial Room and is booth number three in the initiatory, corresponding. Again there are tokens, signs, names, and laws that are there. The God of the terrestrial world is Jesus Christ. So, now when you look at the different officiators, for example, in the initiatory: every time you go into the initiatory room you're going to see a temple worker there. Each one of those people who are ordinance workers are symbolic of a member of the Godhead. So, in that second booth, that person that is officiating there is symbolic of the Holy Ghost. When you move into the third booth, the person there is symbolic of the Son of God because that is the terrestrial world and He is the God of the terrestrial, millennial, third estate world. It's interesting to notice that these various people move from booth to booth. But not just anybody can move from one place to another. There's great meaning in that! If you notice who comes from one place to another place and if you understand that that person represents a God, then you can see a sequence of what they are trying to do. So, when you go into the booth, pay a little bit more attention. It's more than just a temple worker in there performing ordinances. It's actually showing you **your** progress from first to second to third estate.

The great world that's coming up is the millennial world where Christ will reign personally on the earth, and everybody will see Him. This is where you see eye to eye. Here in this world, He is behind the veil. Now, when you move from the third booth into the fourth, you'll notice that the person that's in the fourth booth is the one that comes into the third and presents you there, does something, and introduces you into the fourth room. That's the Father. So, in the fourth booth, you enter into the Celestial Room, and that's the Father. In each one of the sequences you are performing ordinances, receiving names, receiving tokens, receiving signs, and these are all necessary for you to have in order for you to move from one estate to the next estate until you eventually come back into the presence of the Father and receive of His fullness.

So again, God is showing us everything through symbolism, and even your own physical body becomes a great symbol of your progress, moving from a premortal estate through the various stages until you come back into the presence of the Father and receive of His fullness. Last week I told you to look at the human hand. I said that the thumb on the human hand is referred to as the opposer. I hope you looked this up and did a little research into it; it's really interesting. It's interesting that you have four fingers, going from a little finger, on up to the ring finger on down to what they call the pointer, and there's so much to be learned in that. All of the covenants in the temple, all of the signs, all of the tokens, are using your hands. There's a reason for that, and there's a reason why the human hand is fashioned the way it is. Even your hand is teaching you about the progress you make, and that correlates with the temple, four fingers, again representing the four estates. The thumb, which is not a part of the four fingers, called the opposer, represents the opposition necessary for you to go through and successfully complete the four estates. If you'll notice when you put your thumb and little finger together and push on those, then you go through and put your thumb on your next finger and push on those, push on your middle finger, then push on your pointer finger, you'll notice on each one of those that the pressure increases. The little finger is the weakest of the four. And then as you go into each one of these fingers then the strength increases until you get to the pointer finger, which is the strongest.

It's my feeling, and this is me, Mike Stroud, now, that each of those four fingers represents those four estates. You grow from the first estate where you're just beginning your progress as a spirit, haven't even been born into this world yet, and get stronger against the opposer in each estate. But what that's showing you is that the little finger, in my opinion, is the first estate. And the next one is the second estate and so on until you get to the fourth. When you get to the fourth finger, it is the strongest of those four. And so, you can look at different things. We talked about the word *sure,* and how it's used in the scriptures and even in that you can see in your own hand there's

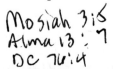
Mosiah 3:5
Alma 13:7
DC 76:4

a possibility for the four fingers to represent four estates, the thumb representing an opposer. I can't talk about this, but you'll remember at certain times on how they give instructions concerning your hand in the temple. You can learn a lot about your progress from estate to estate if you'll just have certain ideas about the thumb. It is the opposer, and in some places, there is no opposition, and in other places, there is major opposition. So, just some fun things to think about as you go through the temple. Any comments on that before we go into what I want to discuss tonight? Those are the questions that came up last week.

I've got a couple of things here that I want to read to you by Brigham Young. This is in the *Journal of Discourses*, Volume 6, pages 274-275. It ties in with what we have been talking about on temple things. As members of the Church, we believe that one of the tenets of the Church is the doctrine called *Eternal Progression*. The early Brethren—Joseph Smith in the King Follett Discourse, Brigham Young in all of his discourses, the Pratt brothers, Orson and Parley, Heber C. Kimball, and all of the early apostles and prophets—taught heavily that the Gods are in a state of progression, that they are progressing and there is nothing ever in eternity that is static. These Gods and Goddesses, the Mothers and Fathers whom we call the Elohim, are always progressing. Elohim is not a single person. Elohim is Hebrew, and it means God. So, the Elohim we are talking about is a society of men and women who have obtained an exaltation. Now, a couple of weeks ago we talked about how exaltation isn't singular; it's plural. If you pay attention to the wording in the sealing ceremony of the temple when men and women are married, you'll see that exaltation is used as a plural. It's exaltations, not exaltation. When we see the writings in the scriptures where it says, "From eternity to eternity, from everlasting to everlasting," it means you can move from a lower exaltation to a higher exaltation, and I'm not so sure there's an end to that. One of the things that the early Brethren learned is the way that the Elohim move or progress and we are following in their footsteps. You can read about this in the first four or five verses of section 88. The Elohim, these glorified, exalted men and women, who are at the upper end of the path that you and I

sealings - "s" kingdoms, principalities?

are on, progress by moving upward and back downward. They progress by ascending and descending. In order for them to go up, they have to go down. The further down they go, the higher they can ascend. Now, that's just two of the motions they make, up and down. The other ones are in and out, entering and leaving. For example, go with me to Helaman 3. There's a phrase that's used in the scriptures, and it's found in several different places. Helaman 3:29-30:

> *Yea, we see that whosoever will may lay hold upon the word of God, which is quick and powerful, which shall divide asunder all the cunning and the snares and wiles of the devil, and lead the man of Christ in a strait and narrow course across that everlasting gulf of misery which is prepared to engulf the wicked—*
>
> *[30]And land their souls, yea, their immortal souls, at the right hand of God in the Kingdom of Heaven, to sit down with Abraham, and Isaac, and with Jacob, and with all our holy fathers, **to go no more out.***

That's a phrase that is used in Alma 7, 29, and 34; *"to go no more out."* It shows that once these people have become a member of that congregation, they come to a point in their progress (at least this progress) and they *go no more out.* They continue to progress, as I'll show you in a minute. This congregation Helaman refers to as the *holy fathers*. Joseph Smith called it *the Elohim*. But, it's not only fathers. It is fathers **and** mothers because there are no fathers there unless there are mothers with them. There is no king there unless there is a queen at his side. There is no priest there unless there is a priestess at his side in this congregation. In the *Book of Mormon* over in 1 Nephi chapter 11, an angel asks Nephi:

> *Knowest thou the condescension of God?*

If you look up the word, *condescend* it's really an interesting word. It connotes voluntarily leaving an exalted place and going to a less than exalted place. And the purpose for that is to go down and gain experience and to **serve others** so that when that period of time is over, you can come to a higher place than you were before you condescended. In progression, it doesn't make any sense to be at a level eight, descend and complete an assignment of ministry or administer and serve, and then go back to a level eight. That doesn't make any sense. So, the Gods are progressing in this way. Let me read this statement. So, again they are progressing in two ways. They ascend and descend, and they enter and leave, they come and go. That will make sense of this Brigham Young statement:

> After men have got their exaltations and their crowns—have become Gods, even the **sons of God**—are made Kings of kings and Lords of lords, they have the power then of propagating their species in spirit; and that is the first of their operations with regard to organizing a world. Power is then given to them to organize the elements, and then commence the organization of tabernacles. How can they do it? Have they to go to that earth? Yes, an Adam will have to go there, and he cannot do without Eve; he must have Eve to commence the work of generation, and they will go into the garden, and continue to eat and drink of the fruits of the corporeal world, until this greater matter is diffused sufficiently through their celestial bodies to enable them, according to the established laws, to produce mortal tabernacles for their spiritual children.

This is the pathway that every man and woman who sits enthroned in an exalted state have gone. There is no other path. It's the same everywhere in all of the universe. It is **the** way. So, when Eve asks, *"Is there no other way?"* And the answer comes back that there is no other way; that is right! They are involved in a pathway that if you deviate from that path, the end result will not take you to where our exalted Mothers and Fathers dwell. I'd like to break this little statement by Brigham Young down first of all; *"After men have got their exaltations and their crowns—have become Gods, even **sons of God**—"* I probably need to give a lesson on this, but there is a difference in becoming *the children of Christ* that Mosiah 5 talks about, and becoming a *son of God* that comes after becoming children *of Christ*. That God that you are becoming a son of is the Son of the

Father, and it's an adoption into His household where you now are an inheritor of all He has. It's not your spirit sonship or daughterhood; all of us are sons and daughters of our Father in Heaven. When you leave His presence and enter into this path, this way, you have to go all the way back, and in the fourth booth and at the veil you are made a *son of the Father* or a *daughter of the Father*. That's what it means to become a *son of God*. Go to section 35 of the *Doctrine and Covenants* and let me show you what this is relating to here. This is not well understood, and it's easy to misunderstand it because there are so many places where it talks about God becoming your Father, and many people say; "How can I become His son when I already am His son?" You have to separate those two things. There are so many scriptures on this that I've got about fifteen different cross references. Go to section 35 verse 2. Here's Jesus speaking:

> *I am Jesus Christ, the Son of God, who was*
> *crucified for the sins of the world, even as many*
> *as will believe on my name, that they may become*
> *the **sons of God**,*

What you want to do is circle that word *God*, and you want to write **the Father**:

> *even one in me as I am one in the Father, as the*
> *Father is one in me, that we may be one.*

Brigham Young says that you come back and you receive your exaltation, and it's because you have obtained this status of a *son of God*. You have to separate that now from what we teach in the elementary beginnings of the Church when we're teaching people what their relationship is to the Father; you are a child of God. You are His son, and you are His daughter. That is not; let me emphasize, <u>NOT</u>, what we're talking about here. This becoming a *son of God*, even according to the Brigham Young quote here, means you've already got your exaltation and your crown, you are already a King of kings and Lord of lords, and that's what it means to become a *son of God*. Over in Psalms chapter 2 verse 7, you can find out what the words are that are spoken to you by the Father when you become His son or His daughter. And the words are:

> *Thou art my Son; this day I have begotten thee.*

That is said when you enter His presence and receive of His fullness.

Now, once you get to that point and you've obtained an exaltation, you are now a god with a small g, not with a capital G. If you look in the scriptures, you will see that when you and your wife get to the first exaltation, you are referred to as gods (with a small g), even the *sons of God* (with a capital G). That small g and that capital G are there for a purpose. You are a small g because you haven't gone through the sequence of events and have been authorized by the Elohim that this statement is talking about. The first authorization you have is that you obtain your exaltation. You and your wife are now celestial beings and have obtained eternal life and an exaltation. The first thing it says is, *"they have power **then**..."* Notice the *then*. Once you're a King and a Lord, a Queen and a Priestess, *"they have power then of propagating their species in the spirit."* So, the first assignment in this progression, after you have obtained your exaltation, is to be given power to beget spirit sons and daughters. Notice that there is no organizing of worlds, no commanding of elements, there's no Garden of Eden. The first thing you do is, you are authorized by those who are in authority over you, to begin having spirit posterity. And that's where we're going to go.

So, after you complete the millennial world, and you learn how to rule and reign in the House of Israel, and you've had practice being a king over a nation of your posterity and others, then the next step after obtaining your exaltation and entering into the celestial world is to begin your spirit family like our Father did. And my spirit inside me is the offspring of that Mother and Father who obtained authority in order to beget my spirit. Now, look at the next interesting thing that's done. Brigham Young says, *"That is the first of their operations with regard to organizing a world."* In other words, you're not going to do anything about organizing a world until you have children that will people that world, to populate it. Then he says, *"Power is **then**..."* So, following when you have your spirit offspring family, and you have a group of sons and daughters who are in a pre-mortal life and looking at you, they see that you have something they don't have. They ask, "How did you get that?

How did you get that body that you have there? How did you get
to be where you are?" Then you start the process with them.
*"Power is **then** given to organize the elements."* That's the next
step. So, you now command element, and it obeys, and you
begin to form an earth. Go with me to Abraham 3 in the *Pearl of
Great Price*, where you can see this sequence. Once you see this,
then when you read the scriptures you will see it all over in here.
It's just marvelous. Abraham 3:22. Here's Abraham looking
back in vision to this premortal world and he says:

> *Now the Lord had shown unto me, Abraham, the
> intelligences that were organized before the world
> was; and among all these there were many of the
> noble and great ones;*

And so, here is Abraham looking back at the spirit family of our
Father in Heaven,

> *[23] And God saw these souls that they were
> good, and he stood in the midst of them, and he
> said: These I will make my rulers;*

There were some who had excelled over others, as this will be
the case with your children. All of them will have an equal
opportunity, but not all of them grow in the opportunities that are
presented. Some excel and in your family, you will have a group
of spirits of whom you will say, "These are the noble and great
ones and these I will make my rulers." Where? Not only there,
but in the new world that you are starting to form, on the new
earth:

> *for he stood among those that were spirits,*

And by the way, He who is standing among those that are spirits
has a body of flesh and bone. It is an exalted, glorified personage
that has a body:

> *and he saw that they were good; and he said unto
> me: Abraham, thou art one of them; thou wast
> chosen before thou wast born.*

Now, look at your next step. See, the spirit family is already
organized in verses 22 and 23; you can see this thing. Now, look
at 24:

> *[24]And there stood among them that was like
> unto God [that would be the Son of God], and he
> said unto those who were with him: We will go*

down, for there is space there, and we will take of
these materials [elements], *and we will make an*
earth whereon these [the spirit family] *may dwell;*
There's your sequence. And it's the same forever. No earth is
created to be dwelled upon until the personages that are going to
dwell there exist. You don't get the cart before the horse here.
So, spirit offspring first, then after a period of time, the second
authorization will be that they can command the elements—
power is given to them. Notice that power is given **to** them.
Notice the authorization to organize the elements here? Then
once the earth is formed, go back down to verse 25:

[25]And we will prove them herewith, to see if
they will do all things whatsoever the Lord their
God shall command them;
[26]And they who keep their first estate
[premortal life] *shall be added upon; and they*
who keep not their first estate [the ultimate
covenant breakers of the first estate were a third
part of the hosts of heaven] *shall not have glory in*
the same kingdom with those who keep their first
estate; and they who keep their second estate
[where we are now] *shall have glory added upon*
their heads forever and ever.

So, now the third thing in this quote by Brigham Young says,
*"Power is then given them to organize the elements, **and then***
commence the organization of tabernacles." Now we've got to
provide bodies for these spirits that are foreordained and
qualified to enter this new earth. Brigham Young asked, *"How*
*can they do it? Have they got to go to that earth? Yes, **an***
Adam..." The first man of all men on every earth bears the title
of *Adam*. Adam is a title. Every first man on every new earth is
called Adam, and the name means, *first man*. By the way, *Eve* is
also a title. Eve means *"the mother of all living,"* according to
Moses 4:26. And Moses 1:34 says:

And the first man of all men have I called Adam,
which is many.

So, every earth has an Adam and that Adam comes down to it.
Now, notice what President Young says, *"...an Adam will have*
to go there, and he cannot do it without Eve; he must have Eve to

commence the work of generation." And notice the first commandment given to Adam and Eve in the Garden of Eden is what? What's the first commandment? Anybody know that?
Student 7: Multiply and replenish the earth.
Mike: That's it! Multiply and fill the earth. And then the second commandment given in the Garden is what? Moses 3:16:

> *Of every tree of the garden thou mayest freely eat,*
> *[17] But of the tree of knowledge of good and evil,*
> *thou shalt not eat of it.*

Over in chapter 4 verse 9, it says:

> *Ye shall not eat of it, **neither shall ye touch it.***

Not only don't eat it, don't even touch it! And this is an interesting little mystery that opens up other questions. So, the first commandment is to do exactly what he is there to do, and that is to provide physical bodies for the offspring of our Father in Heaven. Look at what Brigham says next, *"They will go into the garden, and continue to eat and drink of the fruits of the corporeal world, until this greater matter is diffused sufficiently* [catch this right here] ***through their celestial bodies*** *to enable them, according to established laws, to produce mortal tabernacles for their spirit children."*

So, a question that comes up from missionaries over and over is, "What kind of beings were Adam and Eve when they were in the Garden of Eden?" And the answer to that is, they were celestial beings with celestial bodies of flesh and bone. Brigham Young said that Adam was brought here from an older world and placed upon the new world and that he brought with him his wife, Eve, and they were placed in the Garden. The Garden is a transition zone. The Garden, brothers and sisters, on the new earth, is a terrestrial world. In fact, the great, millennial, third estate that's coming is, as the Tenth Article of Faith says, a paradisiacal world. Another word for paradisiacal is Edenic. The millennial world is similar in many, many ways to the Garden of Eden before the Fall. It's a terrestrial world and a transition zone. All gardens that are prepared by the Gods, by the Elohim, on these new earths fulfill the same purpose. They are transition zones to help a celestial man and woman retransition through terrestrial and down into a telestial world, where they take upon themselves blood and are able to fill the first commandment given in the Garden of Eden, which is to have children and provide physical bodies for spirit offspring; that's what they do. And they live there for one celestial day. One of God's days is a thousand of our measured years and Adam (we don't know about Eve) lived just short of one thousand years in the lone and dreary world, which is **one day**. And notice what the Lord said in Moses 3:17:

> For in the **day** thou eatest thereof thou shalt surely die.

And he lived in that world for one **day**, according to that celestial math ratio that a thousand of our years is **one day** unto God. You can read about that in the *New Testament* in 2 Peter and also in the *Pearl of Great Price*.

And by the way, the reason we do this is, it's the path you and I are on. This is the way we're traveling. This is the way all of the men and women before us have traversed this path. And we now find ourselves in the second estate with mortal, physical bodies clothing our eternal spirits. We received that body through this process of a celestial man and woman descending from an exalted state, passing through a Garden of Eden transition zone, and coming into a mortal state with blood in their bodies, so that physical bodies could be provided for spirit offspring. Does that make sense? I have this under the title "Progression Among the Gods." That's just my title, and this handout by Brigham Young will be there.

What a beautiful plan that is! If you let it sink in, you can see that when you go to the temple and participate in the temple allegory. You can see this statement by Brigham Young all throughout the temple allegory. It shows the progression. It tells you where you are on the path and what you have to look forward to. It gives you knowledge, which provides power to successfully complete the second estate, qualify you to move into the millennial world, and then you better be careful because it is possible to fall in the Millennium. And as we talked about in the past, this sin of the Millennium, according to the temple, appears to be a violation of the law of chastity. We talked about that last week. What's interesting to me is that sexual morality is the great disqualifier in **this** world. It is what's going to keep you from entering into the next world. **The** sin of the telestial world is sexual immorality. And the scriptures list that as one of the great sins, however, it is forgivable. So, if you have committed sexual transgression while in this world, you need to exercise faith, repent, and have the Atonement remove that, so that when it comes time to be judged for your time in the second estate, you can pass that judgment and qualify to enter the next world. Then it's interesting that for the majority of the thousand year period it's a rule and reign of peace. There is no war. Children *"grow up without sin unto salvation,"* and there's no death as we know it; there are no funerals and no need for a police department. But at the end, there is a conflict, a war and in the end, many fall. Satan is loosed one final time to gather his forces, and there's a final conflict. What the temple appears to be teaching us through the third covenant, in the Terrestrial Room, is about morality. The third covenant that you make in the Terrestrial Room, which is the millennial world to come, has to do with being morally clean. With that in mind, I assume that what disqualifies those at the end of the Millennium has to do with human sexuality.

Let me give you another statement here. This is by Orson Pratt. In the temple, in section 76, section 107, 2 Peter 1, and in the Revelations of St. John, it talks about becoming kings and priests. Of course, that is a major part of what takes place in the endowment and the initiatory. Kings and priests: I found this great quote about what that means, and I have used it for quite awhile. I thought I'd share it with you. We'll read this quote and take the last few minutes to talk about it. Again, this will be on your handout for tonight's discussion.

> The priesthood of God is the great **supreme, legal authority** that governs the inhabitants of all redeemed and glorified worlds.

Supreme, legal authority is the keyword I'd like you to tie into. That *legal authority* is divided into two parts. Brother Pratt says that the first one is called the *Kingly authority* and the second one is *Priestly authority*, two authorities. Both of these are part of the Melchizedek Priesthood. Now, think about what goes on in the initiatory. Think about how these words are used in the initiatory and this will give you some ideas. Now, wherever we use *kingly* we're also tying in *queens*, and wherever we use *priestly,* we are also tying in *priestesses*. So, what's taking place in this quote cannot take place with men singly, or women singly because we're dealing with something that the Brethren have referred to in *Doctrine and Covenants* 124 called *"the fulness of the [Melchizedek] priesthood."* That fullness has two authorities.

> *The Kingly authority is not separate and distinct from the Priesthood, but merely a branch or portion of the same. The Priestly authority is universal having power over all things.*

There's your first key. So, when you come up to a point to receive the *"fulness of the Melchizedek Priesthood,"* you are anointed a king and a priest. That takes place in that anointing.

> *The Kingly authority until perfected is limited to the kingdoms placed under its jurisdiction:*

Last week we talked about you being a king and having a ministry to reign over nations, and that begins in the terrestrial, millennial world. None of this is going to take place in this world. You are receiving anointings and promises for the world to come. Now you can, while you are in this world, advance this process through your own faithfulness. It is possible that through the priesthood ordination, called the *second anointing*, for you to be anointed as a king and a priest in this world before you die. It is done in the temple under the direction of the First Presidency, or under the hands of an angel, or God, or a messenger from God who has that authority. That is part of the process called making your *calling and election sure* and you obtain a promise from God that in the world to come you will have eternal life and rule and reign in the House of Israel forever. You obtain that. It's what Bruce R. McConkie said is *"to have the day of judgment advanced."* You are found worthy and judged **before** you die to obtain these promises, these anointings, and these ordinances. And that's happening. It's going on right now. And as we talked about in the past, it is desirable to seek for these things.

Back to the quote:

> *The first* [meaning the Priestly authority] *controls the laws of nature, and exercises jurisdiction over the elements* [think about that last quote by Brigham Young],

> *as well as over men; the last* [which is the Kingly
> authority] *controls men only, and administers just
> and righteous laws for their government.*

So, when we're talking about Kings, we're talking about
governmental administration. It's not the government that we see
at work in the world today, even though the Constitution of the
United States is framed after that heavenly governmental order:

> *Where the two [priest and king] are combined
> and the individual perfected, he has **almighty
> power** both as a King and as Priest;*

So, when you call God *almighty*, or anybody refers to a heavenly
being as *almighty*, it is that they have in them perfected and
combined the two powers of priest and king:

> *The distinctions then, will be merely in the name
> and not in the authority; either as a King or a
> Priest, he will then have power and dominion
> over **all things**, and reign over all. Both titles,
> combined, will not give him any more power than
> either one singly.*

Now, go 1 Nephi chapter 1 and let me show you something
that is interesting. Up at the top, it says, *"THE FIRST BOOK OF
NEPHI,"* and the next words right under it are, *"HIS REIGN
AND MINISTRY."* Now, think about what we have been talking
about tonight. The word *reign* refers to a king, and the word
ministry refers to a priest. What that tells us is that Nephi had
obtained these promises, anointings, and powers. This is not an
earthly king like we're talking about. It is a Melchizedek
Priesthood King and a Priest. Nephi and all of the holy prophets
and kings—Mosiah, Benjamin, all of these righteous kings—had
this authority and were able to function under it. Jacob was
another one. Go with me to Jacob 4. Now, let me show you
something that is interesting. Jacob had this. In fact, Jacob
became the priesthood monarch upon the death of his brother,
Nephi. Priesthood, meaning the authority of the Melchizedek
Priesthood, is the *"great supreme, legal authority that governs
the inhabitants of all redeemed and glorified worlds."* These
men obtained kingdoms on earth, prior to the millennial world
because they had reached up and became Melchizedek
Priesthood Kings and Priests; they obtained the *fullness*. Go with

me to Jacob 4:6 and think about this. Remember that when you are a Priest in this order, Brigham Young said, *"The first* [meaning Priests] *controls the laws of **nature**, and exercises jurisdiction over the **elements**."* Now, look at verse 6:

> *Wherefore, we search the prophets, and we have many revelations and the spirit of prophecy; and having all these witnesses we obtain a **hope**, and our faith becomes unshaken,*

That hope, I would tell you, is more than we think it is. That hope is an **assurance**. Notice that the word in the middle of assurance is *sure*. The hope of the world is out of your control. That is not the hope in Jacob 4:6. This hope has to do with a *sureness* in the Melchizedek priesthood:

> *...our faith becomes unshaken, insomuch that we truly can command in the name of Jesus and the very trees obey us, or the mountains, or the waves of the sea.*

They had this. All of this is available to us. Brigham Young and all the early Brethren understood this, and there are stories of them exercising power over nature and the elements. They could do that because they had attained this level of progress that we're talking about here tonight.

Well, that is what I wanted to chat with you about tonight. These are all things, again, that tie in with the temple. All of this stuff in the temple that we're talking about is alluded to, and once you get a few little keys in your mind and a few little doctrinal points, you can go to the temple, and you can see some wonderful things that they are trying to teach us. You can learn how to come into the presence of the Lord and obtain His kind of life and have an inheritance with Him.

I might mention one other thing that came up last week, and we'll close with this thought. Go with me to Abraham in the *Pearl of Great Price*. Abraham was practicing something that is alluded to in the Kirtland Temple. On April 6, 1836, there were some Heavenly Beings that appeared in the Kirtland Temple; Moses, Elias, and Elijah. The ones that we talk about all the time are Moses and Elijah. We don't talk about Elias. This Elias is not a title that means preparatory; this Elias is an actual prophet, a man who lived in the days of Abraham. We don't know much about him. We know that he lived in Abraham's day and brought back something, or restored the keys of something called the *dispensation of the gospel of Abraham*. It's been my experience that very few people can give a satisfactory idea of what that is. I have pondered on that and wondered about that, and I want to share it with you in closing. This was a question that came up. If you are being taught how to become a king, what good is a king if there is no kingdom? Kings rule over nations and your kingdom right now in this world is your own personal family. You're practicing on your own children, grandchildren, and great-grandchildren. One of the purposes of the Gospel of Jesus Christ is to help you build a kingdom, and you are building your kingdom as you progress up through the gospel. We're learning things now, and the endowment is helping us through the various covenants that we make, how to be successful in organizing our little kingdoms here on this earth and helping to rule and govern our little kingdom through the doctrine of Christ and upon principles of righteousness. We're practicing; that's what we are doing here! So, the beginning of your kingdom is your own family unit. However, when Abraham left the Ur of the Chaldees and traveled with his family he says; *"I took Lot, my brother's son, and his wife, and Sarai my wife...and the souls that we had won."* Interesting, you see, it's missionary work. There are a group of people in this little caravan traveling with them under the direction of God that have been baptized and become a part of the Gospel of Christ through Abraham's instrumentality. So, you've got two groups here. You've got those which are of your own body, the seed of your body, and then you have another group that is a part of your family unit and call you father because of your instrumentality in bringing them unto Christ. And that is what it says in Abraham 2:10:

> *And I will bless them through thy name; for as many as receive this Gospel* [that's your own family **and others**] *shall be called after thy name, and shall be accounted thy seed, and shall rise up and bless thee, **as their father**.*

I would submit to you, that in April 1836 in the Kirtland temple, when Elias brought back the keys to the *dispensation of the gospel of Abraham*, he brought the power to build up your own personal kingdom made up of the seed of your body, and also those who come to Christ because of your instrumentality. That's what we're doing here, but it starts with our own children, and that can be challenging, let alone governing anyone else. Taking care of your family, your children, your grandchildren, your great-grandchildren can be a great challenge, but also a great joy. Your greatest sorrows, your challenges, and your greatest joys are found within your family unit. There's no question about it.

Well, brothers and sisters, that's an hour. I hope that gives you some things to ponder about. A lot of what came out tonight was because of questions from last week's lesson that people called or emailed me about. I wanted to make sure that we covered those things. I will just close by saying that in testimony meeting today, I heard testimonies borne by Latter-day Saints. One thing I heard over and over is that "I know the Gospel is true." I would like to say that not only is the Gospel true, but that the Gospel works. It is a plan, a system. The Brethren say that the Gospel of Jesus Christ is a system that takes the spirit offspring of the Elohim and moves them through schoolroom/classroom experiences called telestial worlds. Step by step, here a little there a little, precept upon precept, line upon line, it purifies and exalts these children so that the children become like the Fathers and the Mothers.

References:
Helaman 3:29-30
Alma 7:25; 29:17; 34:36 "...to go no more out..."
1 Nephi 11:16
Brigham Young *Journal of Discourses*, Volume 6, pages 274-275
Mosiah 5:7 "...the children of Christ..."
D&C 35:2
Psalms 2:7
Abraham 3:22-26
Moses 4:26
Moses 1:34
Moses 3:16-17
Moses 4:9
Moses 3:17
A thousand of our years is one day unto God: 2 Peter 3:8; Abraham Facsimile No. 2, Explanation, fig. 1
Doctrine and Covenants 45:58, "Children...grow up without sin unto salvation."

D&C 124:28 "...the fulness of the priesthood."
Bruce R. McConkie, *Doctrinal New Testament Commentary,* Bookcraft, 1973, 3:330–31.
1 Nephi 1
Jacob 4:6
D&C 110:12, "...dispensation of the gospel of Abraham."
Abraham 2:4, 15
Abraham 2:10

After men have got their exaltations and their crowns—have become Gods, even the sons of God—are made Kings of kings and Lords of lords, they have the power then of propagating their species in spirit; and that is the first of their operations with regard to organizing a world. Power is then given to them to organize the elements, and then commence the organization of tabernacles. How can they do it? Have they to go to that earth? Yes, an Adam will have to go there, and he cannot do without Eve; he must have Eve to commence the work of generation, and they will go into the garden, and continue to eat and drink of the fruits of the corporeal world, until this greater matter is diffused sufficiently through their celestial bodies to enable them, according to the established laws, to produce mortal tabernacles for their spiritual children. Brigham Young **JD 6:274-275**

The Priesthood of God is the great supreme, legal authority that governs the inhabitants of all redeemed and glorified worlds. * * * The Kingly authority is not separate and distinct from the Priesthood, but merely a branch or portion of the same. The Priestly authority is universal, having power over all things; the Kingly authority until perfected is limited to the kingdoms placed under its jurisdiction: the former appoints and ordains the latter; but the latter never appoints and ordains the former: the first controls the laws of nature, and exercises jurisdiction over the elements, as well as over men; the last controls men only, and administers just and righteous laws for their government. Where the two are combined and the individual perfected, he has almighty power both as a King and as Priest; both offices are then merged in one. The distinctions then, will be merely in the name and not in the authority; either as a King or a Priest, he will then have power and dominion over all things, and reign over all. Both titles, combined, will then not give him any more power than either one singly.
[See also 23 July 1843 where Joseph Smith said he would advance from prophet to priest (which happened 28 Sep 1843) and then to king of this earth (which took place 11 Apr 1844). Kings who rule over the different nations, and kings who rule under God in eternity are different functions. The former king has no priesthood, while the latter king holds a fulness of the priesthood. 94. Journal of Discourses, Vol. 2:260; Address delivered in the New Bowery, Great Salt Lake City, by Elder Orson Pratt, April 7, 1855.

Chapter Thirty-Two
Podcast 032 Why Temples

There are questions that have come up that I'd like to share with you. Some people have asked questions about the temple and the initiatory portion of the endowment. We're going to talk a little bit more about that tonight, but one of the questions that came up was concerning the apron as part of our temple clothing. I've had some experiences that might be helpful to you when you go to the temple. It's taken me a long time to learn this. I went to the temple for the first time in September 1963, so for 53 years I've been attending the temple pretty regularly, almost always once a month and sometimes once a week. So, I've grown gradually into an understanding of some things. I want to talk a little more about what I feel is one of the main purposes of the temple. When you go to the temple, you need to go there with questions. If you take the time before you go to formulate specific questions with some real thought and prayer—be specific—and I promise you that you will receive revelation and that the Lord will answer those questions. It is my experience that He is eager to answer our questions and to share with us His mysteries.

I had that experience just on Friday again, and it's fresh on my mind. I had a specific question about why a certain token was given in a certain place. I had about twenty minutes before they started the session to sit in the temple, just sitting in the endowment room, a quiet place, thinking about that. The Lord revealed to me in a very interesting way, even though it didn't take much time, and the thought was complete and what He wanted me to understand was understood perfectly. I rejoiced in that! But, after having an answer to that prayer that I had specifically asked for, He answered two other things that I had not asked for. Reading about Joseph Smith in the History of the Church, I have found that it is very typical. For example, referring to section 76, when Joseph and Sidney were translating the *Bible* they had a question about John chapter 5. Joseph looked at Sidney and Sidney looked at Joseph and said, "I didn't realize there were two resurrections." So, they asked Him the question concerning the two resurrections, the resurrection of the just and the resurrection of the unjust. Because of that one little question, we now have as an answer, one hundred and nineteen verses which are recorded in section 76. And Joseph said that those one hundred and nineteen verses only represent one-hundredth of what they saw in that vision. So, that is typical of the Lord. He is eager for us to ask Him and for Him to be able to reveal to us things that have not been considered and are reserved for personal revelation for those who care enough to spend the time in pondering and meditation, formulating the questions, and taking the questions to Him. It was just a marvelous experience, and I rejoice in it every time it happens.

So, when you go to the temple ask some questions. Here's the nature of some questions you might want to ask. Why do we wear an apron as a part of our clothing? Why is the apron green? Why is Lucifer's apron black? In the living endowment, the person who plays Satan wears a black apron, but you can only see it in some of the temple films. If you look closely in the Manti temple and the Salt Lake Temple, there are some images on that black apron, and that is interesting also. Why are there nine leaves on that apron? Why are they organized in three sets of three? Those are some questions you might want to ask as you go through the temple and you will find out that the Lord is more than willing to answer those questions for you.

When I was in Jerusalem, I had the opportunity to pray at the Western Wall. That ancient wall represents the veil of the Jewish Temple. The reason I say it represents the veil is that they take pieces of paper, and they write prayers on that paper and stick those prayers into the cracks of these huge Herodian blocks. All of those cracks are full as high as a man's arm can reach up, and on the women's side, as high as a woman's arm will reach. They divide it up at the Western Wall; men pray on one side, and then there's a separation, and women pray on the other. Sound familiar?

Student 6: Yeah!

Mike: I watched one Orthodox man come up with a black suit on. He had his Eastern European look, with his large build, a beard, and sidelocks. He was right next to me, and I watched him as he prepared to pray. He removed his black suit coat, put his left arm into the sleeve then tied the right side of that suit coat down around his waist. I thought, "My gosh, there's a Jew that is as close to dressing in the robes of the priesthood, with the robe on the left shoulder, as you'll ever see." He also tied it off with a gartel, which is a garment they wear that is attached around the waist. When I asked, I found out that it separates the human body at the waist; the less spiritual parts of man below the waist, from the more spiritual parts of man from the waist up. I also thought it interesting that they had the robe on the left shoulder, which is an Aaronic Priesthood, preparatory dressing for something higher. How appropriate because all they've ever had for thousands and thousands of years, even prior to the Roman destruction, was Aaronic Priesthood. And I thought about the apron. I thought about how the Lord preserved these things and how fortunate we are, as Latter-day Saints, to be able to have this information, and it answers the question on the apron. Now, you can get a clue as to what the apron represents if you will listen in the endowment when there is an interaction between Lucifer and Adam. Adam says, "What is that apron?" Lucifer gives an answer. Pay attention to his answer, and that will give you some information as to what the apron represents that **we** have on. Think about the colors, green and black, and what they symbolize and you start to get a feel for all these things. So, it's a marvelous experience. Go with questions. The more specific you are, the more specific the answer is and the more likely you are to receive revelation. It requires you to spend some effort in formulating well-thought-out questions that invite personal revelation.

Now, last week's lesson was on *progression in eternity*. I would like to read to you a couple of things here. This is by a man who has received the *Second Comforter* experience, and he said this:

> *Exalted beings sacrifice themselves, and endure punishment on behalf of the guilty. They take upon themselves burdens which they do not deserve. They forgive, they succor, they uplift the unworthy. Pride is incompatible, and selfishness utterly disqualifies a soul from "exaltation." The principles which govern there* [celestial worlds] *are hardly understood here. Most people imagine they will be able to employ means much like Lucifer's to accomplish their expected outcome. They have no concept of the sacrifices and selflessness required to be trusted by the Lord.*

I think that is just a wonderful quote. Here is another one by Chauncey Riddle who was the Dean of Education at Brigham Young University years and years ago when I attended there. This was a CES symposium given in 1989. It's called *The Doctrines of Exaltation*. Think again about progression in eternity, the subject of last week's lesson. He's quoting 1st Corinthians chapter 8 verse five, and Brother Riddle starts out:

> *Though there be gods and lords many, there is but one God, and that God is the priesthood—ordered community of all the righteous exalted beings who exist.*

Let me stop right there and let's look at the definition of the word *Elohim*. We have a feeling that *Elohim* is referring to a single person. The single person is referred to by the Hebrew word *El*, which is a single God. *Elohim* means Gods—plural. So, this will help you in your temple worship if you realize that when we talk about the Elohim, we are not referring to one Man as much as we are to a society or a community of righteous, exalted beings; Men and Women, the Holy Fathers and Mothers:

> *To be invited to join them by hearing the Gospel of Jesus Christ is to receive the greatest message*

in the universe; to be enabled to join them by receiving the New and Everlasting Covenant is to have the greatest opportunity in the universe; to be joined with them is the greatest gift in the universe, which gift is life eternal, sharing with them all the good they have and are.

Now, I want you to listen to this part right here:

This good that they share is righteousness.

There's a definition of righteousness. And I read a similar definition this weekend in the book of Isaiah where the definition of righteousness is to do *things that are right.* Back to Brother Riddle:

Righteousness is that necessary order of social relationships in which beings of knowledge and power must bind themselves in order to live together in accomplishment and happiness for eternity. They bind [seal] themselves to each other with solemn covenants to become predictable, dependable and united so that they can be trusted. They bind themselves to be honest, true, chaste and benevolent so that they can do good for all other beings, which good they do by **personal sacrifice** *to fulfill all righteousness.*

How interesting that is when you contemplate these two quotes and what it is that the Mothers and Fathers, the Elohim, do on behalf of their children from the position of exaltation that they inhabit. Wonderful things!

This past week I was speaking with the stake president in Mongolia. Margie and I served a mission there for two years from 2006 to 2008. My job as a retired CES man was to go and train this new man, who was a district president at that time because he had been employed and hired to be a full-time CES coordinator for the country of Mongolia and he had never had any experience. He received his Ph.D. from the University of Moscow. Even though he is Mongolian, he speaks fluent Russian, and before he joined the Church, he was being trained to be a top communist boss. It's really quite an interesting story. It's been written up in several *Church News* articles and other periodicals from the Church. Quite a story! When I first met him, we sat down, and I asked him one question. I said, "President Odgerel what do you know about the atonement of Jesus Christ?" He had been a member for about ten years.

He kind of tipped his head to one side, and he looked up at me and said, "Elder Stroud, I don't know anything."

I said, "That's a good starting point! While I'm training you on CES policy and procedure, why don't you and I study the gospel together?" And he said that he would like to do that. So beginning within a few days, at a particular time, we isolated ourselves into a room. We took our scriptures and began to discuss the gospel of Jesus Christ. Revelation flowed, and we did that for two years. When I came home from my mission in Mongolia, he asked if we could continue that. So, he and I have been reading, more or less, weekly for ten years, discussing the gospel of Jesus Christ. They don't have access to a temple in Mongolia, and the nearest temple is Hong Kong. He has been to that temple, and he's also been to the temple in Hawaii, but they don't get to go frequently.

And so, as we talked last Tuesday night, he said, "Can we talk about the temple and can you teach me some things about the temple?" So, we began a discussion about the temple. And what that discussion entailed is where I would like to take you tonight.

I'd like to go to section 38 in the *Doctrine and Covenants* and show you what the Lord taught us as we were discussing this. I've used this scripture over and over to show that one of the purposes for the temple and the endowment in the temple is to be endowed with power. President Odgerel is now the Stake President in Mongolia. One of the things that we talked about was that it was my impression that somewhere along the line after we receive our own personal endowment, we get the feeling that for us, the temple experience is now complete and that every time we attend thereafter, it's in the form of providing a service for somebody who is deceased. And we chatted about that. If you were to ask a group of Latter-day Saints why they go to the temple after they have received their own temple endowment blessings, why they continue to go, my experience and my feeling is that the majority would say, "I go there to do work for the dead." Even though that is a great purpose of the temple, what I would like to say tonight is that the primary purpose of temple attendance—your first time and every time thereafter—is primarily for you. If we slip into thinking of the temple as a holy service project for the deceased, then my feeling is that we're missing out on something tremendous and very, very essential. I know that this is the way it was for me. When I went to the temple 53 years ago, as a 19-year-old man getting ready to go to Germany on a mission, I knew absolutely nothing. And for almost 40 years after that, I went to the temple basically for two reasons: number 1, to do work for our deceased ancestors and others; and number 2, to return to that holy place because when I was there I could feel the difference inside that building, versus the atmosphere and environment outside. It was easy for me to see that there was something special, something to be desired about being inside there. And when I came out, the difference between inside and outside was stunning. That was enough to keep me coming back. In the last 14 or 15 years, I've come to understand some different things about the temple, and now I feel that every time I go through the temple, it should be first and foremost for me and the welfare of my eternal soul. And then secondarily, as a project to help those who cannot help themselves, which don't get me wrong, is sacred and is holy. What I'm just saying is that we, as a people, have kind of slipped over into an area where we're missing out on way too much.

In President Nelson's 2016 Conference talk on priesthood, he talks about one of the ways to obtain *power in the priesthood* is to be able to go to the temple and to ask certain questions about *power in the priesthood*. He goes on, and he says:

> *Are you willing to worship in the temple regularly?*

This week I talked to a man who for several months has been attending the temple daily, and it was this talk by President Nelson that has inspired him to do that. He said that this talk changed his life. President Nelson goes on and says:

> *The Lord loves to do **His own** teaching in His holy house.*
>
> *Imagine how pleased He would be if you asked Him to teach you about priesthood keys, authority, and power as you experience the ordinances of the Melchizedek Priesthood in the*

holy temple. Imagine the increase in the priesthood power that could be yours.

I emphasize that what President Nelson is doing is pointing us to our regular temple attendance doing something **for us**. Even though you may have received your endowment blessings years ago, the President of the Quorum of the Twelve is pointing the members, men **and** women, back to the temple so that you can get something holy and significant **for you**.

Now, let's go over to section 38 for just a minute. Let me show you a little exciting thing in the scriptures. So, we ask the question, "Why do I go there?" And the answer is in verse 31. The Lord says:

And that ye might escape the power of the enemy,

There is your first reason for you to go to the temple. You will see that that is a part of temple worship when we get to verse 32:

and be gathered unto me a righteous people.

Put your finger there and let's go over to 1 Nephi chapter 10 for just a minute, and let me show you what the *Book of Mormon* says about the gathering of Israel. And then I will read to you what Joseph Smith said. 1 Nephi 10:14:

And after the house of Israel should be scattered they should be gathered together again; or, in fine, after the Gentiles had received the fulness of the Gospel, the natural branches of the olive tree, or the remnants of the house of Israel, should be grafted in, or [and here is why the gathering takes place] *come to the knowledge of the true Messiah, their Lord and their Redeemer.*

So, the purpose of the gathering is to bring people into a situation where they can come to a knowledge of the true Messiah. Now, this is what Joseph Smith said. This is in *Teachings of the Prophet Joseph Smith*, pages 307-308.

What was the object of gathering the people of God in any age of the world?

Think of the word *gathering* now anytime you read about the gathering of Israel. This is a great principle now that should enlighten our minds in a little different direction. Joseph said:

The main object, was to build unto the Lord a house whereby He could reveal unto his people

> *the ordinances of His house and the glories of his*
> *kingdom, and teach the people the way of*
> *salvation; for there are certain ordinances and*
> *principles that, when they are taught and*
> *practiced, must be done in a place or house built*
> *for that purpose.*

In Ehat and Cook's book called, *Words of Joseph Smith*, on page 215, the Prophet Joseph Smith said:

> *The purpose of the gathering and building the house of*
> *the Lord is to bestow the fullness of the Melchizedek*
> *Priesthood.*

Now, the *fullness of the Melchizedek Priesthood*, brothers and sisters, is when you are chosen, called up, and anointed a king and a priest, a queen and a priestess. And as we've talked about in the past, that *fullness of the priesthood* can be bestowed under the direction of the First Presidency through an ordinance called *the second anointing*, or it can be bestowed by immortal hands, by either God's own hands upon your head (I'm speaking literally), or by having messengers sent from Him for that purpose. The interesting thing is that the purpose of temples is to obtain the *fullness of the Melchizedek Priesthood*, to have your *calling and election made sure*, and to pass through the veil and enter into the presence of the Lord. Going back to section 38, notice that another reason listed is *"that ye might escape the power of the enemy, and be gathered unto me a righteous people."* Now, you see that we have a feeling for what that gathering is. The purpose of the gathering in all ages according to Joseph is to build a temple and reveal certain things that cannot be revealed anywhere else. Now, look at the bottom of verse 31:

> *And be gathered unto me a righteous people,*
> *without spot and blameless—*

There are three reasons for temple attendance that are built into verse 31. This is what they are and what they can do for you:

Number 1- It can empower you to *"escape the power of the enemy."* Even if that is the only reason, wouldn't that be wonderful as we live in this war zone called the telestial world, that when we go into the temple, we are endowed with power, through knowledge and ordinances, so that we can escape Lucifer's power in this world?

Number 2- *"Be gathered unto [the Lord] a righteous people."*

Number 3- That you become *"without spot and blameless."* Those are two different things. Being blameless—the term used there is *justified*. Go over to section 20 in the *Doctrine and Covenants* and let me show you a little bit about that. *Justification* is a legal term that is used in connection with judges, lawyers, advocates, and the bar of judgment, etc., etc., and in section 20, if we go to verse 30 Lord says this:

> *And we know that **justification** through the grace of our Lord and Savior Jesus Christ is just and true;*
>
> *[31] And we know also, that **sanctification** through the grace of our Lord and Savior Jesus Christ is just and true, to all those who love and serve God with all their mights, minds, and strength.*

Here you have two terms, and one precedes the other. You can look this up and do a little study on it. *Justification* is a term all over in the *Book of Mormon*. In *The New Testament* Paul talks about it extensively. Justification means to be brought to a place through faithfulness and the atonement of Christ, to where you are innocent, pronounced not guilty and held blameless before the judgment bar of God and the demands of the *law of justice*. That means that if you come up to a state of *justification* and you were to die while in that state, the demands of divine justice have no claim on you. In essence, you are pronounced innocent and *blameless*. You obtain that state when you receive a forgiveness of your sins. And there is a difference between the **forgiveness** of sins and a **remission** of sins. That's another thing we'll talk about. Now, back in section 38, *blameless* is to be *justified*, and to be *holy, without spot* is to be **sanctified**. Let's go over to Moroni chapter 10 for just a minute. *Justification*, which is being held blameless, not guilty, or made innocent through the atonement of Christ, **precedes** *sanctification*. Verse 33 is the next-to-last verse in the *Book of Mormon*:

> *And again, if ye by the grace of God are perfect in Christ, and deny not his power, **then are ye***

> *sanctified in Christ by the grace of God, through the shedding of the blood of Christ, which is in the covenant of the Father unto the remission of your sins, that ye become holy, without spot.*

So, over in section 38 when the Lord says, *"that ye might escape the power of the enemy, and be gathered unto me a righteous people,"* into the temple, and be *"without spot and blameless,"* He's talking about these two terms. Being *justified* and *without spot* means to be *sanctified*. Now, with that in mind, every time you go there it builds on those three things. Verse 32:

> *Wherefore,*

Meaning because of everything in verse 31:

> *Wherefore, for this cause I gave unto you the commandment that ye should go to the Ohio;*

The Church is in New York at this time and the Lord commands the whole Church to uproot and move to Ohio. Why move to Ohio?

> *and there I will give unto you my law; and there you shall be endowed with power from on high;*

There is your endowment. If you are *blameless* and *justified*, your temple worship can help you retain that status you hope to obtain every time you and I go to the temple. And every time you go to the temple, especially in the initiatory, you become *sanctified* as the purpose of the temple and the power of God descend upon you there; it further *sanctifies* you and makes you *holy, without spot*. In essence, *"endowed with power from on high."* I asked the stake president why he thought that it was necessary for elders and sisters, before they go on a mission, to go to the temple. Why was that necessary? Why not when they have had a year and a half and up to two years experience out preaching the gospel. Why endow them before? As we went over this, it became obvious that these elders and sisters on that call have a big target planted on them; a big target is drawn upon them, from the dark forces because they are the endowed, ordained, emissaries of Christ to preach His gospel. They become primary targets and need that protection. They need to have the garment on. They need to have the information that goes on there. And even though our young men and young women don't understand a lot about the temple, when they enter in and take upon themselves, or accept those covenants that are offered to them, there is a huge degree of protection that distils upon them as they go into the world to preach the gospel. And so, the thought then is that the endowment is a gift. That's one of the feelings I have as we go to the temple, those three things.

They call it the **endowment** ceremony and endowment means gift. So, when people have gone through and received their temple blessings, we ask, "What is the gift that you got? Obviously, you have received something that you didn't have prior to participating in this ceremony. What did you receive?"

And most of the people that I've talked to about that, myself included before I had a feel for this, would sit back and say,

"Gosh, I don't know. Knowledge?"

"Knowledge about what?"

"Knowledge about the creation?"

By the way, the creation account in the temple is different from the creation account in Moses and different from the account in Abraham. You have to ask yourself the question, why do we have three different accounts of the creation? One is a spiritual creation; one is a physical creation, but what's the one in the temple because it does not match in significant places with either of these scriptural records of the creation.

So anyway, is our endowment knowledge? The early Brethren taught that the signs, tokens, and various things you receive in the temple are what is called the *keys of the priesthood*. And in the lecture at the veil that they used to give, they would say, "This information is what is known as the *mysteries of godliness*." Brigham Young taught, in the Nauvoo temple, that when you went through the temple and received your endowment blessing, you received the key to access knowledge from the past, you received another key to access knowledge in the present, and you received a third key to access knowledge in the future. I will put that quote from the Nauvoo Temple minutes in your handouts. If what Brigham Young taught is true, then what you received as you went through the temple, was your own personal Urim and Thummim. You received a gift on how to inquire as to things in the past, things in the present, and things to come. You see, brothers and sisters, everything in the temple is designed to teach you how to come and obtain a *Second Comforter* experience. Everything is designed to take you into the presence of the Lord Jesus Christ, who is called the *Second Comforter*. The *First Comforter* is the Holy Ghost, and His job is to prepare you in all things so that you can have a *Second Comforter* experience. Everything in the temple, from the beginning initiatory ordinance on through to when you enter into the presence of the Lord, is designed to teach us how to do that here on this side of the veil. As we've mentioned in the past, nothing in the temple endowment is talking about after physical death, nothing. Even the scriptures when the Lord talks about the *Second Comforter* and obtaining it in this life, have prerequisites that you have to do in order to get there, indicating that He's inviting you to obtain that and have that experience while still in mortality. So, when you're praying in the temple just prior to entering the presence of the Lord, you're being instructed on how to do that for real. The temple isn't the real thing. The temple is teaching you how to obtain the real thing. That's what that is. So, the more that we can go with that in mind, then greater are going to be the opportunities for us in this life. Can you see the value now in going there and trying to determine what the temple is teaching you? One thing that it tells men and women is that you should consider yourself to be Adam and Eve. That should be a great indicator right there. So, as I look at my first ancient parents, who are going through a telestial world experience and seeking to be redeemed from the Fall through the atonement of the Lord Jesus Christ, they are portraying a step-by-step system on how to do that. All of the various things that we read in the scriptures about being born again, the mighty change of heart, the baptism of fire and the Holy Ghost, the ministration of angels, the visitations of angels, and of dreams and visions; all of these things are steps along the way, mile markers, to measure your progress. At each level of the endowment, whether it's a booth or a room, certain privileges and also obligations are lined out about what you can obtain at this point to help you access the end result, which is the *Second Comforter*.

The purpose of the *Second Comforter*, brothers and sisters, does not stop there. When you have obtained an audience with Jesus Christ, face-to-face—literal, not symbolic—He has a specific mission, and that is to now prepare you to enter into the presence of the Father. The Holy Ghost takes you to the presence of the Son, and the Son takes you to the presence of the Father. And when you enter the presence of the Father there is a ceremony there. In that ceremony, the Lord speaks certain words. You can find these words in Psalms chapter 2. When the Father adopts you, through His Son, so that you become a joint heir with Christ in all that the Father has, then in Psalms 2:6-7 are these words:

> *[6] Yet have I set my king upon my holy hill of Zion.*
> *[7] I will declare the decree: the Lord hath said unto me, Thou art my Son* [or Daughter]*; this day have I begotten thee.*

When you stand in the presence of Father, having been brought there by the Son, the Father says, *"This day have I begotten thee."*

This gives a different meaning to the words that were spoken at the baptism of Christ that is mentioned in Matthew:

> *This is my beloved Son, in whom I am well pleased.*

So, we start to get a feel for those kinds of things. Any questions or comments on that?

Student 6: Why does He need to adopt us? Why does He need to adopt us when we are His children already?

Mike: Great question. I struggled with that for years and years. Go over to section 35. We are His children, and as a child, as a spirit child, you have the privilege of coming up and being an heir. Not all children become heirs. There's a process in order for you to come up and inherit or become an heir. Under the priesthood order, the patriarchal order, in the family there's only one legal heir. In our family, in the family of our Father, Christ is the legal heir. There is a reason for that. It has to do not only with His place of birth, His birth order; but more than order of birth, it has to do with the person He has become as a result of His progress and experience. So, this adoption is not re-adopting you as a child of God. What you are doing is, you're being adopted into His family as a legal heir. It's obvious that of God's children, who are all His spirit offspring, very few, comparatively speaking, are going to come up and be able to qualify for an inheritance with Him, in other words, eternal life. Section 35, verse 2:

> *I am Jesus Christ, the Son of God, who was crucified for the sins of the world, even as many as will believe on my name, that they may become* **the sons of God,**

And you will note that the word *sons* is a small letter **s** and the letter **G** is a capital **G**.

> *even one in me as I am one in the Father, as the Father is one in me, that we may be one.*

So, there is a whole process where you can come up and do that, and it begins with baptism by water. We've talked about the ordinances. You go up through the various steps of what the endowment symbolizes; after baptism of water must be the baptism by fire and the Holy Ghost. That takes place, by the way, in the second booth, which symbolizes the telestial world. There is a second ordinance that is performed in the second booth. When you go to the temple think about that. There are actually two People who come into that booth, and one of them is coming down to perform the second ordinance performed in this world, which is baptism by fire and the Holy Ghost. Go with me to the *Book of Mormon* in 3 Nephi 12, to see who performs that ordinance necessary for this progress. Here you can see these two steps; baptism by water in verse 1, and then go toward the bottom of verse 1. It says:

> *and after that ye are baptized with water, behold* **I** [Christ speaking] *will baptize you with fire and with the Holy Ghost;*

Those two baptisms are symbolically represented in the second booth of the four booths of the initiatory. Go to verse 2:

> *And again, more blessed are they who shall believe in your words because that ye shall testify that ye have seen me* [that's us by the way], *and that ye know that I am. Yea, blessed are they who shall believe in your words, and come down into the depths of humility and be baptized* [with water], *for they shall be visited with fire and with*

> *the Holy Ghost, and shall receive a remission of*
> *their sins.*

Remember earlier we talked about the difference between the remission of sins and the forgiveness of sins. You can have your sins forgiven. Joseph Smith had his sins forgiven multiple times, but the **remission** of sins takes place with the ordinance of baptism of fire and the Holy Ghost. It's a whole different game. It's a step up. Also, with the baptism of fire and the Holy Ghost, you experience the mighty change of heart and are born again. If you go to Mosiah chapter 5 we can see the process of being born again; *Book of Mormon* born-again. They have this baptism of fire and the Holy Ghost, and then an indicator that this has happened is that they have a desire to make covenant to be obedient to the Lord for the remainder of their lives. Verse 7:

> *And now, because of the covenant which ye have*
> *made ye shall be called the children of Christ,*

So, along the road, you also must be adopted into the royal family of Christ. Through the *baptism of fire and the Holy Ghost,* you become **His** children. Notice what it says:

> *his sons, and his daughters; for behold, this day*
> *he hath spiritually begotten you; for ye say that*
> *your hearts are changed through faith on his*
> *name; therefore, ye are born of him and have*
> *become his sons and his daughters.*

So, there is a previous step along the way before you can ever become a son or daughter of the Father, you must, first of all, become a child of Christ and be adopted into the royal family of Christ through His atoning sacrifice. That opens the door for being able to converse with the Lord through the veil. And *conversing with the Lord through the veil* is receiving what we call *the more sure word of prophecy.* And through that experience, you obtain something called *making your calling and election sure.* Now, you're coming up to the *fullness of the priesthood* where you obtain promises from the Lord. It comes from His own mouth to you, not through anyone else because He is the keeper of the gate *"and He employeth no servant there."* So, even though you can obtain blessings and experiences and privileges through the Church of Jesus Christ of Latter-day Saints, if you want these precious promises of eternal life and exaltation they will not come from an employed servant at the gate. They come from the Savior Himself, from His own mouth. That's your next step, that's called *conversing with the Lord through the veil.*

Now, think of your temple experience. There's a place where you come with your temple endowment ceremony, and you desire to converse with the Lord through the veil. That's receiving your *calling and election made sure* through the ordinance of the *more sure word of prophecy.* We talked about that in some detail. After that, it now turns the key for you to be able to enter into the presence of the Lord and sets the stage for you to be introduced to the Father. There are people who have had this experience and have gone all the way into the presence of the Father. I know of one who also saw Heavenly Mother. These are very real promises that are available to all of us. And the temple is a template. I suspect that the real power to all of the blessings that we talk about isn't obtained through institutional membership. That power isn't obtained by going through any ceremonies. It's the membership and the ceremonies that are teaching you that the power that God talks about resides in Him and His Son and other exalted, holy beings that are on the other side of the veil. So, isn't it interesting that the endowment ceremony ends with the veil and you entering into the presence of the Lord? What's that teaching us? It's teaching us to seek for what's on the other side. There are persons on the other side that have information that you and I cannot obtain in any other way. It's interesting wording that Moroni uses with the brother of Jared in Ether 3 and 12 when he says that he could not be kept from *within the veil.* If you're not able to step outside of that veil and access those people who are there, then the privileges, promises, and blessings that they have, that have your name on them and are reserved for you, if you don't access them then you can't obtain that information, and you forfeit that. That is what the temple is all about. Every step is a step-by-step process, one step building on the other, one preparatory for the other; Aaronic Priesthood before Melchizedek Priesthood, portions before fullnesses, faint things before sure things. Everything is pointing toward that crowning experience of stepping from *within the veil* and accessing what's waiting for us.

So, in answer to your question, and you asked a great question, you're already a child of God in that your spirit was begotten by Heavenly Parents. But, that doesn't make you an heir. To become an heir, there is a ceremony, and that ceremony has certain words that are spoken, certain ordinations that are done, and certain ordinances performed in order for you to be recognized in eternity as an heir/son or daughter of our Father in Heaven.

Well, we've been at it for an hour. Those were just some thoughts tonight on the question; Why temples? Why does the Church build temples and why do they want all of their members to go through them? I hope this is not misunderstood because certainly, the work for our deceased ancestors is critical. Joseph Smith said that the greatest obligations that have been laid upon us by the Lord are to search out and do the work for our deceased ancestors. I mean, there's no way you can minimize that. I just fear that after we've gone through for the first time that we somehow lose something that could be a blessing to us every time we go through. And that is: What am I supposed to learn here? How does this help me in the battleground of the telestial world? Does that make sense?

Student 6: Yes. I was just wondering how this relates to our own family, you know because everything is a pattern. The pattern here is the pattern in heaven or vice versa.

Mike: Right.

Student 6: Anyway, that's just a question I have. You gave a lot of good things that I can think on. Thank you.

Mike: I hope that helped. Any other comments?

Student 2: I have a question. You know, I'm confused about patriarchal blessings and the lineage that we receive through those blessings so that we can come to an understanding. Is it just some people that are adopted into the house of Israel, or is the adoption that came up today, is it this same adoption?

Mike: It all depends on how we define the word *gentile*. When Joseph taught about adoption into the house of Israel, he was referring to gentiles who are adopted into the house of Israel, and it literally changes their blood. Now, he takes that literally; it changes their blood. But, in this case, a gentile would be a person who has no claim on descendance through the house of Israel. I might mention that I've talked to several patriarchs over the years, and very few pure gentiles are joining the Church today.

Student 2: Ok, thank you.

Mike: Very few. And so, I hope that helps.

Student 2: Yes, that does.

Mike: You have people from all of the tribes of Israel that are joining the Church. The majority, obviously right now is Ephraim and Manasseh, and will be until we have the return of that large group of people out of the north, as one body coming down to the children of Ephraim to receive their endowment blessings that section 133 talks about. There are two groups of people that comprise the ten lost tribes of Israel. You are a part of one of those groups because Ephraim and Manasseh and Joseph, are one of the lost tribes of Israel. They were a part of the kingdom of the north that was led away into Syrian captivity. So, here you are as members of the Church of Jesus Christ of Latter-day Saints, and if you are Ephraim and Manasseh, you are a member of that group called the lost ten tribes. Now the groups that you come from are groups that went north and then turned west at the Assyrian captivity and went into what today we call Western Europe and intermarried with the peoples there. There is another complete body of people, that right now will number in the millions, that have not intermarried with gentile races. See, Western Europe is considered the great gentile nations of the earth.

Student 2: Okay.

Mike: And the members of the Church that come into the Church today are gentiles in the sense that their descendancy comes out of Western Europe. So, it all depends on how the word gentile is used, and there are four or five different ways that it can be used. Unless you get the context on that right, it can be really confusing.

We who are Ephraim and Manasseh and members of the Church today, or any of the other tribes that are gathering into the Church, are not a part of that separate body of people that were led away and remained a distinct and separate group of people that by this time will number in the millions. When you want to read about their return, go read *Doctrine and Covenants* 133. When they come down, it will be one of the greatest miracles ever in the history of the world. In fact, it says in Jeremiah that it will be such a miracle when they return, that the Lord says you will no longer talk about Moses and the parting of the Red Sea and the children of Israel going through the Red Sea. You won't talk about that. You will only talk about the return of the tribes out of the north. So, this miracle that we are on the edge of will eclipse the greatest biblical miracles anywhere that's ever been spoken. And that's coming up in our day.

Now, for those of us who are Ephraim and Manasseh that have been gathered to the Church and have access to the temple, when this huge body of people come down from the north, Wilford Woodruff said that they do not have their endowment blessings; they are baptized, they have the gift of the Holy Ghost, they been taught the gospel of Jesus Christ, and they have prophets among them, but they have not received their temple endowment blessings of the initiatory and endowment. They come down to receive these blessings under the hands of their brethren, Ephraim, and that is us. So, there are some marvelous things are coming, and I think we are on the cusp. You can see a great cleansing period that is almost on us. And out of that great cleansing period will come forth the *remnant* who are sanctified, and in some cases translated, so that they can perform the miracles necessary previous to building the New Jerusalem. Anyway, that's the thought, did that help?

Student 2: Yes, immensely. So the Arabic people are true gentiles?

Mike: Well, I wonder how many true gentiles there are, meaning there is none of the House of Israel's blood in them. I think that we have been so intermarried, intermingled, and mixed up, that it would be difficult. But, they certainly are in a state of apostasy and worshiping a false God.

Student 2: Now, I have another question. I hope you don't mind.

Mike: Go ahead!

Student 2: I've been trying to figure this out, and I think you can really enlighten me. We've discussed *fullness*; fullness of the priesthood, fullness of the gospel. Is there more than one *fullness of time*?

Mike: *Dispensation of the fullness of time*: this is my opinion. There is one dispensation of the fullness of time, but it's broken up into different segments. I believe that the *Day of the Gentile* that we are in right now is one portion of the *dispensation of the fullness of time*. But the *Day of the Gentile* will end, and there is another segment that is about to come out, and it will be called the *Day of the House of Israel*. In <u>my opinion,</u> both of these are a part of what the Lord calls in the *Doctrine and Covenants* as the *Dispensation of the Fullness of Time*. In order for you to have time fulfilled and everything revealed from Adam up to the present, which is the definition of the *Dispensation of the Fullness of Time*, we have to have the House of Israel gather and obtain and receive their temple blessings. And we're not doing that yet. We're still in the *Day of the Gentiles*.

Student 2: I just know that often, when it refers to Christ's birth in the *Book of Mormon,* it will talk about *"in the Fullness of Time."* Not the *Dispensation of the Fullness of Time,* but in the *Fullness of Time* Christ will be born.

Mike: I think that's probably referring to the same thing because the *Fullness of Time* is the last dispensation of this earth's life before it enters a terrestrial world.

Student 2: So, it's about a 2,000-year segment?

Mike: I think the *Dispensation of the Fullness of Time* started with Joseph Smith and the Restoration.

Student 2: Well, you know in the *Book of Mormon* when it speaks about Christ being born and Nephi seeing what was happening?

Mike: Oh, I see what you mean. *

Student 2: The angel says to him *in the Fullness of Time*.

Mike: Yes, that's interesting. Good point. Good point.

Student 2: Okay, that was just a question I had. Thank you so much, Mike.

Mike: Excellent question, good comment. Anybody else before we end for tonight? Thank you so much! I hope that was helpful tonight.

*Mike follows up with further information on this student's question in the next lesson. See the beginning of chapter 33.

References:
Isaiah 45:19 "...righteousness...things that are right."

April 2016 General Conference, "The Price of Priesthood Power" by Russell
M. Nelson
D&C 38:31
1 Nephi 10:14
Teachings of the Prophet Joseph Smith, pages 307-308
Words of Joseph Smith, page 215; Ehat and Cook
D&C 20:30-31
Moroni 10:33
D&C 38:32
Psalms 2:6-7
Matthew 3:17 "This is my beloved Son, in whom I am well pleased."
D&C 35:2
3 Nephi 12:1-2
Mosiah 5:7
2 Nephi 9:41 "...and he employeth no servant there."
Ether 3:19-20; Ether 12:19 "...within the veil..."
D&C 133
Jeremiah 16:14-15; return of the lost ten tribes greater than the miracle of
parting the Red Sea

The New and Everlasting Covenant by Chauncey Riddle
given at The 1989 Sperry Symposium on the Doctrine and Covenants

The gods.
We begin with the concept of our God. We know of three beings
who are our God: the Father, the Son and the Holy Ghost>>1.
These three are individuals, yet they are also one, and
furthermore, they invite every human being to become one with
them>>2. The good news of the Restored Gospel of Jesus Christ
is that God is our Father and invites us to become as he is and
one with him through his son Jesus Christ.

Though there be gods and lords many, there is but one God, and that God is
the priesthood – ordered community of all the righteous exalted beings who
exist.To be invited to join them by hearing the Gospel of Jesus Christ is to
receive the greatest message in the universe; to be enabled to join them by
receiving the New and Everlasting Covenant is to have the greatest
opportunity in the universe; to be joined with them is the greatest gift in the
universe, which gift is life eternal, sharing with them all the good they have
and are.
This good which they share is righteousness. Righteousness is that necessary
order of social relationships in which beings of knowledge and power must
bind themselves in order to live together in accomplishment and happiness for
eternity. They bind themselves to each other with solemn covenants to

become predictable, dependable and united so that they can be trusted. They bind themselves to be honest, true, chaste and benevolent so that they can do good for all other beings, which good they do by personal sacrifice to fulfill all righteousness.

The contrary of this good is evil. Evil is departing from God's order of righteousness by twisting and/or diminishing it. Evil enables one being in a social order to fulfill his own personal desires at the expense of others, thus to be a law unto himself.

December 28, 1845 [Instructions of Brigham Young from General Record of the Seventies, Book B; three other records of these instructions are William Clayton Minutes, 28 December 1845; Heber C. Kimball, Diary, 28 December 1845, as kept by William Clayton; and, John D. Lee, Diary, 28 December 1845.]

. . . the name that was given to Adam was more ancient than he was the first man—but his New Name pertained to the Holy Priesthood & as I before stated is more ancient than he was—there are 4 Penal Signs & 4 Penal Tokens and should I want to address the Thorone (sic) to enquire after ancient things which transpired on Plannets that roledaway before this Plannet came into existence, I should use my New Name which is Ancient & refers to Ancient things—Should I wish to Enquire for Present things I should use my own Name which refers to present things & should I want to Enquire for Future things I would use the 3rd Name which refers to the first token of the Melchizedek Priesthood—or is the 3rd token that is given—& refers to the son—the 2nd Token of the M. Priesthood is to be given only in one place and nowhere else—but these signs & tokens that pertain to the Priesthood should never be given any where only in such places as belong to the P.H. & that too by none but such as belong to the order of the Priesthood.
(General Record of the Seventies, Book B, 28 Dec 1845

Chapter Thirty-Three
Podcast 033 The Law of Justice

Well, it's been an interesting week. We've had multiple comments from people who have listened to the podcasts. I'd like to take just a few minutes and address some of the things that had come up that I think are interesting and informative. First of all, last week [Student] asked a question, and as I listened to the podcast, I didn't answer the question correctly. She referred to a *Book of Mormon* prophecy that mentioned that Christ would come in the *fullness of time,* and she wondered how that could be when the *dispensation of the fullness of time* was not open until the Prophet Joseph Smith and the restoration took place. I think that the *fullness of time* that's referring to that period when Christ comes, the New Testament period, is different than the *dispensation of the fullness of time.* So, it refers to His coming at that particular time, which is referred to as the *meridian of time.* A meridian doesn't necessarily mean the middle of time. It can, but it doesn't necessarily, and it can also mean the *high point* or the *zenith of time.* In other words, the sun at its highest point in any given day is referred to as the meridian. So, the *dispensation of the fullness of time* begins with Joseph Smith, and we're in it now. It's also my opinion, this is me, that this dispensation is broken up into at least two different segments and that we're in the first segment of that, preparing for the end. Those segments take place before the Second Coming of Jesus Christ. The first segment is called *the day of the*

Gentile and the second segment is called *the day of Israel.* We have not entered into the second segment yet, but I think that we are nigh unto it. It's been a controversy back and forth in the Latter-day Saint community, that the fullness of the Gentiles has come to an end and *the day of the Gentile* has finished, and we've made that leap and that bridge into that. I'm not so sure that that's happened yet, but it's just a matter of personal opinion.

Another question that came up two or three times this week had to do with the sacrament prayer when it talks about *"always have his spirit to be with them."* We taught that the Spirit that is being talked about in the sacrament prayer is the light of Christ, the Holy Spirit, the Spirit of Christ, and is not the Holy Ghost. A couple of you sent me references from general conference talks over the last two or three years, where it was specifically pointed out that the Spirit spoken of in the sacrament prayer is the Holy Ghost. So, there seemed to be a contradiction there on what we were teaching and what had been taught in general conference. Let me just explain to you my feelings on that. It is my feeling that the Church of Jesus Christ of Latter-day Saints, today, is for us what the Law of Moses was for the Nephites in the *Book of Mormon.* It's preparatory. It's Aaronic Priesthood. It's preparing you for something higher and something deeper, something that has to do with Melchizedek Priesthood Orders. We've talked about the various priesthood orders. General conference is coming up and everything that you'll hear in the Church— general conference addresses, all lesson manuals, all correlated material, everything that we were exposed to today in Church— is what the *Book of Mormon* refers to in Alma 12— as *"the lessor portion of the word."* That's not a negative at all. It's a necessary, preparatory step for something higher. Remember that everything in the gospel of Jesus Christ is designed to move from lower to higher, from lesser to greater, from portions to fullnesses. Everything is designed. And so, the Church has made a decision that what it presents in its general conferences and in its correlated material (lesson manuals and everything) is designed for the convert level member of the Church. And rightly so, and that's the way that it should be. I've heard statistics in the past that the majority of the membership of the

Church is in the convert category, meaning that they've been members less than five or six years. So, everything that we have that's given *generally*, in *general* conference by *general* authorities, *general* handbooks, *general* teaching manuals, are designed to specifically instruct those members of the Church that have not been members for a significant period of time. They need to be nurtured in this.

Now, the other thing that I want to talk to you about is that when the Nephite disciples in 3 Nephi 19, were in the presence of the resurrected Christ, in essence, they had had a *Second Comforter* experience, which is something that we should all seek for, and it's right that we should seek for that. But, after He left the first day and before He came back the second day after they had this experience, the disciples/apostles broke the people into groups and knelt down with them and taught them how to pray. You can read about this in the beginning verses of 3 Nephi 19. While they were in the midst of praying, at the beginning of the second day, He came. The scriptures say, *"They did pray for that which they most desired,"* which was the Holy Ghost. Now, the Holy Ghost is preceded by the Light of Christ. Elder Packer addressed this more than any other general authority in modern times. Now, Elder Bednar has started speaking more about it, showing there is a distinction between these two Spirits. On page 90 in *Preach My Gospel* Elder Packer says this:

> The light of Christ should not be confused with the personage of the Holy Ghost, for the light of Christ is not a personage at all. **Its influence is preliminary to and preparatory to one's receiving the Holy Ghost.**

Now, that's an important concept, especially when you talk about it in terms of the sacrament and in doctrine. Brother Packer goes on and says:

> It is important for a...missionary...to know that the Holy Ghost can work through the Light of Christ. A teacher of gospel truths is not planting something foreign or even new into an adult or a child. Rather, the missionary or teacher is making contact with the Spirit of Christ already there. The gospel will have a familiar 'ring' to them.

198

Now, to a general group of people who are learning the basics and the fundamentals of the gospel, it's not necessary for there to be a distinction between the Holy Ghost and the Light of Christ. However, when you start to progress and learn more, it behooves you to learn the difference and how it applies to you in your day-in and day-out experience here in the telestial world. So, let's look at this for just a minute. When I partook of the sacrament today, I had specific doctrinal things in my mind as to what was going on. When I partook of that sacrament, I made an obligation to take upon myself the name of Christ, always remember Him, and keep His (Christ's) commandments, that I might always have His (Christ's) spirit to be with me. What does that mean for me over the next seven days? The light of Christ, the Spirit of Christ is a compass. It is one of the two spindles in the Liahona. It's designed to point the direction and give you guidance—those two words, guide and direct—every day that you're here in the telestial world. That's the purpose. So, when I partook of the sacrament and took those three obligations upon me, I expect that for the next seven days, I will have this compass, this guide, to do the following things for me. It will say, "Go here and don't go there. Do this and don't do that." It is very elementary, but can, in time, become a huge flow of revelation. Remember that Brother Packer said the Holy Ghost can work through the Light of Christ, but the Light of Christ is preliminary. So, when I hear that the Brethren, in their general conferences addresses, as they address the **general** membership of the Church, are not making the distinction between the Light of Christ and the Holy Ghost, I'm okay with that. I understand that they are speaking to a convert level of membership and it's not necessary to make that distinction at this point. Actually, this quote in *Preach My Gospel* doesn't come to an Elder or Sister until they have grown up enough in the gospel of Jesus Christ to be going out as emissaries now, and teach the gospel and they need to start to understanding these principles. You are not going to have the Holy Ghost come to you unless you have been obedient and become experienced in the revelations that come through the Holy Spirit. The Holy Spirit is given to everybody. The Holy Ghost is more unique and has a different set of ministerial powers that are reserved for people who have been tried and tested and obedient in the Light of Christ. So, basically, what happens is, if I take upon myself that covenant, I have the promise of the guidance of the Holy Spirit, which is not a person. If I'm obedient over the next seven days to that, and I have that experience and that revelation, then within that seven days, I can also qualify for the greater revelations, the greater sanctifying power, and the greater purifying power of the Holy Ghost, the one preceding the other.

Go with me to *Doctrine and Covenants* 93:19 and let me show you why this is important. Here, the Lord makes a distinction on why we should know these things. The Lord says this:

> *I give unto you these sayings*

Think about all the doctrine and everything that is revealed. Think about what's available to us if we will avail ourselves to this. Think about the vast universe of untapped knowledge as it comes to us through revelation. Then the Lord says this:

> *I give unto you these sayings that you may understand and know **how** to worship, and know **what** you worship...*

Those two things: how to worship and to know what you worship. All of these things that can come to us through revelation, through the scriptures, and any light and knowledge are designed to let you know how to worship and what you worship. For what purpose? Why is it important to know how and what to worship? When I say my prayers, I use doctrine I know to be true. In my prayers, I verbally express thoughts and feelings concerning the Holy Spirit and the Holy Ghost. I make a distinction between those two. The more exact I can be in my prayers, and in the truth I am expressing in my prayers, the more I can unlock the powers of heaven and access what's on the other side of the veil. There is a difference between general and specific. Now, notice at the end of verse 19, the Lord tells us why it's so important to know how and what you worship:

> *that you may come unto the Father in my name, and in due time **receive of his fulness.***

Now, you're never going to receive the fullness of the Father with generalizations in doctrine. Never! It will not happen. So, I don't find a conflict with what one prophet teaches and what appears to be expressed as a contrasting doctrine by another prophet. I don't find a problem with that. And that's also a trap that's on the side of the borrow pit of this life's road. Satan is always waiting in the pits to cause a crisis of faith, to accuse, and find fault. We're just not in the business of doing that. We're not going to do that. So, what you do is learn the doctrine just as exactly as you can. The Lord wants you to be exact. You're going to take this knowledge into eternity with you, and the more specific and more exact your experience and knowledge, the greater the advantage you are going to have in the world to come.

In the garment you wear as a temple-attending member of the Church, there is a sign that the word *exact* is associated with. It behooves us, especially as endowed members, to move forward and learn doctrine with exactness and get it just as correct as we possibly can. So, that was another thing that came up this week. I'm glad it came up because it caused me to do some pondering and thinking on it. Pray about it and find balance. I will say this, and I mentioned this to the brother and the sister that had this question; I told them that as you move further and further and do what Joseph Smith said—

> *I advise all to go on to perfection, and search deeper and deeper into the mysteries of Godliness. A man can do nothing for himself unless God direct him in the right way; and the priesthood is for that purpose.*

—you will find that the Lord hides some of His greatest secrets, some of His greatest mysteries in **paradox** and in **contradiction**. You have to be prepared to do whatever the Lord tells you to do. Remember what Joseph Smith said, that he had learned that whatever God says, is right. He learned that from sad experience. The template for the organization of the Church, of apostles and prophets—you have fifteen men, and in a couple of weeks we will sustain them as prophets, seers, and revelators—they are a template for each man and each woman and you should seek to have the same gifts in your life that these men exercise as leaders in the Church. Joseph Smith said that each man is encouraged to become a true prophet within his own stewardship, within his own realm. And what we're doing there, we're watching these men, as our leaders, and observing them, so that we can learn how to, within our own realm, within our own stewardship, pattern that very thing for our family and for our loved ones and for those who look to us for some guidance and help. So, that's the purpose of that. I might also say that the Church, as an institution is never ever going to take you into these deeper things. Joseph Smith said:

The things of God are of deep import.

You're never going to get that from the Church. It's not designed to do that. The Church is training wheels. It's preparatory. It's Aaronic. It's preparing you for something more, as everything in the gospel is doing. So, if you want to get the things of God which *"are of deep import,"* then Joseph listed five things in order to do that. He said:

*The things of God are of deep import; and **time**, and **experience**, and **careful** and **ponderous** and **solemn thoughts** can only find them out.*

Did you get those things? Time, experience, and careful, solemn and ponderous thought are the only way to access the deep things of God. That's what we want to do. It's a wonderful thing to pursue that and go after that.

The last comment that came up was on the podcast on *Devils and Unclean Spirits*. I got a note from a lady today, that shared with us some of her personal experiences. Her question was whether we thought these were unique to her or if this was happening more generally. Our experience is that you'd be surprised how much affliction these organized, evil, intelligent beings cause among mortal men and women in this life. You may not even know about it within your own family, within your ward, within your stake, and within society in general, and you'd be absolutely amazed. It's my feeling, that as we move forward now, closer to the Second Coming of the Savior, that this is not going to lessen. It's going to become more blatant and more dangerous. But, here's the neat thing: we live in this day of the internet. The internet is a great societal *Urim and Thummim*. Everything is available: the good, the bad, and the ugly! But, if you are searching for certain areas, for example, the Urim and Thummim, and you're looking into seer stones, you would get a feeling of how those kinds of things can benefit you, individually, even in your own day. The power of Urim and Thummim and seer stones are not limited to apostles and prophets only, or people we read about in church history and in the scriptures. You may not have an actual stone, but you can have those powers in your life. You can seek for those things so that the Lord can bless you with these discerning powers, and the power to be able to see things that are not seen generally in the society around you. That's the definition of a *seer*. So, each member of the Church, as you look at these things, can claim some of these blessings. I've found out that the Lord is anxious to give us whatever we desire in righteousness, and according to *Doctrine and Covenants* 88, *"is expedient for you."* What is expedient for you is that you be preserved, that you and your family be preserved in a darkening, dying world. So, if you can discern that the things that God has used in the past to bless his sons and daughters, would be of value to you in the present, then ask for them. Again, the great secret that's hidden in plain sight is, we don't have these gifts simply because we don't ask for them. One of the great secrets hidden is to ask, seek, and knock. That's a sequence. It begins with asking. Asking leads to seeking and seeking leads to knocking. That's a great pattern for opening up the veil and accessing the tools and the gifts of the spirit that each one of us needs in order to move forward. So, in regard to *Devils and Unclean Spirits:* if any of you would like to chat specifically on that, you can call or email me. The phone number is on the podcast home page, and so is the email address. I will be glad to share with you some experiences that we've had. We're in the process of learning. It is a developing adventure.

I'd like to talk to you for a few minutes about justice, the *law of justice*. The companion to the *law of justice* is the *law of mercy*. It's interesting that when the Lord speaks about justice, He uses the male pronoun, and when He speaks about mercy, He uses the female pronoun. You can skip with me over to Alma 42:24, and I'll show you where that is:

> *[24] For behold, justice exerciseth all **his** demands, and also mercy claimeth all which is **her** own; and thus, none but the truly penitent are saved.*

You can see a pattern of justice and mercy within the family unit between a husband and a wife, at least if you're like my family. The male, the husband, is justice, and the female, the wife, is mercy. Justice wants to exact recompense. Mercy wants to nurture. So, every once in awhile, when the kids want to act up, mom will defer justice to dad, and once dad starts to mete out justice, then mom steps in and wants to lessen the effect. So, even in the man/woman relationship, there is a pattern of justice and mercy.

When we read about justice in the *Book of Mormon* and the writings of Paul in the *New Testament*, those are probably the two best sources for the doctrine of God's justice anywhere in the scriptures. But, the *Book of Mormon* sheds light and knowledge that the *New Testament* doesn't. Paul certainly had a grasp of it, but I believe there are things that have been altered and changed and lost, so the *Book of Mormon* fills in the gaps. Here's how it works, if I understand it correctly. We're going to go to Alma 34 as kind of our reference tonight for what we're talking about. The symbol for justice in the world is a woman. We all know how that woman is: she's blindfolded, she has a sword in one hand and scales in the other. I'm not so sure that that's doctrinally correct. I wonder if that should be a man up there instead of a woman, but it doesn't matter. Justice is black and white. It's exact. It's very impersonal. Justice, in the scriptures, is a term that refers to a courtroom setting. Mercy is more of a term that fits into a home setting—mother nurturing in the home and dad in a justice setting in a courtroom. In the courtroom, you have a bar, and you have a judge who sits at the bar. You have advocates, which is an old English name for lawyers. You have prosecuting and defense. You have the words guilty or not guilty, innocent or guilty. And, another word that fits in with the *law of justice* is blameless. So, either to blame or blameless, guilty or not guilty, innocent or guilty. Those are the terms you see in the courtroom. They all apply to the *law of justice*. The *law of justice* is an eternal law that exists in eternity and that all of the Elohim, all of the Mothers and Fathers that have been through the process to get them where they are, are perfectly aligned in their residence in the eternal worlds with justice and mercy. There is not, nor can there be, a violation of the *law of justice* and as the *Book of Mormon* says, that those that enjoy the title God, would cease to be. So, these Beings, these Men and Women, the Holy Mothers and Fathers, walk a very razor-fine edge of aligning themselves perfectly, never violating this *law of justice*, which basically does two things. Again, it exists in eternity. It doesn't originate with any particular Man or Woman. It's just something that *is*. And, that Being who has perfect alignment with this law, is considered a just Man or a just Woman. They live in a state of *justification*. They're perfectly aligned with this eternal law. God's commandments are also eternal and don't originate with any one particular Person. All of the commandments, all of the ordinances, everything that you and I have been through or will go through, have existed in eternity and is the same path that all of the men and women have walked upon, in order to become exalted Mothers and Fathers. So, when it's asked, *"Is there no other way?"* There is no other way. **This is the way**. As a matter of fact, the early followers of the gospel of Jesus Christ were not called Christians until we get up into Antioch, later in the book of Acts. Prior to the book of Acts, when Jesus ministered, the gospel that He taught and ministered was called *"The Way."* The people who were followers of that were referred to as *"Followers of the Way."* They weren't referred to as Christians. And, it is the only way. So, when Jesus says in John 14:6, *"I am the **way**, the truth, and the life: no man cometh unto the Father, but by me,"* and, "He is the way," exemplifies the eternal pathway that all the Gods, the Mothers and Fathers, have trod in order to get to where they are in their exalted state, and there is no other way. And that *way* says that whenever a commandment of God is obeyed, it always results in a blessing. That's a part of the *law of justice*. We sometimes think that the *law of justice* is always negative. In essence, it's not; it's two-sided. Obey the laws that are eternal in nature and are designed to bring happiness, peace, and progress to the children of the Elohim, and receive blessings, every time. It's eternal in its nature. The other side of that is that disobeying that law always results in a punishment and a consequence for disobedience, always. That's how the *law of justice* works. It dispenses blessings for obedience and punishments or consequences for disobedience. It's very impersonal, just like a courtroom situation. It simply analyses what is, and makes a judgment based on what is.

So, you and I come into this world, and it doesn't take very long for us to make enough wrong decisions with the use of our agency, to violate God's law, and we find ourselves in a sinful, polluted, lost, and fallen state. That's the *Fall of Man*—all of it for a plan; all of it necessary. I keep thinking about what Eve says to Adam after he partakes of the fruit and she explains to him the necessity of it, and he then sees *"that this must be so."* Then, I just love how in a couple of the films, she takes him by the hand when he's looking at Lucifer, she twists his face so that he's looking into her eyes, and she says, *"It is better for us that we should pass through sorrow that we may know the good from the evil."* And that's true! So, it is all designed to do this.

In a priesthood class today, they were talking about the terror, the blood, and horror, that exists in the telestial world. We attended a banquet last night for an organization called Living Hope that provides facilities and resources for young girls who find themselves pregnant and sometimes homeless outside of wedlock. Some of the stories we heard there were just heart-wrenching. It just shows how brutal the telestial world schoolroom can be. And yet, with that, it's a part of the plan. It's important to understand, brothers and sisters, that the darkness and evil in this world are controlled. It does not operate independently from a higher part, which is God, our Father in Heaven. Again, in the temple, you'll hear the words, *"We will **allow** Lucifer, our common enemy..."* Underline the word allow. That's a great insight. So, evil has its place. As a matter of fact, there are no people, Men or Women, among the Elohim, among the exalted Mothers and Fathers, that could have gotten there without the presence of evil in a telestial world classroom. You can't do it. *"It is **better** for us to **pass through** sorrow,"* and they both recognized that. Notice the keywords of that are *"pass through."* We're passing through. You have entered into a classroom; you're going to attend the class, complete the curriculum, graduate, and leave this place. Hopefully, your experience will give you an advantage in the world to come, and when you leave the class, you leave it advantaged and not disadvantaged. Of course, that depends on us.

So, here we are in this world, with the *law of justice*, now, and it has a claim on every one of us. We've been indicted. See, it's a courtroom situation. There is an indictment made against us because we have committed sins and now find ourselves in a place where justice has a claim. What's the claim because of sin? The claim is punishment. Okay, so because of us being in this world under these circumstances, the *law of justice* now has a claim upon us. We've been indicted and found guilty of disobedience to God's commands. That's the way justice works. Let's go to Alma 34:15 for just a minute. This talks about deliverance from the *law of justice*. We need an Intercessor, Someone to come and place Themselves between us, who have been indicted and found guilty of violating God's commands, and the *law of justice*, which now has a legitimate claim upon us to dispense punishments for disobedience. That's how it works. Now, God has provided a way for us to escape that punishment. So, we have in the scriptures, the word *Intercessor*, which means a Person who intercedes on our behalf. We have words called Mediator, Intercessor, Redeemer, Savior. All of these words are indicating the need for a rescue. It's interesting that each one of us leaves the Father's presence, comes into this world, and He loses every one of His children because this world quickly and effectively puts us in a position where we cannot be in His presence because of what we've done. Again, I emphasize, it's all a part of the plan. It is as it should be. In the temple, They say that if Adam and Eve break these commandments, *"We will provide a Savior for them."* The purpose of that Savior is, under certain conditions (and the *Book of Mormon* uses the word through certain **means** and conditions), these children who are indicted and are under the full effects of the *law of justice*, can be reclaimed and redeemed and brought back into the presence of the Lord. That doesn't mean that in the process they aren't going to experience some suffering because suffering, even through redemption, leads to experience that can promote and give birth to wisdom. So, there needs to be some suffering, but not the suffering that the *law of justice* would afflict upon you, otherwise, if you remain in a disobedient and rebellious state. Even through repentance, there's going to be some suffering. President Kimball said that there is no repentance if there is no suffering. But this suffering is the suffering that Eve talked about, *"It is better for us to pass through sorrow."* You're going to have some sorrow. Even the Redemption isn't going to take away sorrow and suffering and pain because all those things are necessary for you to gain the experience that the telestial world is designed to give you. Otherwise, what's the purpose of being here?

So, now we'll talk about Alma 34:15:

> *And thus he...*

He is the Intercessor, the Person who steps in, and He steps in because there are two criteria. First of all, He wants to, and second, He's **able** to. So, the Intercessor not only has to be willing, but **able**. Now, the **able** part disqualifies everyone else. There may have been many who were willing, but there was only one who was **willing and able** because of who He is and because His own experience uniquely qualifies Him to intercede on behalf of the Father's other children, who find themselves in a perilous situation, in jeopardy, in need of a rescue. Without a plan, they would be hopelessly lost forever with no chance of ever being reclaimed. This is the doctrine that the sons of Mosiah and Alma the younger taught the Lamanites. If you look at the doctrine, you'll see they taught it in an exact way. They taught, first of all, the creation. They taught the purpose of the telestial world. We have a podcast on the telestial world that teaches what the purpose of this world is. It's very unique and intimately designed to give each person exactly what they need in order to leave this schoolroom advantaged. And so, he says in verse 15:

> *And thus he shall bring salvation to all those who*
> *shall believe on his name; this being the intent of*
> *this last sacrifice, to bring about the bowels of*
> *mercy, **which overpowereth justice,***

Now, you're going to find in Alma 34 and 42, that without an Atoning One, without an Anointed Savior sent on a rescue mission, there is no mercy; there is only justice. So, without Christ, the whole plan of mercy, which overpowers justice in our behalf, could not take place. That's *Book of Mormon* doctrine:

> *and bringeth about **means** unto men that they may*
> *have faith unto repentance.*

> *[16] And thus mercy **can** [not will] satisfy the*
> *demands of justice;*

Why is it not **will**? The **can** is there pointing back to the **means** that are required for this whole thing to happen, and that **means** depends on your choice. In Alma 42, it's called the *"conditions of repentance."* These conditions and **means** have to be in place in order for mercy to begin to overpower justice. Go back to verse 16:

> *[16] And thus mercy can satisfy the demands of*
> *justice, and* [mercy] ***encircles them in the arms***
> ***of safety,***

That's a big phrase you want to circle. Brothers and sisters, we do not want to be exposed to the demands of justice. It goes on further:

> *while he that exercises no faith unto repentance*

That's the **means**. Those are the conditions:

> *is exposed to the **whole law** of the demands of*
> *justice;*

The other day when I was reading that, the Spirit whispered and said, "If there's a **whole** law, if there's a **whole** exposure to the *law of justice*, then there must needs be a **partial** exposure to the *law of justice*." You can't have a whole without its opposite, which is a partial. The partial exposure to the *law of justice* is the consequences that we experience in this life for our poor choices which are not circumvented. Mercy will save you from the demands of the whole *law of justice* and its demands, but it's necessary for you to experience **some** of that exposure. Otherwise, there's no learning experience that can lead to **wisdom**, which is highly prized by the gods:

> *therefore only unto him that has faith unto*
> *repentance is brought about the great and eternal*
> *plan of redemption.*

Now, look at verse 17. We have a mistaken idea in the Church, and I taught it for years as a Church Education instructor, that repentance is like a book on the shelf that has written on its cover, "Repentance," and anytime you have a notion or a feeling, you can go and simply take that book off the shelf, read its words, and benefit from its wisdom. I would like to share with you that repentance is a *gift of the Spirit*, and like all other gifts, has to be sought for, there has to be a desire for it. If you want any of the other *gifts of the Spirit*, for example, *the gift of discerning of spirits*, you have to have a desire for that and then seek for it. It's probably not going to come to you easily. It's going to be something that you'll have to work at in order for you to get that gift. Repentance is a *gift of the Spirit*. If there's no desire to repent, there is no repentance. It's granted to you as one of the gifts of God. You get a feel for that in verse 17:

> *[17] Therefore may God grant unto you, my*
> *brethren, that ye may begin to exercise your faith*
> *unto repentance, that ye begin to call upon his*
> *holy name, that he would have mercy upon you;*

That's the *law of justice*. It's very personal and exacting and painful! There are at least two portions of that: #1 is exposure to the whole law, and #2 is partial exposure to the demands of justice. Let's go to *Doctrine and Covenants* 19, and we'll get a feeling of what it would be like to be exposed to the whole demands of the *law of justice*, and why the Lord wants to prevent us from experiencing that and wants to save us and to hold us in the arms of safety. In verse 4, the Lord says this:

> *[4] And surely every man must repent or suffer,*
> *for I, God, am endless.*

Now, you understand that repentance is the means whereby you can escape exposure to the whole demands of justice. That's what we want to do. You want to be found in a place through the Atonement, through your faith, and through your repentance, to where you are *justified*. We talked about that last week. *Justification* fits in with this whole thing—the *law of justice*, the demands of the law, escaping exposure to the demands. So, when you exercise repentance and faith in Christ to the degree that you receive a forgiveness of your sins, at that point, you are *justified*, meaning that the demands of justice have been answered on your behalf by Christ, through His atoning sacrifice, and that law has no more claim on you. In essence, the judge in this courtroom has declared you *blameless*, *not guilty*, and *innocent*. Those are the three words that describe *justification*. So, when we read in the scriptures that certain men were *just men*, there's a deeper meaning to that. That means that the *law of justice* has no claim on them and has been satisfied through the Atonement of Christ because of the repentance, conditions, and means that you've exercised for you to be delivered from exposure to the whole law. That's the *law of justice*. It's eternal. Now, we'll end the discussion tonight on Alma 42. You can see how this all starts to play out and how it starts to work. This all makes sense now. Alma 42:13:

> *Therefore, according to justice, the plan of redemption could not be brought about, only on conditions of repentance of men in this probationary state,*

You can't get freed from that law, only on conditions of repentance.

> *yea, this preparatory state; for except it were for these conditions,*

Which is what? Faith in Jesus Christ and repentance. The fruits of that are forgiveness of sins and the *gifts of the Spirit*, and when you come to that point where your sins have been forgiven, and you're endowed with the *gifts of the Spirit*, you are in a state of *justification*. The demands of justice, on your behalf, have been answered and you're *"[encircled] in the arms of safety"*:

> *mercy could not take effect except it should destroy the work of justice. Now the work of justice could not be destroyed; if so, God would cease to be God.*

Let's go back to section 19 and look at verse 4 again. It simply states:

> *...every man must repent or suffer...*

You see that the suffering comes from the divine *law of justice*, and repentance is designed to deliver us from the demands of that law. Let's continue in section 19 and look at verse 15:

> *[15] Therefore I command you to **repent—repent**, lest I smite you by the rod of my mouth, and by my wrath, and by my anger, and your sufferings be sore—how sore you know not, how exquisite you know not, yea, how hard to bear you know not.*

You now see why mercy encircles us in the arms of safety? Here is the Savior, who is commanding us to repent, so that we don't experience the sufferings He's talking about here, with exposure to the whole *law of justice*:

[16] For behold, I, God, have suffered these things for all, that they might not suffer if they would repent;

[17] **But if they would not repent they must suffer even as I;**

And then He describes a God's experience with exposure to the whole demands of the *law of justice*. Not for just one person, but for humankind:

[18] Which suffering caused myself, even God, the greatest of all, to tremble because of pain, and to bleed at every pore, and to suffer both body and spirit—and would that I might not drink the bitter cup, and shrink—

[19] Nevertheless, glory be to the Father, and I partook and finished my preparations unto the children of men.

[20] Wherefore, I command you again to repent...

That's a feeling for the *law of justice*, and all of us are under that indictment.

Now, here's the thing. Christ has paid the demands of justice. The debt has been paid in full. Whether you accept Him or not, the debt has been paid. That's the Atoning Sacrifice made by the One Anointed to be the *Savior of the World*. Now, when you find out about this, when God puts you in a position where you have knowledge given to you of what He has done for you, and you understand sufficiently that you can repent and access this gift, and you **choose not to**, knowing—not supposing, but knowing—then what you do is place yourself in a position where you, as a rebel, with that knowledge, will have to pay the price for those sins a second time, which were already paid for sufficiently once, by your Redeemer. So, the sin has already been satisfied, and because of your rebellion and rejecting the gift, you'll be placed in a position where justice makes a claim on you. This exacts an unnecessary payment. This is what is referred to in the *Book of Mormon* as *"[trampling] under [your] feet the Holy One."*

Brothers and sisters, I hope that gives you a little feeling for the *law of justice*. It ties into the category of "the fall of man."

The great missionaries of the *Book of Mormon* taught the gospel in a three-segment process. The teaching process they used was:
#1 The Creation.
#2 The Fall.
#3 The Atonement.
The *law of justice* fits into the Fall/Atonement categories. You have to understand why Christ's mission is a rescue. Without that rescue, what happens to each one of us?

That kind of bridges the gap with last week's lesson on *justification* and how that fits in with the *law of justice*. All of these things are wedded together, and I hope we've been able to discuss those in a way tonight that gives you a better feel for what the forgiveness of sins does. Now, the remission of sins is a higher level. Forgiveness of sins is associated with this preparatory step. Forgiveness of sins is preparatory to the remission of sins. Forgiveness of sins puts you in a place where the *law of justice* has no claim. If you were to die in that state, then that law has been appeased and satisfied and does not exact the payment that it otherwise would. A remission of sins is something higher and deeper. A remission of sins includes with it a healing process that makes a person whole. We'll talk more about that in the future.

So, to end our class tonight on our discussion of justice and mercy, let's turn to Mosiah 2:36. Verses 36-39 should make a lot more sense out of this principle of justice:

> *[36] And now, I say unto you, my brethren, that after ye have known and have been taught all these things,*

These are people now, who have the knowledge of the Atonement, the knowledge of the Fall, the knowledge of their need to be rescued:

> *if ye should transgress and go contrary to that which has been spoken,*

In other words, you reject it. You rebel against that which you know to be true:

> *that ye do withdraw yourselves from the Spirit of the Lord, that it may have no place in you to guide you in wisdom's paths that ye may be blessed, prospered, and preserved—*

> *[37] I say unto you, that the man that doeth this,*
> *the same cometh out in open rebellion against*
> *God; therefore he listeth to obey the evil spirit,*
> *and becometh an enemy to all righteousness;*
> *therefore, the Lord has no place in him, for he*
> *dwelleth not in unholy temples.*

Now, think about all of our discussion tonight as we read verses 38 and 39:

> *[38] Therefore if that man repenteth not,*

In other words, you make a conscious choice not to meet the conditions of repentance and the means provided to be rescued and saved:

> *and remaineth and dieth an enemy to God, the*
> *demands of divine justice do awaken his immortal*
> *soul to a lively sense of his own guilt, which doth*
> *cause him to shrink from the presence of the Lord,*
> *and doth fill his breast with guilt, and pain, and*
> *anguish, which is like an unquenchable fire,*
> *whose flame ascendeth up forever and ever.*
> *[39] And now I say unto you, that mercy hath no*
> *claim on that man; therefore his final doom is to*
> *endure a never-ending torment.*

So, if you know these things, and you choose to reject them, then you you trample the Holy One of Israel under your feet and the sins that have already been paid for, as a gift by Christ through His Atonement, make a claim against you through divine justice, and you have to pay a second time for the same sin; an unnecessary second payment.

References:
Alma 12:10, 11 "...the lesser portion of the word..."
3 Nephi 19:9 "And they did pray for that which the most desired..."
Brother Packer page 90 in *Preach My Gospel.*
Section 93:19
Teachings of the Prophet Joseph Smith, Section Six 1943-44, p. 364
History of the Church, 3:295–96; from a letter from Joseph Smith and others to Edward Partridge and the Church, Mar. 20, 1839, Liberty Jail, Liberty, Missouri.
D&C 88:64 "...expedient for you."
Alma 42:24
Alma 43:14 "...God would cease to be God."

John 14:6

Mosiah 3:17 "[the] **means** whereby salvation can come…"

"If there is no pain and suffering for the errors, then there can be no repentance." Spencer W. Kimball from "What Is True Repentance?" May 1974

Alma 34:15-17

Alma 42:13 "…conditions of repentance…"

D&C 19:4

D&C 19:15-20

Helaman 12:2 "…and do trample under their feet the Holy One…"

Mosiah 2:36-39

Chapter Thirty-Four
Podcast 034 Temples: The Purpose of Gathering

Tonight, brothers and sisters, I have a couple of things I want to cover with you. The first goes to a statement by the Prophet Joseph Smith that he made in *Teachings of the Prophet Joseph Smith*, page 307-308. It has to do with the gathering of Israel. There is a scripture from 1 Nephi that I want to use also. I'll come to that in a minute. First, Joseph said this:

> *What was the object of gathering...the people of*
> *God in any age of the world?*

Now, the Tenth Article of Faith talks about the gathering of Israel under the keys that were restored by Moses in the Kirtland Temple. The gathering has been the main subject of the Restoration in The Church of Jesus Christ of Latter-day Saints, but Joseph gives us a little different view. He says:

> *The main object was to build unto the Lord a*
> *house whereby He could reveal unto His people*
> *the ordinances of His house and the glories of His*
> *kingdom, and teach the people the way of*
> *salvation; for there are certain ordinances and*
> *principles that, when they are taught and*
> *practiced, must be done in a place or house built*
> *for that purpose.*

Every time you read the word *gathering*, as it pertains to now in the present, and in the future, and really for the past also, the purpose is to bring a group of people together for the purpose of building that temple, so the Lord could reveal ordinances in His house that could only be done there. One of the ordinances I want to talk to you about is called *the fullness of the Melchizedek Priesthood*. In the book, *The Words of Joseph Smith,* by Ehat and Cook, on page 215, the Prophet Joseph Smith said that the purpose of the gathering was to bestow the *fullness of the priesthood.* So now, you have two things that point towards the purpose of temples and the gathering of Israel in any age of the world. That gathering is still going on, and even greater gatherings are going to take place, especially after the world falls into chaos, as has been prophesied. Then there will be a group of rescuers that we refer to as the 144,000, and others, who will be sent out into a chaotic world, in the middle of anarchy and blood and horror. Their job will be to gather pockets of stranded people who qualify to come to a safe place called the New Jerusalem, and to bring them there *"with songs of everlasting joy upon their heads."* Isaiah talked a lot about that. We're talking tonight about the *fullness of the priesthood*, and the Prophet Joseph Smith said that the *fullness of the priesthood* can only be revealed in temples built for that purpose and that the purpose of the gathering is to bring people together to build the temple, so that the *fullness of the Melchizedek Priesthood* can be bestowed upon them. I want to read a scripture to you. It's *Doctrine and Covenants* 124:26-27. This section was given October 27, 1838. It was almost winter time, and the Latter-day Saints had been driven out of Missouri and had crossed the river. They came to Quincy, Illinois for a while, then moved on up to Commerce, Illinois. Commerce would later be called Nauvoo. They hadn't been there very long when they received this. You can read the previous verses that tie into this. It is a **call to gather** people, and the Lord says:

> *[26] And send ye swift messengers, yea, chosen messengers, and say unto them:* **Come ye,** *with all your gold, and your silver, and your precious stones, and with all your antiquities; and with all who have knowledge of antiquities, that will come, may come, and bring the box tree, and the fir tree, and the pine tree, together with all the precious trees of the earth;*

[27] And with iron, with copper, and with brass, and with zinc, and with all your precious things of the earth; and build a house to my name, for the Most High to dwell therein.

See, it's a call to gather there and build a temple in Nauvoo, Illinois. For what purpose?

[28] For there is not a place found on earth that he [God/Christ] *may come to and restore again that which was lost unto you, or which he hath taken away, even the fulness of the priesthood.*

There's that quote: *the fullness of the priesthood.* Now, here's a little statement answering the questions, "What is the *fullness of the priesthood*? What does that mean?" Actually, it's a term that ties in with several other terms that we've talked about in these classes. Let me read to you this little statement by Joseph Fielding Smith, from a conference report in April 1970. He talks about the *fullness of the priesthood.* He says this:

In 1841 the Lord revealed to the Prophet that "the fullness of the priesthood" was available to men only in the temple, in "a house" built to his name. And in 1843 the Prophet said: If a man gets a fullness of the priesthood of God, he has to get it in the same way that Jesus Christ obtained it,

Isn't that an interesting statement? Again, following the footsteps of the Savior:

and that was by keeping all the commandments and obeying all the ordinances of the house of the Lord.

Some people have questions as to whether Jesus was married. Well, that statement right there, for Latter-day Saints, should lay it to rest. Jesus received the *fullness of the priesthood,* and He received it by keeping **all** of the commandments and observing and obeying **all** the ordinances in the House of the Lord. Well, what's the most sacred ordinance performed in the temple? The sealing between a man and a woman. So, that lays that to rest! That quote is from *The Documentary History of the Church* Vol. 5, page 244. Then, President Joseph Fielding Smith goes on and says:

*Let me put this in a little different way. I do not care what office you hold in the Church—you may be an apostle, you may be a patriarch, a high priest, or anything else—but you cannot receive the fullness of the priesthood and the fullness of eternal reward **unless you receive the ordinances of the house of the Lord**;*

You want to understand that. Do you see how important it is for you to go and receive your initiatory ordinance; how important it is for you to obtain the endowment blessings of the temple? President Smith says that if you want a **fullness** *of the Melchizedek Priesthood,* these ordinances and what takes place in the House of the Lord are absolutely necessary. President Smith continues and says:

*and when you receive these ordinances, the door is then open so you can obtain all the blessings which **any man can gain**.*

Do not think because someone has a higher office in the Church than you have that you are barred from receiving the fullness of the Lord's blessings.

I want to add, also, that because you are a woman, do not think that you are barred from receiving these blessings:

*You can have them sealed upon you as an elder, if you are faithful; and when you receive them, and live faithfully and keep these covenants, **you then have all that any man can get**.*

There's a question that comes up as to whether the blessings of the *fullness of the priesthood* are available to women separately. The blessings of the *fullness of the priesthood* are as follows: You obtain a promise from God, from His own mouth, spoken to you, calling you by name, that you shall have eternal life. The judgment day is advanced on your behalf. You can obtain that promise through the *more sure word of prophecy,* which is another way of saying, "conversing with the Lord through the veil." You can have your *calling and election made sure* as a separate man or a separate woman. You can obtain the *Second Comforter* blessings as a separate man or a separate woman. Now, in order to enter into the Celestial Kingdom and obtain all that the Father has is going to require a **couple** to have that sealing blessing of husband and wife and one of those blessings is to have the blessings of eternal increase (meaning spirit children in and after the resurrection of the dead). But these other blessings—to see the face of the Lord in this life, to embrace with Him, to have a personal encounter with Him, and part of that is to discuss and converse with Him through the veil and then obtain these blessings—single women and single men can obtain those blessings. President Smith goes on and says this:

> There is no exaltation in the kingdom of God without the fulness of the priesthood, and every man who receives the Melchizedek Priesthood does so with an oath and a covenant that he shall be exalted.
>
> The covenant on man's part is that [#1] he will magnify his calling in the priesthood, and that [#2] he will live by every word that proceedeth forth from the mouth of God, and that [#3] he will keep the commandments.
>
> The covenant on the Lord's part is that if man does as he promises, then **all** that the Father hath shall be given unto him; and this is such a solemn and important promise that the Lord swears with an oath that it shall come to pass.

So, the purpose of gathering in all ages of the world is to bring people into a place that they can go to the temple, and they can see the face of God and have all of these blessings bestowed upon them, while still mortals in this life. I want to share with you what happened this week. I was reading in the *Book of Mormon,* and I'd like you to go over to 3 Nephi 8:1. If you know these principles, then you can start to see things in the scriptures that are just magnificent. Scriptures come alive! This is that chapter where the prophecies of Samuel the Lamanite are actually fulfilled. We have a physical fulfillment of the prophecies of Samuel the Lamanite. Think back on our lesson last week on *justification.* Remember what we taught? If you can't remember, you might want to go back and review it, but look at what this verse says:

> *[1] And now it came to pass that according to our record, and we know our record to be true, for behold, it was a **just man***

There's that clue. Whenever you hear that term, this is a person who has been *justified* through the atonement of Jesus Christ, and we talked about that:

> *who did keep the record—*

Now watch, here's what a **just man** and a **just woman** can do:

> *for he truly did many miracles in the name of Jesus;*

Justification opens the door for miracles to occur.

> *and there was not any man who could do a miracle in the name of Jesus*

Now, keep in mind what *justification* means when we look at this last sentence:

> *save he were cleansed every whit from his iniquity—*

That is a great scripture that shows you certain things: what a **just man** is, what they can accomplish, and why.

I want to throw in here a little quote by the Prophet Joseph Smith. It goes into our discussion here tonight, overall. Speaking to Latter-day Saints, he said:

> *I advise all to go on to perfection,*

Now, we have a podcast on being perfect in Christ. There might be a little confusion because a lot of Latter-day Saints will teach, and we hear it all the time, that it's impossible to be perfect in this life, but when Jesus said:

> *Be ye therefore perfect, even as your Father which is in heaven is perfect.*

Or in 3 Nephi when He says:

> *Therefore I would that ye should be perfect even as I, or your Father who is in heaven is perfect.*

We want to push that on into eternity and say, "Well, that's impossible to do in this life." No, it's not. Actually, you have a commandment to **be perfect in this life**, and we gave a whole lesson on that. I want you to notice the correlation between the miracles and what we are going to read here. So, the Prophet Joseph Smith says this:

I advise all to go on to perfection, and search deeper and deeper into the mysteries of Godliness.

Now, if you look at that comment, and you go to the last two or three verses of Moroni 10, you can see that it's a commandment to obtain perfection:

*[32] Yea, come unto Christ, and **be perfected in him**....*

That's not referring to after this life, or into the spirit world, or into some assigned kingdom after the resurrection of the dead. We have a commandment to be perfect in this life. Joseph is talking about how perfection is tied into knowing the *mysteries of God*. In other words, you could reverse that and say that the perfection that the Father and the Son want their children to obtain in this life **cannot** be obtained without a knowledge of the mysteries. We've hit on that theme several times. Let's go back into 3 Nephi 8:5, referring to the record that this *just man* is keeping:

*[5] And it came to pass in the thirty and fourth year, **in the first month**, on the fourth day of the month, there arose a great storm, such an one as never had been known in all the land.*

Notice that it is at the **beginning** of the thirty-fourth year, whatever that is according to Nephi. That's all we know that it's their thirty-fourth year, in the first month that this storm arises. Of course, we know what happens: you have tremendous lightnings, tempests, fires, and you have huge mountains that are picked up and they bury cities. Verse 12 comes out and says:

*[12] But behold, there was a more great and terrible destruction in the land northward; for behold, **the whole face of the land was changed**, because of the tempest and the whirlwinds, and the thunderings and the lightnings, and the exceedingly great quaking of the whole earth;*

This storm and destruction go on for a period of three hours. I love it in the middle of verse 19 where it says:

*[19] ...they did last for about the space of three hours; and **it was said by some that the time was greater**;*

Ha-ha! I thought that was an interesting thing. But:

> *nevertheless, all these great and terrible things were done in about the space of three hours—and then behold, there was darkness upon the face of the land.*

Have you ever been in a situation where you were in stress or turmoil, and someone pointed out that it lasted about ten minutes, but to you, it seemed like about five hours? I was in the 1994 Northridge, California earthquake. I was on the twelfth floor of the Marriott Hotel on Century Boulevard across from LAX, not far from where the center of that earthquake was. I do not go back to California easily because I was so traumatized in that huge earthquake. I can't even explain to you what it was like to be in that room at 4:30 A.M. when that 6.7 earthquake hit. I fully expected that when it finally settled down, to open the door to our hotel room and look twelve floors straight down into the parking lot. I just could not see how the rest of the building could withstand what we'd just gone through. It seemed like it would never end. And yet, the whole thing only lasted about twenty-two seconds! It seemed to go on and on, so I relate to this deal. Now, in verse 23 it says that the darkness lasted for three days. I did a *Book of Mormon* class in the Philippines on numerology, and it's always interesting to me that these numbers have significance. You had three hours, and then you had three days. There's a reason why it's three hours and not four hours, and it's three days and not six days. God uses numbers to teach us certain things, but that's another lesson. So, now I want to show you something. They hear the voice of Christ in the darkness. If you look at your heading for chapter 10, it says:

The voice of Christ promises to **gather His people**

That's a significant thing. I had never seen this until I studied it this week and the Holy Spirit pointed this out to me, and I knew I needed to share with you. We've been talking about the gathering tonight, and notice here you have this tremendous destruction that takes place, then after that, the people hear a voice in the darkness. When you hear the voice of God, but don't see Him, if that happens to you, no matter where it is, you are obtaining what is called *the more sure word of prophecy.* You are on a track very close to obtaining the *fullness of the*

Melchizedek Priesthood and having a very, very intimate and significant encounter with the Lord, Jesus Christ. Well, after that darkness passed away, if you look at 10:9 it says:

> *[9] And it came to pass that thus did the three days pass away. And it was in the morning, and the darkness dispersed from off the face of the land,*

In those previous verses, though, the Lord comes out, and starting in 10:4 He says:

> *[4] O ye people of these great cities which have fallen, who are descendants of Jacob, yea, who are of the house of Israel,* **how oft have I gathered you**

Now, think about what we've talked about gathering. All through time, from Adam up to this point, the purpose of gathering is to bring people together, to build a house, a temple, wherein the fullness of the ordinances of the Melchizedek Priesthood can be bestowed on the people's heads. Notice what he said:

> *how oft have I gathered you as a hen gathereth her chickens under her wings,* **and have nourished you.**

Interesting statement:

> *[5] And again, how oft* **would I have gathered you...**

And then the top of verse 6:

> *[6] O ye house of Israel whom I have spared, how oft* **will I gather you**... *if ye will repent and return unto me with full purpose of heart.*
> *[7] But if not,*

Watch what happens if you refuse the call to gather, either in the past or the future:

> *O house of Israel, the places of your dwellings shall become* **desolate**

Desolate means *void of life.* You lose everything that you could have had or the promises that were available to you because you will not harken to the voice of God; you rebel, harden your heart and do not come to Him. Now, in chapter 11 we have the appearance of Jesus Christ among the Nephites. Here's something interesting that a lot of people don't know. Go to 3 Nephi 10:18. Think about what we've done:

*[18] And it came to pass that in the **ending** of the thirty and fourth year,*

So, from 3 Nephi 8:5 where the storm ends at the **beginning** of the thirty-fourth year, you're almost a year later in 3 Nephi 10:18 where it's in the **ending** of the thirty-fourth year:

behold, I will show unto you that the people of Nephi who were spared, and also those who had been called Lamanites, who had been spared, did have great favors shown unto them, and great blessings poured out upon their heads, insomuch that soon after the ascension of Christ into heaven [you can read about that in the book of Acts] *he did truly manifest himself unto them—*

[19] Showing his body unto them, and ministering unto them;

Brothers and sisters, here's the thing: you've got almost a year between when the storm starts and when Christ appears among the Nephites. There was almost a complete year between that period of time. That's something that a lot of people haven't seen, and it's just a fascinating thing. Then you ask yourself this question, "What took place in that year?" Between the time when the three-hour storm ends, and then the darkness disperses after three days, it's eleven plus months, and they gather in a different place, in a place called Bountiful, which is a temple city. See, you have a political capital, and you have a religious capital among the Nephites. It's the pattern of Zion in the latter-days. You have a place where just laws are administered or should be. In this case, Zarahemla was destroyed by fire, along with many other places. Their political system had corrupted itself to such a degree that the Lord just completely wiped them out and started over. There was one other city there called Jacobugath which was especially deplorable to the Lord because it says in 3 Nephi 9:9:

...it was they that did destroy the peace of my people and the government of the land;

So, the failure of their political system started in this place and, like a cancer, spread throughout the whole Nephite system until the Lord had to come in and wipe it all out. We read in 3 Nephi 11:1:

And now it came to pass that there were a great
multitude gathered together, of the people of
Nephi, round about the temple which was in the
land Bountiful;

See, this is almost a year after the destruction ends. Chapter 11 is going to tell us that they all came forward, one by one, and we know how many people were in this multitude because later on in 3 Nephi it says there were 2,500 people. They find themselves on this day, eleven months after the darkness disperses and the destruction ends, gathered at the temple city among the Nephites, which is Bountiful. So, you've got to ask yourself these questions: Why were they there? What brings these 2,500 people to the temple? What takes place? It goes on and says:

and they were marveling and wondering one with
another, and were showing one to another the
great and marvelous change which had taken
place.

We think that took place after three days. The way we teach it, and I taught it for years in seminary classes, is that after three days of these people howling and bawling and lamenting about the darkness, it disperses and Christ comes down in a beam of light and appears on the steps of the temple at Bountiful. In reality, it's a year later. These are not all the Nephites that were spared, as we're going to find out in the next two or three days. Christ is there for the first day and leaves, which starts in chapter 11, and the people don't sleep that night. They go throughout the whole area and *"noise it abroad"* and gather people for the next day when the Savior said He would come back. There were 2,500 people that had a special privilege bestowed. And, again, here's the question: Out of all the surviving Nephites, what brought them to the temple place a year later?

So, where am I going with this? The exciting part is in chapter 11, verse 3. Here are these 2,500 Nephites that are at the temple. Remember what the Lord says, "How often have I tried to gather you? How often will I gather you? etc." And, as we said, the purpose of the gathering is to bring people to the temple so that they can receive the *fullness of the Melchizedek Priesthood.* I'm going to show you an ancient example, among the Nephites, the descendants of Joseph, where this very principle that Joseph Smith was teaching is playing out. Then I want to see what that means to us in our day. In verse 3 they hear a voice, and they don't recognize it. In middle of verse 3 it says:

> *it being a small voice it did pierce them that did hear to the center, insomuch that there was no part of their frame that it did not cause to quake; yea, it did pierce them to the very soul, and did cause their hearts to burn.*

And they hear it again, for the second time in verse 4. In verse 5, they hear it a third time. Then in verse 7, the voice says:

> *[7] Behold my Beloved Son, in whom I am well pleased, in whom I have glorified my name—hear ye him.*

Then, in verse 8 we see the descension of Christ as He comes down in a shaft of light to the Nephites. This is a *Second Comforter* experience. Isn't it interesting that these people experienced *conversing with the Lord through the veil* during the three days of darkness? They hear the voice of Christ talking to them, but they don't see Him. That is *conversing with the Lord through the veil.* That is obtaining *the more sure word of prophecy.* Then, a year later this small group finds themselves **gathered** to the temple in Bountiful. As they are gathered, they heard the voice of the Father and saw Christ face to face. In verse 14, He invites them to come up:

> *[14]Arise and come forth unto me, that ye may thrust your hands into my side, and also that ye may feel the prints of the nails in my hands and in my feet, that ye may know that I am the God of Israel, and the God of the whole earth, and have been slain for the sins of the world.*

And 15 says:

> *this they did do, going forth one by one until they had all gone forth, and did see with their eyes and did feel with their hands, and did know of a surety and did bear record, that it was he, of whom it was written by the prophets, that should come.*

So, what's the point? These 2,500 people have an advantage over others in this society who were spared, who do not find themselves at the temple. The advantage that they have is that they hear the voice of the Father. If you look in the middle of verse 3 again, it says:

> it did pierce them that did hear to the center, insomuch that there was no part of their frame that it did not cause to quake; yea, it did pierce them to the very soul, and did cause their hearts to burn.

Only those 2,500 people, out of all the surviving Nephites, a year after the destruction, find themselves at this place to have this experience. From this point on, in the record of 3 Nephi, no one else who gathered after this first day has that experience. Think of the second and third day. He's among the Nephites three days (there's that number three again). Only on the first day do we have a record of them hearing the voice of the Father, and they are invited one by one to come up, in what is a solemn priesthood recognition ceremony, to receive an apostolic witness of the resurrected body of the Lord, Jesus Christ. You don't read about that happening on day two and day three. They see Him, but there is an advantage of having been there on the first of these three days. Could it be, brothers and sisters, that they understood this doctrine of the gathering? The voice of the Lord was speaking to them in the darkness, and He talked about gathering. Did they understand the principle that Joseph Smith taught, that the purpose of the gathering in any age is to build a temple? Did they have that doctrine taught among them, and as a result of that were they gathered at the temple eleven and a half months later looking for something that they thought would happen because of the doctrine they understood? I've heard all kinds of speculation as to why they were gathered at the temple there, and they all may be right. I'm just showing you how exciting it is to show that these people who found themselves at that temple when Christ appeared there, had some advantages that the other people who came later on, did not experience. Anyway, it's just a fascinating experience to me on how to see the scriptures unfold. The Lord showed me that this week as I was reading.

Student 1: Can I ask a question?

Mike: Sure.

Student 1: If the land was all destroyed, did they build that temple during the eleven months? They went to the temple. Where did the temple come from?

Mike: The temple was there. It existed during the destruction. How much damage or destruction was done to the temple complex or to that area around the city of Bountiful, I don't know. I'm sure there must have been some damage, just like when we have tornadoes or earthquakes or something like that, some of our buildings get damaged. Then again, maybe the temple was preserved completely. I don't know. Here's the thing, though: they were gathered there marveling one with another about the mighty changes that had taken place. We automatically think those changes had to do with the physical destruction and real estate damage that was done among the Nephites, and what if that isn't what it was all about? What if they were not marveling and wondering so much about physical damage? What if they were wondering about the change that had taken place in their life, as a result of surviving this and finding themselves at the temple? What if that is the thing they were marveling about? It says, *"they were marveling and wondering one with another, and were showing one to another the great change which had taken place."* It's just a thought. What if those changes were not physical or geographical or real estate? What if they were changes of the heart? Because those people who have gone through this, I'll guarantee you, are not the same people that went into it. There were some huge changes.

Now, back to the *fullness of the priesthood*. What have you gathered here today? You have to have a temple place in order for these ordinances to be bestowed. Now, we talked about how *calling and election* and *more sure word of prophecy* can be bestowed upon you by God, and it can be done personally, wherever He chooses. It does not have to be inside a temple. It appears from what the prophets have written, the ordinances of initiatory and the endowment ceremony, and everything that takes place, and the knowledge that is gained in there, are necessary for you to come to a point where you converse with the Lord through the veil. It's interesting that it doesn't take place until the initiatory is done, symbolically, in the temple. You don't obtain the *more sure word of prophecy*, you don't obtain the *fullness of the priesthood*, and different things like that, without the temple ordinances. That's what the prophets have spoken. That's what they've said. You enter into a new order of things through the temple. So, anyway, I wanted to share that with you. It's something that's yet to happen.

Tonight, I want to talk to you about another temple. Go to your *Bible Dictionary* and look under the word *temple*. I want to share with you something there, and this will take the remainder of our time. Just the first paragraph is all I want to talk about. It says this:

> *A temple is literally a house of the Lord, a holy sanctuary in which sacred ceremonies and ordinances of the gospel are performed by and for the living and also in behalf of the dead. **A place where the Lord may come**,*

You ought to triple underline that! I don't think there are any of us that don't have a witness that every dedicated temple when it's accepted by the Lord—and I assume all the temples that have been dedicated by the First Presidency have been accepted by the Lord—that He has set His foot in those buildings. He has personally been in those buildings. It says:

> *A place where the Lord may come, it is the most holy of any place of worship on the earth. **Only the home can compare with the temple in sacredness.**

Now, you want to look at that paragraph right there. So, I'd like to talk to you a little bit about the home. I gave a lesson a couple of weeks ago in priesthood and it was about protecting the family. We discussed that the family is the most sacred unit in eternity and that ideal family life on Earth is patterned after family life in heaven. Of all the terms that God the Father is referred to—and He has many, He is a Man of many names—the one that He prefers is *Father*. I might also add that Husband is right up there; Husband and Father. We got to thinking about what are the holiest places on Earth? When the Lord says in section 45, *"stand in holy places, and...not be moved."* We talked about what holy places means and what these holy places are. Of course, the temple is rated right up there, and some men in the High Priest Group said homes should be holy places. I agreed with that. Actually, a holy place is anywhere a holy man and a holy woman, who have been *justified, sanctified,* and cleansed from sin, stand. Anywhere they place their feet is holy ground. We asked the question, "Out of all these places, where is the place that children spend the most time—temples, stake buildings, ward buildings, or in the home?" The obvious answer was in the home. The job is to protect the family in the degenerating circumstances of the world. And, it is. It's deteriorating before our very eyes. The place where children have the greatest exposure to their parents is not in the temple. It's in the home. So, I got to thinking about this principle and wondered what we can do, then, brothers and sisters, to turn our home into a temple place? The *Bible Dictionary* says that *"Only the home can compare with the temple in sacredness."* I'd like to give you a little thought. The word *temple* also has within it the meaning of *template.* A template is a pattern. Could it be that the temples are designed to be a pattern and a template so that we can make our homes temple places? A man once told me, and I agreed with him, that the temple is not the real deal. That's not taking anything sacred away from it, but it's emphasizing what the temple is trying to do. The temple is not the real deal; the temple is pointing us to the real deal. If we start to contemplate what's going on in our temple worship, we can see that it's pointing us somewhere, always upward. It's a template.

So, for years and years, you could not dedicate your home through a priesthood ordinance, until that home was paid for and any financial obligations and mortgages on it were paid off. That was in the handbook of instruction for years and years. Over the last few years as a missionary, I've had the opportunity to have access to the blue handbook of instructions. There is a red handbook for general leadership, and then there's the blue handbook that's only for bishops, stake presidents, mission presidents, general authorities, etc. I've had the opportunity to read that book several times. One of the things it says is that now you can dedicate your home, through a priesthood ordinance, without it being paid off. So, that was a change from earlier handbooks. You can dedicate your home. I would like to talk to you tonight about starting the process of turning your home into a temple place, every bit as sacred and purposeful as any temple built and dedicated by The Church of Jesus Christ of Latter-day Saints. In my mind, I can see the need for no difference between those edifices and our home. It all depends on whether you start to look at this concept.

Now, if you're talking about "for the living," that's one thing. Of course, we don't do vicarious work for the dead in our homes. I'm talking about making your home a temple safe place for you and your family, each mother and father presiding over those who have a claim on this home as a sanctuary and a safe place; and then spreading that out so it goes out to your posterities so that when they get married they do the same things. Zion, as a principle, is not going to be established by The Church of Jesus Christ of Latter-day Saints. It's not going to do it. It's teaching us concepts and principles that when you act on them as individual members of the Church, who have access to church membership conference and canons of scripture, that when a man or a woman can come up to a Zion status, wherever they are, you have Zion. Zion is the pure in heart. It has nothing to do with buildings, institutions, or real estate, at least, in the beginning. It begins with a man and a woman coming up and obtaining these things we're talking about tonight and in every podcast. One of the central messages of Isaiah is the establishment of the cause of Zion. If, as you're reading this and the Spirit weighs upon you, and you have views concerning yourself, your family, and the Zion concept, you can consider yourself as having received the call to Zion, because that call is issued through the Spirit. It is not issued through any kind of decree sent out from an institution. It is spiritual in nature. There is a gathering taking place right now, and people are feeling and hearing this call to Zion. As you listen to general conference and one of the prophets or one of the Brethren say something that is Zion-centered, you may have the Spirit of the Lord distil upon you and have a view of you and the future that you've never had before. That is a call to Zion. To answer that call begins with individual sanctity. All the things we've been talking about begin with you becoming clean through the atonement of Christ and having a new heart in Christ. What help is your environment?

Let's talk about you dedicating your home. Now, sisters, this is a Melchizedek Priesthood ordinance. If you don't have a husband, you can have someone you trust, someone that's a Melchizedek Priesthood holder, come in and perform this ordinance for you. Margie and I have done this a number of times because we were gone on missions, and our home that had been dedicated had been defiled. So, we had to re-dedicate our home, and we've done that several times. Let me just share with you things you may want to consider. How do I proceed on this? The ordinance is done like all ordinances in the Church. The ordinance begins by addressing the Father and ends in the name of Jesus Christ. The only other thing in there that's used is, as you address the Father and begin the dedication of your home, you call upon the authority of the Melchizedek Priesthood. Then, simply speak the words, or you can read the prayer from that point forward, then end it in the name of Jesus Christ. That is all of the guidance you need in order to do that. Now, what's in between is the interesting part.

Here is something that I would recommend that you do. I was talking to the Stake President in Mongolia the other day. He said he wanted to dedicate his home and we talked about some of these things. He had not done it and wanted to do it. "How do I proceed?" I asked what his favorite temple was. He said it was the Laie, Hawaii temple, but his temple district is Hong Kong. I told him to go online, and you can find all the dedicatory prayers for all LDS temples, including the Salt Lake Temple, the St. George temple, etc. The Kirtland Temple is your foundational one, in *Doctrine and Covenants* 109. Find the dedication prayers for your favorite temples and read them; study them. Let that be a study for you. Go over them and get a feeling for the flow of what an inspired dedicatory prayer feels like. What does it feel like? What's included within the words? You'll get a feel for that. Maybe you'll want to do two to three of those. I know when I did this, I read five or six of them. I just went online and found the one for the Salt Lake Temple, the Mesa Arizona Temple, the Snowflake Arizona Temple (which is my temple district), and I looked at these. Then Margie and I began a fast, and before the fast was ended, I sat down at my computer, said a little prayer, and asked the Lord to reveal to me the words of the dedication for the Mike and Margie Stroud residence. As I sat down, I was fasting and had that prayer, and the words just flowed. This is a wonderful experience, brothers and sisters! This is so to be desired. It is revelation that comes to you in the spirit of fasting, and you have the Spirit to dictate to you, word for word, sentence for sentence, and paragraph for paragraph, and it just flows. When I was through, there were two complete pages written, single-spaced. I took it to Margie and asked her to proofread it and see if she could see any errors in it or any places I need to make some changes. And I don't know, Margie, were there any changes?

Margie: No. I couldn't find anything.

Mike: So, she went through it, as it was given to me. It probably took me about thirty minutes to write that prayer down, and it stood as it was given. After we had received that dedication prayer, we made an appointment with each other for when we would dedicate it. So, during another time of fasting, we simply went upstairs and knelt down next to our bed. I put the written prayer on the bed in front of me, read the prayer, and dedicated our home. I can tell you that it makes such a difference in the atmosphere of the home. It makes such a difference. I might also say that you may want to consider going through your home and having a good housecleaning before this dedication. Clean it up because our God is a God of order and not a God of confusion. You don't want angels to come to your house and be ashamed and cover their face because the environment is not Godly. So, what you can do now is dedicate your home and place a shield around it. Let the Spirit guide you. This is one reason why you look at all these prayers of LDS temple dedications. You get a feeling for what the wording is from the prophets and apostles that helped dedicate these holy places. That's the beginning of turning your home into a temple place. In my mind, it should be every bit as sacred. Even with little children, I know that it's more difficult, but you should be able to enter into that home and feel the atmosphere in your home that you sense when you go into a temple of the Lord.

Student 1: It's interesting, last Sunday we had a Stake Priesthood meeting, and I was told that the first counselor encouraged them not just to bless their homes, but to actually dedicate the home. And he also mentioned something else; I guess it's quite a problem in the Church with men, and he was talking about the power of the priesthood. He said you do not dedicate it with the power of the priesthood; it is the authority. So, it's just interesting that you bring this up and here, our stake encouraged brethren to dedicate their homes.

Mike: Thank you. I appreciate that. I think we're going to hear more and more of these kinds of things through instruction from our church leadership because I believe that we're going to need to have that protection and that atmosphere. You'll find out that angels will come, seen and unseen, and will reside in your home. If you look at the temple ceremony, there is a pattern there of angels, who are sent from Christ, down to observe what is going on in the telestial world. They observe, and then they go back and say, "Lord, this is what we've seen." They return and report. Then the Lord brings this word to the Father. That's a correct principle. Here's a promise I want to make you. As you draw nearer to the Lord and you start to make these moves, you start to act in ways that the Spirit directs you, to sanctify your home and everything in it, it is something that is so rarely done in the telestial world that it will attract the attention of angels. They will come and see something being done in your home that is so rare, not only in the Church but especially in the population of the world, that they will immediately return and report to the Lord and say, "Master, we have been down as thou hast commanded and what we've seen, we feel You need to see. You need to come and see this." Angels open up the way for the Savior to come down and observe what's going on in your home. Angels are the precursor to a personal visit from the Lord, Jesus Christ. They are the ones that clear the way. As I said before, there are examples of where they've come into the dwelling space of mortals and have to cover their eyes and are ashamed at what they see. We don't want that. We want to turn that around. We want them to come and observe the conditions in our homes and then return to the Lord, Jesus Christ and say, "Master, You need to see this." Then He comes and observes that and then presents it to the Father. That is the key that opens the door for all of the blessings of the *fullness of the priesthood*. This should be a personal, revelatory experience. The difference in your home is stunning. That's the word I would use. It's a stunning difference to compare before the dedication, and after. And, the more effort you put into this to be spiritually prepared, the greater the experience you're going to have. But, it is a stunning difference before and after. Boy, do we need that sanctity in the days that are unfolding! I think, brothers and sisters, there is no time to lose. I don't know about you, but I feel a quiet urgency. No panic and not to be done in haste, but I feel a quiet urgency that we need to be about, first of all, obtaining Zion status for ourselves and our family. Anything we can do in the environment where they reside to help that is only a tremendous benefit. That's the purpose of homes.

So, thank you very much. I think it will be a help for all of us to pursue that and to make our homes holy places where we can stand and not be moved, as the Lord commands in section 45.

References:
Teachings of the Prophet Joseph Smith, page 307-308.
The Words of Joseph Smith, page 215, by Ehat & Cook 1980
Isaiah 35:10 "...with songs of everlasting joy upon their heads..."
D&C 124:26-27
Joseph Fielding Smith April 1970 (*Documentary History of the Church*, Vol. 5, p. 244.)
D&C 124:28,31
Documentary History of the Church, Vol. 5, p. 244.
D&C 84:39
3 Nephi 8:1
History of the Church, 6:363; from a discourse given by Joseph Smith on May 12, 1844, in Nauvoo, Illinois.
Matthew 5:48 "Be ye therefore perfect, even as your Father which is in heaven is perfect."
3 Nephi 12:48 "...be perfect even as I, or your Father who is in heaven is perfect."
Moroni 10:32
3 Nephi 8:5, 12, 19
3 Nephi 10 Heading
3 Nephi 10:9; 4-7; 18-19
3 Nephi 11:1, 3, 7; 14-15
Bible Dictionary: Temple
D&C 45:32, "...stand in holy places, and shall not be moved;"

Chapter Thirty-Five
Podcast 035 The Remnant of Jacob

Well, tonight brothers and sisters, I would like to talk to you a little bit about what the scriptures refer to as *the remnant of Jacob*. *The remnant of Jacob* is a theme that has its origin in the book of Micah in the *Old Testament*. You can read about it in Micah chapter 5, beginning with verse 7 and going through 15. When the Savior appeared on the American Continent, toward the end of the second day of His three-day visit there, He quoted this prophecy from Micah. He quotes it in 3 Nephi chapters 20 and 21. It's really interesting because of all of the *Old Testament* prophets that the Savior could quote when He visits the Nephites in ancient America, Micah, and this particular prophecy is the one that He mentions. It pertains to our day. It's happening right now and what I would like to do, with the help of the Holy Ghost, is break this down and see if we can identify the fulfillment of this prophecy right now in the world news that's going on. The majority of the prophecy is going to find its fulfillment in a day that's coming upon us. *The remnant of Jacob,* right now, is being martialed. It is found in many different places throughout the world. Its purpose is to scourge the Gentiles. Now, scourge is a Hebrew word that means whip. I'd like to go over to 2 Nephi chapter 5 for just a minute. What the Lord does all through the scriptures is that He uses other nations as a whip, a scourge, to get His people (In this case, those that have the blood of Israel) to repent and return to Him. 2

Nephi 5:25 we have an example of how this is going to be done. Speaking of the Nephites and the Lamanites:

[25] And the Lord God said unto me: They [the Lamanites] *shall be a scourge unto thy seed* [the Nephites]*, to stir them up in remembrance of me; and inasmuch as they will not remember me, and hearken unto my words, they shall scourge them even unto destruction.*

That was Nephi speaking. This is when he is an old man and about ready to pass his ministry and reign to his brother Jacob. You can see that in verse 26:

[26] And it came to pass that I, Nephi, did consecrate Jacob and Joseph, that they should be priests and teachers over the land of my people.

Now, in the latter-day, one of the scourge nations that the Lord is going to use, spoken of all through Isaiah, is a modern-day counterpart to the ancient nation of Assyria. The Assyrian Empire is the one that attacked the Northern Kingdom of Israel about 721 B.C. They took that kingdom and killed many of the tribes of the Northern Kingdom, and took the rest captive back into Assyria. The Northern Kingdom of Israel, which was their land of inheritance, was left as a place where gentile nations would come in and inhabit that land. They were a mixture of Israelites who survived and managed to stay there with non-Israelite nations, intermarry with them, and then became known as the Samaritans. So, after the Northern Tribes of Israel were carried away captive, any remnants of that group who managed to survive, or who were later allowed to come back there and resettle that land by the Kings of Assyria and intermarry with other conquered nations that were not Israelites, they became known as the Samaritans. The Jews at the time of Jesus really looked upon the Samaritans with disdain. They looked at them as subhuman because they were a mixture of the Northern Kingdom of Israel, the Ten Tribes in the north, with other people that had been conquered by the Assyrians and intermarried with them. So, they were looked upon as inferior because they did not keep their bloodlines pure. They intermarried, violating the law of Moses and the commandments that Moses gave to not intermarry with non-Israelite people. So, the Assyrians in 721 B.C. were a scourge to the Kingdom of Israel and eventually scourged them even to destruction, as 2 Nephi 5:25 says. A generation or so later, the Southern Kingdom of Judah would also have another nation that would scourge them to destruction. The Southern Kingdom was Judah and Benjamin, along with many others from the Northern Kingdom who fled there for safety when the Assyrians attacked. The Babylonians came in, scourged that kingdom, and many were killed. That was in the day of Lehi and what you are reading about in the opening of the *Book of Mormon* is the Babylonian scourge that came down.

So, God uses these nations to scourge His people when they are in a state of disobedience and apostasy. It's important to know this because we are going to see a replay of that and it's building up right now. We are living in a day of fulfillment of ancient prophecy concerning a nation of people that are going to scourge the United States of America and the Gentile nations of the world. Let's look at a couple of references on that. I am going to take you to *Doctrine and Covenants* 87 and show you an interesting reference to what's coming. Section 87, of course, is the prophecy concerning war. Look at the heading:

> *Revelation and prophecy on war.*

If you look at the heading it gives us a little feeling for what was going on:

> *This section was received at a time when the Brethren were reflecting and reasoning upon African slavery on the American Continent*

This part right here is key:

> *and the slavery of the children of men throughout the world.*

We have a tendency to think that this is referring to black slaves in America, and it certainly makes reference to that, but it's anywhere in the world where God's children find themselves enslaved for whatever purpose. So, you could have Russia, you could have China, you could have any of these nations in the past, but this is a revelation concerning the latter-days. The first three verses talk about the beginnings of the Civil War and the rebellion that takes place beginning in South Carolina. Verse 2:

> *And the time will come that war will be poured out upon all nations, beginning at this place.*

That's when the first shots are fired on Fort Sumter in South Carolina. So, that's the Civil War beginning in America, but it's also a sign for the beginning of war and conflict to be poured out upon the whole world. Look at verse 4:

*[4] And it shall come to pass, **after many days**,*

Now, verse 3 talks about the Southern States calling upon the nation of Great Britain and other nations to help them during the War of the States, then it says, *"after many days."* So now the Civil War is long past. We are long past 1865 in verse 4:

slaves shall rise up against their masters,

We think that's Civil War again, but it's not. The uprising of slaves against their masters was so isolated during the Civil War that it can't fulfill that prophecy. This has to be something that's going on in our day:

> *slaves shall rise up against their masters, who shall be marshaled and disciplined for war.*
>
> *[5] And it shall come to pass also that the remnants who are left of the land will marshal themselves, and shall become exceedingly angry, and shall vex the Gentiles with a sore vexation.*
>
> *[6] And thus, with the sword and by bloodshed the inhabitants of the earth*

See, there's your feeling that we're not talking about an isolated civil war in the United States. It's talking about what will eventually consume all the nations of the earth, including the United States of America. It has been well prophesied that the United States of America, as a government, as a republic will cease to exist. Verse 6 talks about that:

> *with sword and by bloodshed the inhabitants of the earth shall mourn; and with famine, and plague, and earthquake, and the thunder of heaven, and the fierce and vivid lightning also, shall the inhabitants of the earth be made to feel the wrath, and indignation, and chastening hand of an Almighty God, until the consumption* [that means consumed] *decreed hath made a full end of **all** nations;*

You want to circle that word **all** because that includes the United States of America. Now, the principles that made America great, the Constitution of the United States and the doctrines of the Founding Fathers, will survive this holocaust. I don't know what else to call it. We are looking at a train wreck that's coming at us. When the Lord says that there's a consumption of all nations decreed, and it will happen by war and by earthquake and thunder and lightning and famine and plague, I take Him at His word. This is what's coming at us. Now, on top of all that, on top of the natural cataclysmic events that are taking place in this time, there is also a scourge that has been decreed upon America and upon the Gentile nations of the earth. That scourge is the object of our lesson tonight. And that scourge is known as **the remnant of Jacob**.

The scriptures talk about the need for us, in a coming day, to be found in holy places. Let's go over to section 45 for just a minute and let's look at what the Lord says there. All of these things come together now. If you get a feel for what's happening, you will see the fulfillment of many of these prophecies. Now, let's look at section 45 verse 30, and we are going to see an end to the Gentile nations of the earth. What the scriptures and the Lord refer to as "The time of the Gentiles being fulfilled." You've read that in the scriptures; it's all over. Look at verse 30, here it is again:

[30] And in that generation shall the times of the Gentiles be fulfilled.

That has not yet happened. This is the important part; there's a controversy throughout the Church, among members, that the time of the Gentiles has been fulfilled. No, it has not been fulfilled. We will get into that, look at the next verse:

[31] And there shall be men standing in that generation,

"That generation" is meaning when the time of the Gentile has been fulfilled. The beginning of the time of the Gentile begins with an uprising of people in the Gentile nations. There is a social disorder, there's an **uprising** (that's a good word to use for it), not only in America, but in all of the latter-day Gentile nations, and I'll identify those for you in a minute:

that shall not pass until they shall see an overflowing scourge;

Now, that overflowing scourge is mentioned many places in the
scriptures. Notice the semicolon after that:
for a desolating sickness shall cover the land.
Desolating means *left without life.* Overflowing scourge:
remember the word for scourge is whip. What's the purpose of
the whip? To get God's people to turn to Him. That's the
purpose of it. I remember President Benson and his great talk on
pride. After he talked about pride as a universal sin, he said that
the cure for pride is humility. Then he made this great statement:
> God will have a humble people. Either we can
> choose to be humble or we can be compelled to be
> humble.

Now, what we are talking about tonight is what's going to
happen when we choose not to humble ourselves, which we are
not doing. As a people, whether it's the Latter-day Saints or the
people of the world, whatever it is, we are not choosing Christ on
the whole. Back to section 45:
> [32] But **my disciples** shall stand in holy places,
> and shall not be moved; but among **the wicked**,
> men shall lift up their voices and curse God and
> die.

Do you see the division there? You've got a division between
"My disciples" and *"the wicked,"* a fulfillment of another *Book
of Mormon* prophecy. Go over to 2 Nephi 30 and let me show
you another one. All of a sudden these scriptures come together,
and we want to see if it has happened or is it yet to happen. How
close are we in the sequence of events, so that we can identify
and better prepare ourselves? 2 Nephi 30:10:
> [10] For the time speedily cometh that the Lord
> God shall cause a great division among the
> people, and the wicked will he destroy; and he
> will spare his people, yea, even if it so be that he
> must destroy the wicked by fire.
> [11] And righteousness shall be the girdle of his
> loins, and faithfulness the girdle of his reins
[another word for kidneys].

Then he talks about millennial reign. There's a great division
coming here. I don't believe that you could ever stand on neutral
ground, but you can sense that if there ever was a time where it

appeared that you could, that day is gone and it's never coming back. Because of events that are happening and escalating every day, you are required now to make a choice *"Who's on the Lord's side? Who?"* It's that great hymn we have in the Church.

Let's go over to 3 Nephi for just a minute and look at some of these prophecies the Savior talked about. We're going to spend time in 3 Nephi 20 and 21 tonight. It really helps when you read these prophecies and what's going on, to ask: of the three days that Christ was here, which day was this prophecy given, what were the events that led up to this prophecy, and what are the words and sayings that follow it? I want to go to verse 11. Now, this is before *the remnant* prophecy. And by the way, Isaiah also speaks of *the remnant,* but the original one comes from Micah. The prophet Micah was a contemporary with Isaiah; they lived at the same time down in the Southern Kingdom with Judah and Benjamin. Micah was a righteous prophet-king. Isaiah was a great statesman, prophet, and poet. Look at what the Lord says in 3 Nephi 20:11 as he begins this whole subject on *the remnant of Jacob:*

> *[11] Ye remember that I spake unto you, and said that when the words of Isaiah should be fulfilled—behold they are written, ye have them before you, therefore search them—*
> *[12] And verily, verily, I say unto you, that when they shall be fulfilled then is the fulfilling of the covenant which the Father hath made unto his people, O house of Israel.*

Now, the main body of that covenant which He has made with the house of Israel is that, with love and kindness, He would gather them a second time from their dispersed and scattered state. Look at verse 13:

> *[13] And then shall the remnants,*

Notice the key word there has an **s** on the end of it: *remnants.* In this prophecy, we are just speaking about *the remnant of Jacob.* But, there are other peoples of the house of Israel that have been taken away and scattered, and will need to be gathered:

> *And then shall the remnants, which shall be scattered abroad upon the face of the earth, be gathered in from the east and from the west, and*

> *from the south and from the north; and they shall*
> *be brought to the knowledge of the Lord their*
> *God, who hath redeemed them.*

Now, we gave a lesson here a few weeks ago about the gathering, temples—the purpose of the gathering. As we look at this, let's remember that Joseph Smith taught that the purpose of the gathering was to bring the scattered remnants of the house of Israel into the covenant of the gospel, and eventually get to the temple where they could be taught the true points of the Savior's doctrine and receive the *fullness of the Melchizedek Priesthood.* That is the purpose of the gathering in any age, no matter when. It's to bring people to a Holy place (in our day, temples) where the *fullness of the Melchizedek Priesthood* can be bestowed upon the scattered remnants of Israel and be brought home.

Who are the Gentiles? Let's identify them and then we will identify *the remnant.* Anciently, if you go back far enough, the simple definition of Gentile is *non-Israelite.* We've got three groups of people here that the scriptures talk about: Gentiles, Israelites, and heathens. Heathen nations, historically, are the non-Christian nations of the earth. Anciently, they were idol worshipers and did not worship the True and Living God. The Gentiles, in our day, are the descendants of the Holy Roman Empire. That would include Eastern and Western Europe, some of Asia, America, and Australia, which were colonized by Europeans. So, there are your Gentile nations in the modern day. These nations came out of the Roman Empire and can be found in those places. Now, are the Latter-day Saints Gentiles? There's a question for you, see? Are we, as Latter-day Saints, considered Gentiles? Let's go over to the Title Page of the *Book of Mormon* and see if we can answer that. There's a huge section of prophecy in the *Book of Mormon* concerning the Gentiles, and sometimes it's difficult to understand who that is talking about. Who are these Gentiles? On the Title Page of the *Book of Mormon* it says;

> *AN ACCOUNT WRITTEN BY THE HAND OF*
> *MORMON UPON PLATES TAKEN FROM THE*
> *PLATES OF NEPHI*

The first paragraph, second line says that it was:

*Written to the Lamanites, who are a remnant of
the house of Israel; and also to Jew and Gentile—*
The *Book of Mormon* is not written to the heathen nations of the earth. Then look at what else it says:

*Written by way of commandment, and also by the
spirit of prophecy and of revelation—Written and
sealed up, and hid up unto the Lord, that they
might not be destroyed—To come forth by the gift
and power of God unto the interpretation
thereof—Sealed by the hand of Moroni, and hid
up unto the Lord, **to come forth in due time by
way of the Gentile**—*

Well, who was it that brought the *Book of Mormon* out of the Hill Cumorah and translated it? Joseph Smith.

The interpretation thereof by the gift of God.

The *Book of Mormon* title page identifies its translator and the person who brings it out of the ground **as a Gentile**. And yet, Joseph, in his writings said that he was a pure Ephraimite. That gets a little confusing, doesn't it? So, those of us who have received patriarchal blessings, and that patriarch lays his hands on our head and declares our lineage, the vast majority of the members of the Church are going to be declared to come from one of the tribes of Israel, one of the twelve sons of Jacob. Another way of describing the house of Israel, one would simply say, the family of Jacob. Jacob's name was changed to Israel. He had twelve sons and one daughter. So, the descendants of all those twelve sons and that one daughter, which are called the family of Jacob, another name of it is the house of Israel or the family of Jacob. Now, it's important to know that Latter-day Saints who receive their patriarchal blessings and have a lineage declared through one of the tribes of Israel are also Gentiles. We are Gentiles. Almost all the Latter-day Saints can track their immigration of their forefathers and their ancestors from the Gentile nations of the earth that we've identified tonight—those Christian nations of Western and Eastern Europe, America, Australia, etc. and some parts of Asia. And we'll talk about Asia a little bit tonight. Asia is really an interesting place when it comes to the house of Israel.

Go over to section 109 and let me show you something else. This is the Kirtland Temple dedication. I had a sister write me this last week and ask some questions concerning all this, and it's a confusing deal. It can be confusing! *Doctrine and Covenants* 109:60. Here's the prophet Joseph Smith and he's praying on behalf of the Latter-day Saints and the establishment of Zion. In verse 60, he and comes out and says this:

> *[60] Now these words, O Lord, we have spoken before thee, concerning the revelations and commandments which thou hast given unto **us**,*

Who's the **us**? The Latter-day Saints, right? Look at the next one:

> *who are identified with the Gentiles.*

These members of the Church are Gentiles. In fact, the Church of Jesus Christ of Latter-day Saints, which is filled full of members who have received patriarchal blessings that identify them as Israelites, the Church is a Gentile church. Why is it a Gentile church? Because it was restored and established in a day called *the day of the Gentile.* Now, you remember back in the days of the *New Testament* Church, that the gospel of Jesus Christ was taken by the leader in that dispensation only to the remnants of the house of Israel. And you'll remember that the Savior said, in the *New Testament* in Matthew, *"I am not sent but unto...the house of Israel."* And you have people that were not Israelites that periodically took the Saviors time and tried to glean from Him blessings and power and information, for example, the woman at the well; this is a classic example. She's a Samaritan; she's a Gentile according to the society of that day. And He sits and talks with her, and it amazes her that He, being a Jew, would talk to her who is a Samaritan. And the disciples came up, and they saw Him talking to this woman, and they reasoned amongst themselves, "What is He doing talking to this woman? She's subhuman." And by and large, throughout the whole *New Testament*, Jesus avoided the Gentiles or those who were not members of the house of Israel. And that changed when Peter has a vision in Acts 10, down at Simon the tanner's place in Joppa on the Mediterranean coast and that whole thing with Cornelius and his household. Peter sees a vision of the great sheet with all the four-footed beasts that are unclean on it. The

Jews are forbidden to eat these animals listed. (According to Leviticus chapter 11). The Lord lowers this great sheet, and a voice says:

Rise, Peter; kill, and eat.

And Peter says:

Not so, Lord; for I have never eaten any thing that is common or unclean.

And then the voice says:

What God hath cleansed, that call not thou common.

And at that point, we have a new dispensation opened because the house of Israel rejects the gospel, so the gospel is taken to the Gentiles, and Paul becomes the great Gentile apostle. Even that eventually ends in apostasy, but not before the *New Testament* Church obtains the *Church of the First Born* and the *General Assembly,* and the ministration of *just men made perfect.* So, they did have some success even though it ended in apostasy. When you take these two groups, Jew and Gentile, or house of Israel and Gentile, you can see that in Christ's time, the first to receive the gospel was the Jew/house of Israel and the second to receive it in Christ's time, the last to receive it was the Gentile. In our day, the gospel was restored first to the Gentile, and at some future time that we're on the edge of, it will be taken again to the house of Israel. And *the remnant of Jacob* plays a role in the transition from Gentile to the house of Israel. So, the first, the Jews in Christ's day, will be the last in our day. And the last in Christ's day, the Gentiles, were first in our day. *"The last shall be first, and the first shall be last."* And that's how that fits with these two big groups. So, the Latter-day Saints are Gentiles. We belong to a Gentile church. And it doesn't take anything away from us, however, that we have the blood of Israel flowing in our veins which have been identified by revelation through a patriarch.

So right now, we're in a state where the house of Israel is scattered. You know that if you are a descendant of Joseph, through Ephraim and Manasseh, you are numbered with the ten lost tribes that were taken into the north country by the Assyrian emperors. This is something a lot of Latter-day Saints don't think about. You have family that has been led away and lost, and they

are called the lost ten tribes. Now, without going into it too
deeply, these lost ten tribes that were taken north from the
Northern Kingdom into Assyria, eventually found themselves in
two groups. One group continued north led by prophets through
miraculous means. They parted the water; they passed through
ice, etc. They went north, and we've not heard of them since.
They are the lost ten tribes of Israel. Then there was another
portion of this group that didn't go north, but went northwest and
eventually moved over to Scandinavia and into Western and
Eastern Europe and intermarried with those people living there.
Those are our ancestors. That's where we come from. This is
where the Gentiles come from, and this is why the Gentiles have
the blood of Israel in their veins. Of the ten tribes, there are two
groups: those that intermarried with the Gentile people, who are
our ancestors; and there's another isolated, separate group that
were taken north, and they are called the **lost** ten tribes. Now,
sometimes in the Church, we think that the lost ten tribes are lost
because they are intermingled among the nations of Western and
Eastern Europe and that the gathering of the ten tribes of Israel
from the north is happening as those people join the Church and
receive their patriarchal blessings. That is not correct! Almost
90% of those that are coming into the Church today are through
the house of Joseph—Ephraim and Manasseh, the majority being
Ephraim. These are the people coming out of Western Europe
who have been intermingled with the Gentiles. That's why we,
who are in the Church today, are identified with the Gentiles.
Joseph's ancestry came out of Great Britain, so did mine.
[Student], you are there from Switzerland, you're coming out of
that group too. But this is not the ten lost tribes that Moses is
talking to Joseph and Oliver about in section 110 of the *Doctrine
and Covenants*. Let's go to section 110, and we'll come back to
3 Nephi in just a minute. This is so fascinating. As we start to get
a feel for it, it makes a lot of sense. *Doctrine and Covenants*
110:11:

> *After this vision closed, the heavens were again
> opened unto us; and Moses appeared before us,
> and committed unto us the keys of the gathering of
> Israel from the four parts of the earth,*

See you've got two groups here:

and the leading of the ten tribes from the land of the north.

Now, it's true that those of us who come out of the Gentile nations come out of the northern countries; they're in the Northern Hemisphere. But, there's another group who went further north and when they return that group will come in the millions.

Let's go to Jeremiah, for example. Let me show you a fascinating scripture. I'm giving all this background so that we can get a feel for what's happening among us because I'm telling you brothers and sisters, every day in the news you see the fulfilling of this prophecy we're talking about. This may take a little longer than an hour tonight, but I'll try to keep it short. Go to Jeremiah 16:14. This is a good one for you to underline and mark:

[14] Therefore, behold, the days come,

Anytime you see the *Old Testament* speak about—*in those days, the days come, at that day, in the latter day, in the last days*—it is always referring to our day:

saith the Lord, that it shall no more be said, The Lord liveth, that brought up the children of Israel out of the land of Egypt;

Now, think about that. What's the greatest *Old Testament* miracle recorded in that volume? The parting of the Red Sea, right? And even to this day, when we think of miracles we think of the deliverance of millions of Israelites out of Egyptian captivity by this huge miracle. It is still a major miracle in all of scripture. But, notice in verse 14 Jeremiah says we won't talk about that anymore. The day is going to come when we don't talk about that anymore. Verse 15:

[15] But, [so instead of talking about that, we're going to talk about] The Lord liveth, that brought up the children of Israel from the land of the north, and from all the lands whither he had driven them: and I will bring them again into their land that I gave unto their fathers.

The lost tribes of Israel (especially those that were taken into the north and did not assimilate with the Gentile nations, as our ancestors did), when they return, the miracles that accompany their return will eclipse the parting of the Red Sea to a point where people won't even talk about that anymore. Instead, they will talk about the return of the tribes from the north and from all other lands whither He has driven them. In Isaiah chapter 29, he talks about *a marvelous work and a wonder.* And the LeGrand Richards book, *A Marvelous Work and a Wonder,* referred to the restoration of the gospel through the Prophet Joseph Smith in the 1830's. And certainly, that was a marvelous work. I'm not taking anything away from that. The coming forth of the *Book of Mormon* was a part of it and was certainly a marvelous work and a wonder. I want to testify to you that the *marvelous work and a wonder* that Isaiah is talking about hasn't happened yet. But, you and I are on the edge of it. All of the events are now in place and starting to happen for the establishment of Zion and what the Lord calls, in *Doctrine and Covenants, "my strange act."* In Malachi 3:17 He says:

> And they shall be mine, saith the Lord of hosts, in that day when I make up **my jewels**; and I will spare them, as a man spareth his own son that serveth him.

So, this *"strange act"* will happen when the Lord gathers His *"jewels."* Isn't that interesting?" That's what's coming. And the miracles that you read about in the scriptures are going to be eclipsed, brothers and sisters, by the miracles we are going to see in our day. Nothing like it, ever, in the history of the world.

When the Lord pours out fantastic, unspeakable knowledge and power, there has to be the opposite that takes place. Hence the cataclysms the scriptures speak about—lightning, thunder, earthquakes, plagues, war, and all those things—are happening at same time when God is pouring out knowledge upon the heads of the Latter-day Saints. Knowledge that is unspeakable and has never been uttered or spoken of since the foundation of this world is now coming in our day. The things we talk about on these podcasts, the *mysteries of Godliness,* are part of things that have been reserved to come forth in this day. And with that revelation of great knowledge, you're also going to have great upheaval. That's okay! Now, let's go back to 3 Nephi 20:16:

> Then shall ye, who are a remnant of the **house of Jacob**,

That's that group. We've identified the Gentiles, and now we're talking about the second group in the fulfillment of this:

go forth among them;

"*Them,*" meaning the Gentile nations, not only in America. But, this is the point I want to bring to you tonight that we don't talk about much in the Church. We want to limit this prophecy of *the remnant of Jacob* to America. But it's not America, and if you read about it, "*Then shall ye, who are a remnant of the house of Jacob, go forth among them,*" you'll see that it's not just American Gentiles. That's the Gentile nations of the whole world. And I want you to grab hold of that because, after tonight, it's going to make sense to you. You're going to look and say, "Oh, my gosh, this is what's going on in Germany. Oh my, this is what's happening in France. This is what's happening in Sweden. This is what's happening in America." And you'll see that this *remnant of Jacob* isn't limited to just what's going on in America, but *the remnant of Jacob* has to do with something that scourges all of the Gentile nations in our day. So, grab hold of that thought and don't limit it to America. Certainly, there's going to be a cleansing take place. Now, this cleansing will ultimately result in the consummation of all nations. Nations that exist today, national borders, national sovereignties, national identities, are going to be completely done away with, and a new order will come out of this. The old order is going to pass away, and a new order will come. The new order I am talking about is an order among nations that survive this scourge and that new order will be a Zion Order. Now, Satan has a counterfeit to that, and he calls it the New World Order, which is satanic. It's Babylonian. Now, look at 3 Nephi 20:16 again. It says:

[16] Then shall ye, who are a remnant of the house of Jacob, go forth among them; and ye shall be in the midst of them who shall be many;

So, there's the key that right now this remnant of Jacob is found within the populations of the Gentile nations of the earth. They're already there. Now, "*those who shall be many*" are the Gentiles. It says that:

[the remnant of Jacob] shall be in the midst of them who shall be many; and ye shall be among

*them as a lion among the beasts of the forest, and
as a young lion among the flocks of sheep,*
These *"beasts of the forest"* and *"the flocks of the sheep"*
identify the Gentiles. We've divided the Gentiles into two groups
because it's referencing them. A lion among these two groups:
one lion among the beasts of the forest and another lion among
the flocks of sheep. It's interesting to contemplate that if you
take the Gentile nations of the earth, how could you divide them
up in such a way that one group would be referred to as *beasts of
the forest* and the other one as *flocks of sheep?* Something to
ponder, you see? Continuing verse 16:
*who, if he goeth through both treadeth down and
teareth in pieces, and none can deliver.*
This is not some little civil strife. This is a major, national, global
uprising among the nations of the Gentiles. Look at what it says
in 17:
[17] Thy hand [meaning *the remnant's* hand]
*shall be lifted up upon thine adversaries, and all
thine enemies shall be cut off.*
Any of these Gentiles that try to go up against this *remnant* will
be destroyed. There's no deliverance.
*[18] And I will gather my people together as a
man gathereth his sheaves into the floor.*
[19] For I will make my people [this is *the
remnant*] *with whom the Father hath covenanted,
yea, I will make thy horn iron, and I will make thy
hoofs brass.*
In Isaiah imagery, an iron horn and brass hooves have reference
to warfare. When it goes through, nothing can survive this.
Anciently you had nations that used iron and brass, which are
two metals of warfare. You even take epics of time in
humankind and divide it according to these two metals—the Iron
Age, and the Brass or Bronze Age—and you start to get a feel.
Israelites who were in the field and went against their enemy
who had chariots of iron, could not survive against this warfare
machinery. The only way they could survive this was if Jehovah
Himself came down and fought their battles because their
enemies were always in a position where their weaponry out did
the Israelite weaponry. Israelite weaponry in the *Old Testament*

was always inferior to non-Israelites. These people were metal workers, and they made chariots of iron with bronze, and brass weaponry. The Israelites, at best, were copying them from what they saw. And it was that way on purpose so that God's people would learn to rely on Him instead of upon their own arms to make weapons of war that would match or supersede their enemy. Look at the rest of 19:

> *I will consecrate their gain unto the Lord, and their substance unto the Lord of the whole earth. And behold, I am he who doeth it.*

Now, it appears that this *remnant of Jacob,* when they're acting as a scourge among the Gentiles, does not know, for the most part, that they are a remnant of the covenant people. The Lord is simply using them as a scourge, so they don't have an identity of "I'm being used by the God that I worship." These are people who are fulfilling a scourge purpose prophesied in the scriptures, and they don't really know who they are yet. After the scourging has taken place and we make an end to the Gentile nations(*the remnant of Jacob* is going to do that throughout the world, not just in America), the only Gentiles that will survive this are those who repent and come to the Lord; they are the only ones who will survive this scourging, this uprising, this massive destruction. This is so large, brothers and sisters, that it leaves the Gentile cities desolate. *The remnant of Jacob* doesn't know who they are. They are just acting out as an instrument, in this case, of destruction in the hands of the Lord to destroy the Gentile nations of the earth. After the scourging and they have their identity revealed to them, those Gentiles who repent and are not destroyed will be numbered with *the remnant of Jacob.* That is an important part of the prophecy. They'll be numbered with *the remnant of Jacob.* Look at 3 Nephi 20:20:

> *[20] And it shall come to pass, saith the Father, that the sword of my justice shall hang over them* [the Gentiles] *at that day; and except they repent it shall fall upon them, saith the Father, yea, even upon* [here's your key] *all the nations of the Gentiles.*

All of them! Verse 21:

> *[21] And it shall come to pass that I will establish
> my people, O house of Israel.*
> *[22] And behold, this people will I establish in
> this land, unto the fulfilling of the covenant which
> I made with your father Jacob; and it shall be a
> New Jerusalem. And the powers of heaven* [city of
> Enoch] *shall be in the midst of this people; yea,
> even I will be in the midst of you.*

That's the establishment of the New Jerusalem, but before that happens, *the remnant of Jacob* is going through the Gentile nations, as what? As a lion among sheep and none can deliver.

Let's try to identify *the remnant of Jacob* here for just a minute. I think we're at a point where we need to do that. In America, *the remnant of Jacob* would be the descendants of the Nephites and Lamanites that Jesus was speaking to in the verses we just read. This would include American Indians and those with significant Indian blood, i.e. many people from Mexico, Central America, and South America. I want you to go back now and think about what it said over there in verse 16:

> *Then shall ye, who are a remnant of the house of
> Jacob, go forth among them; and ye shall be in
> the midst of them who shall be many;*

Now, Gentile America has 300 million people in it coast to coast. Do we have any of *the remnant of Jacob* in the midst of our population at this time? Can you see Native Americans? Can you see people from Mexico, Central America, and South America within the borders of the United States of America? Are they here? Do they represent a significant, societal, political force? Is there anything going on with American politics that has to do with immigration? Is there any concern about that? These people in America might also include some people from the Eastern Hemisphere who have immigrated to America. Is that going on? Are there people from the Eastern Hemisphere, the Middle East? As we're going to see, *the remnant of Jacob* is also found in the Middle East. Are there any of those found in the United States of America? Is the remnant here, amongst us, in the midst of us? Is the plan set in motion? What about the Gentile nations in Europe? Think about what's going on there right now with the immigrants that are coming primarily from the Middle East,

Africa, and Southern Asia. Could these people that we're talking about, i.e. the ones in the news, mostly Syrians, could they also be considered *the remnants of Israel*? And do they find themselves in the midst of the Gentiles of Europe, and in some cases, Asia?

Here are some things to think about: The tribes of Israel spent their first four hundred years in the nation of Egypt before Moses' deliverance. What was the likelihood of intermarriage? Do you think any of those Israelites intermarried with those Egyptians in 400 years? What was the likelihood of assimilation into Egyptian society? Here's a good question: what percentage followed Moses out of the land of Egypt during the exodus? Do you think that all Israelites left with Moses? So, there's a group of Israelites that possibly could have intermarried. Following the exodus, the tribes of Israel centered in Palestine but eventually split into two kingdoms. They were carried away to Assyria, and eventually, some of the captive Israelites escaped into the north countries, but there was no mass return to their homeland. We've talked about that tonight. Again, what's the likelihood of intermarriage and assimilation? What percentage of Israelites left Assyria? What percentage stayed there and intermarried? Because ancient Assyria can be identified in modern nations today.

Here's another one: there were other scatterings of Israelites. *The Book of Mormon* speaks of two such groups, the Lehites, and the Mulekites, leaving in the 6th century. Apocryphal scriptures and historical records speak of or at least hint at the fact that there were other peoples who left and made their homes in other lands. I don't think that in all of North and South America at the time of the *Book of Mormon,* that it was only Nephites and Lamanites. I don't believe that. This is Mike Stroud now, I believe that there were other people, and there seems to be some evidence coming around to support that. There were other people besides the Nephites, Mulekites, and Lamanites, in the Americas that had been brought there by the hand of the Lord. We only have the record of the Lehi colony—the Nephites and Lamanites. We don't have a record of anybody else, except the Jaredites were there. What this means is that the nations in the Middle East, Africa and, Southern Asia, are likely filled with the blood of Israel, and many of their people could be considered *the remnant of Israel*. For example, if you'll turn to Isaiah 11 for a minute, let me show you something. Here's a great scripture that helps us. We're looking to see if these people coming out of the Middle East and out of Africa, into the Gentile nations, have Israelite blood in their veins; and it appears that they do, big time! Do they know that they are Israelites? No, we just simply assign them saying, "Oh they are coming out of the Arab countries, those are not Israelites." You know there was intermarriage all through this. I tell you that when these Arab people start joining the Church we're going to be amazed at what their Patriarchal Blessing lineage is identified as; they are going to be the blood of Israel. Go to Isaiah 11; we're going to look at verses 11 and 12:

[11] And it shall come to pass in that day,
There's your key that always points toward the latter-days:
that the Lord shall set his hand again the second time
The first time was to gather the children of Israel out of Egyptian bondage and bring them unto a promised land. The second time:
to recover the remnant of his people, which shall be left,
Now, look we identify ancient lands:
from Assyria, and from Egypt, and from Pathros, and from Cush, and from Elam, and from Shinar, and from Hamath, and from the islands of the sea.
[12] And he shall set up an ensign for the nations, and shall assemble the outcasts of Israel, and gather together the dispersed of Judah from the four corners of the earth.

That is happening with the Jews more and more. If you're a Jew and you leave a nation and immigrate to Israel and seek to become an Israeli citizen of that land, it's called Aliyah. That is happening so much that Israel and the Jews of the world set up an emigration fund, a lot like the Perpetual Emigration Fund of the Latter-day Saints, which is Joseph's side. The Jews have their own perpetual emigration fund for Jews from throughout the world to "make Aliyah" and come to Israel. Now, I did a little homework on these nations. Cush is thought to be the nations that surround the Red Sea. So, if you go today and look at the nations around the Red Sea, they would be identified with ancient Cush. Pathros would be southern Egypt. Elam is western Iran. Shinar refers to Babylonia, which would be Iraq. Hamath is located in west central Syria. Anything going on there today? Assyria is the empire that included Egypt, the western part of the Mediterranean Sea, northern Iraq, northeastern Syria, southeastern Turkey, and northwestern Iran. In short, the blood of Israel is scattered throughout all of these nations. And where are they going? Look at the migration of these nations; where are they heading? They are going to the Gentile nations of the earth.

Let's go over to 3 Nephi 21 for just a minute. The first 11 verses talk about a sign that the Lord is going to give that the events we're talking about now are about to happen. That sign is broken up into some things; it talks about the restoration of the gospel, the coming forth of the *Book of Mormon*, and the gathering of the tribes of Israel from the various places. Let's go to verse 12. Here's another reference to *the remnant*. This is the purpose of the lesson tonight.

[12] And my people who are a remnant of Jacob shall be among the Gentiles, yea, in the midst of them as a lion among the beasts of the forest, as a young lion among the flocks of sheep,

You've got to ask yourself a question; why is the Lord referring to these scriptures twice? He did it over in chapter 20, and He's doing it again in chapter 21. Whenever you see Him refer to something twice in two scriptures, we ought to have a heads up on that. This is an important event that we, as Latter-day Saints, have access to because we have the *Book of Mormon*. If you don't have the *Book of Mormon*, you don't have this additional knowledge. You've got Micah 5, and you've got Isaiah 11 and a couple of other places. So, it's really giving us some good insight. Let's look at verse 13:

[13] Their hand shall be lifted up upon their adversaries, and all their enemies shall be cut off.

This is the part that was not found in chapter 20. Now we're getting some additional information, here we go, verse 14:

[14] Yea, wo be unto the Gentiles except they repent;

Now, I'm going to include the Gentiles in the Church of Jesus Christ of Latter Day Saints because we've got problems in the

Church. A person will not be saved from the scourge that is going to take place among the Gentiles just because they've been baptized. They have to make the choice to align themselves with Christ and keep their covenant relationship. Remember that the only Gentiles who escape what's coming here, whether they're members of the Church or whether they're not members of the Church, are the ones that repent *"and they shall be numbered among my people, O house of Israel."* It doesn't matter what your patriarchal blessing says. It doesn't matter that you are a member of the Church. Right now, we have nine to eleven million members of the Church that are not attending church. I know that'll be startling to you, but Margie and I have traveled on three missions throughout the world, and we got a pretty good feel for what's happening around the world. Now, unless those of you who live along the Wasatch Front and the states of Utah, Idaho, and Arizona, those strong established stakes, have gone out on a member/leader support mission, the MLS missions like we have, you may not notice the inactivity in the Church. In Mongolia, the percentage of active members attending church is 27%. The Church has been in the Philippines for 50 years; when we were there, we celebrated the 50th anniversary in Cebu. If you go there, you're going to find out that the active membership percentage is 12%. That means that 88% of the members of the Church in the Philippines are not attending any church. Now, when I travel to these places, I want to find out what's happening out there because a member/leadership support missionary's job is to go out and reclaim and rescue members of the Church who have ceased activity. That's your whole job. It's a rescue mission to go out and get what we call "the low hanging fruit." And "the low hanging fruit" means you're going out to rescue people who have already entered into a covenant, at one time felt the Spirit, but lost that. The low hanging fruit" are the easy ones to get, right? You don't need to reach up there with tools to go out and get those who have been close at one time and wandered away. Well, in New Jersey it was 24%. So, look at verse 14 again:

Yea, wo be unto the Gentiles except they repent;

And that is including members of the Church for one reason or another that have walked away from activity. Your covenants mean nothing if you're not **in** your covenants. Brother Ballard said that you want to die in your covenants and stay there so you can be pronounced safely dead. Continuing verse 14:

for it shall come to pass in that day, saith the Father,

If they don't repent, if the Gentiles continue to reject Christ and His Gospel:

that I will cut off thy horses out of the midst of thee, and I will destroy thy chariots;

Let's talk about that for just a minute. If you're an ancient prophet looking down on 2016 and you saw trains, interstate trucking and mass transportation in these Gentile nations, what would you think? Transportation in the Gentile nations is the best of anyplace in the world. You go out of the Gentile nations and from that point on transportation goes downhill. And I have been on some of the roads and driven in some of those places. Anciently, what moved their vehicles were horses. Isn't it interesting that the power that moves it in our day is referred to as what? Horsepower. What could possibly happen that would cut off the horses and destroy the chariots? What would happen if we were to lose electricity? What would happen if we were to be cut off from oil supplies? We're dependent on foreign nations for the oil reserves for the oil we have right now. What if there was an electromagnetic pulse? What if there were a cyber hack that cut down the grid? How quick would trucking come to a stop if there was no electricity to pump the fuel out of the tanks that runs the truck? Did these prophets see that? Look what else it says:

[15] And I will cut off the cities of thy land,

Well, I'll tell you that if you cut out the transportation, we'd be in trouble! Right here in little Eagar, Arizona, we rely on a Safeway truck coming up over that 8,000-foot mountain pass between Show Low and Eagar every night, and we've had the experience of having our little city cut off because no transportation could get in here:

and throw down all thy strongholds;

You can let your mind ponder on what these prophets saw coming in 2016 to 2020. How did they describe it? By using all of this imagery. Verse 16:

[16] And I will cut off witchcrafts out of thy land, and thou shalt have no more soothsayers;

A soothsayer is a person that ascends to something less than the truth. They are Satan's seers. A soothsayer is a dark seer, with dark gifts. They had that. There was the witch of Palmyra. When Joseph was translating the *Book of Mormon* there was a woman that had a stone and she could look into that stone and she could see where Joseph had the plates and Joseph was having to move the plates from one place to another constantly to stay ahead of this dark seer, this woman who had a stone which showed her where Joseph was hiding the record. Interesting stuff! Let's go to 17:

> *[17] Thy graven images I will also cut off, and thy standing images out of the midst of thee,*

Graven Images, what's that? Well, you'll know by looking at the rest of verse 17:

> *and thou shalt no more worship the works of thy hands;*

What is it we worship most in this world in the Gentile nations? Money! What is it that Satan says to the messengers when they go to Adam and Eve? "You can have anything in this world for money." Boy, that describes the world. And don't you know that money is graven? You know that the plates that prints the Federal Reserve notes are called "engraving plates?" And the money we use is a graven image using metal plates to do it; just a possibility. Look at verse 18:

> *[18] And I will pluck up thy groves out of the midst of thee; so will I destroy thy cities.*

Anciently, the groves were places of prostitution, ritual prostitution, and immorality in the grossest forms:

> *[19] And it shall come to pass that all lyings, and deceivings, and envyings, and strifes, and priestcrafts, and whoredoms, shall be done away.*

Now, you want to ask the question, what is it that's doing away with all of these things? Go back up to verse 12, and look at what's causing all of this turmoil, collapse, and change. It's *the remnant of Jacob* among the Gentile nations:

> *[20] For it shall come to pass, saith the Father, that at that day*

The scourge of *the remnant of Jacob* makes a full end of the Gentile nations and, by the way, the end of *the day of the*

Gentiles is when this *remnant* goes through and, in the uprising, destroys the national identities of these countries:

> *whosoever will not repent and come unto my Beloved Son, them will I cut off from among my people, O house of Israel;*
>
> *[21] And I will execute vengeance and fury upon them* [the Gentiles], *even as upon the heathen, such as they have not heard.*
>
> *[22] But if they will repent and hearken unto my words* [this is the Gentiles], *and harden not their hearts, I will establish my church among them, and they shall come in unto the covenant and be numbered among this the remnant of Jacob, unto whom I have given this land for their inheritance;*

And *they* means the repentant Gentiles because the rest of them are gone. They are gone, like a lion among the sheep:

> *[23] and they shall assist my people, the remnant of Jacob, and also as many of the house of Israel as shall come, that they may build a city, which shall be called the New Jerusalem.*

Well, brothers and sister, we've got some stuff coming at us here! Unbelievable! Can you feel it? I've had several people ask me about the *call out.* The *Call Out Principle* that is advocated on some LDS sites and by some Latter-day Saint groups is a true principle. That is a true principle. It's obvious that it's a true principle. It's all through the scriptures that the Lord will take His people, those that repent and honor their covenants with Him, out from among the nations of the wicked and gather them to holy places, safe places **before** He pours out vengeance and judgment on those who refuse to repent. In the New Testament times, after Christ's death, He warned them. He said to let those who are in the fields flee; let those in the cities flee, and if you don't and you get caught in that day and you're pregnant, it's going to be tough on you. But, if you flee you're going to flee to a place of safety. Now, before the Roman destruction of the Jews in 70 AD, the priesthood leaders among the Church there warned the members to get out. There was a *call out,* and they went north to a little city called Pella that is now located in modern Jordan. The members of the Church in the New Testament time who harkened to that *call out* and went to Pella survived the Roman destruction of Jerusalem in 70 AD. The destruction was so devastating that it is said that the blood of the Jews ran up to the bridles of the Roman soldiers' horses. It marked the end of the Jewish nation, the last temple the Jews ever had, and they were then scattered among all the nations of the world. This is what's called the great Jewish Diaspora. It was only in May of 1948 that it started to turn around. But the members of the Church heeded the call of their leaders, went to Pella, and were able to survive that Roman holocaust. And we can see that all through the Church. Latter-day Saints went right out of the United States into Mexico; they were *called out*. The Jaredites were *called out*. The Nephites were *called out*. It's just one after another! It's a true principle. Whether the Church is preparing holy places or not, I don't know. But, I do know that if you are in tune with the Spirit, you are already picking up messages that you should be doing something to prepare for this cleansing experience that we've talked about tonight, *the scourge of the Gentiles, the remnant of Jacob*. I know that some of you who have lived in metropolitan areas have shared with me that you have made decisions to get out. And you got out, not knowing how you were going to do it. It was financially and feasibly impossible for you to do, but you heeded that Voice and the Lord prepared the way. You've shared your testimonies with me that what happened to you was truly miraculous. So, that's going on now, this *call out*, and you don't have to look for that to happen. It's happening right now, and people are being told by the Spirit that they need to go here or go there, do this, or do that because we've got a train wreck coming at us. And the Church cannot take care of its membership; can't do it! All of Welfare Square in Salt Lake City is not going to do the job. So, it's left up to individual members of the Church, mothers and fathers, either singly or together, to harken to the voice of the Spirit and to do what it says. It comes back to the theme of these podcasts: Put your trust in no man. 2 Nephi 4:34:

> *I will not put my trust in the arm of flesh; for I know that cursed is he that putteth his trust in the arm of flesh. Yea, cursed is he that putteth his trust in man or maketh flesh his arm.*

Trust in the Lord. Take the truth and the Holy Spirit as your guide. These are they who will stand when the Lord appears.

I hope that's been helpful. I hope that now you can look at the news today and look at *the remnant of Jacob* and say, "My gosh, it's happening all around us." You can see the stage is being set with all of these Syrian refugees, all of these problems in Europe, with Germany, Sweden, France, and here in America and all of the talk of illegal immigration. They are amongst us now; *the remnant of Jacob* is here. And if you're a German citizen you would definitely say, "*The remnant of Jacob* is here." Now, what are you going to do with the prophecy?

Sorry it took so long, but I needed that much time to just lay this out. I hope that feels right. I'd like to read a little something that someone wrote about this and conclude with it:

> The current invasion of Gentile nations by foreigners appears to be the beginning of the sore vexation *the remnants of Jacob* will bring against the Gentiles. At the very least it is setting the stage for the prophesied uprising of a people that will be as a lion among the beasts of the forest. This uprising will begin the destruction of the Gentile nations.

And by the way, the destruction of the Gentile nations is the end of *the day of the Gentile* and the beginning of *the day of Israel*. The *dispensation of the fullness of times* can be divided into two parts. Part A is *the day of the Gentile,* and part B is *the day of Israel*. We are ending *the day of the Gentile* and about to go into *the day of Israel*, which are both parts of *the dispensation of the fullness of times*. Back to this statement:

> Most of *the remnant of Jacob* who tread down the Gentiles will probably not realize that they possess the blood of Israel and can become heirs of the covenant and promised blessings on condition of their faithfulness. They will be used to do the Lord's work in removing the wicked Gentiles from the land and then will be given the opportunity to learn and follow the gospel of the Messiah. If they do not respond to the call to gather to the Lord's Gospel, they too will find

themselves swept up off the land. However, the scriptures seem to indicate that a great many [this is *the remnant of Jacob*], if not the majority, will embrace the gospel of Jesus Christ. What can be done? We must remember that God is preparing the world and a people for the second coming of Christ and his millennial reign of peace. The earth is being changed and a loving God is calling his children to repentance, so that they might meet their Savior when He comes. The only way for Gentiles and *remnants of Israel* to not be cleansed from the land is to fully turn to the Lord and truly become His people in the way they think, speak, and act.

I thought that was a great statement to conclude our lesson tonight. Thank you, brothers and sisters. I hope that's helpful to you. Bless your hearts and let's just stand in Holy Places, love the Lord, keep His commandments, seek for the cause of Zion and all will be well. In the name of Jesus Christ, amen.

References:
Micah 5:7-15
2 Nephi 5:25-26
D&C 87 section heading
D&C 87:2, 4-6
D&C 45:30-32
General Conference April 1989, *"Beware of Pride"* by Ezra Taft Benson
2 Nephi 30:10-11
"Who's on the Lord's Side?" *Hymns of the Church of Jesus Christ of Latter-day Saints*, hymn 260
The Book of Mormon title page
D&C 109:60
Matthew 15:24 "... I am not sent but unto...the house of Israel."
Leviticus 11
Acts 10:13-15
1 Nephi 13:42 "The last shall be first, and the first shall be last."
D&C 110:11
Jeremiah 16:14-15
Isaiah 29:14 "...a marvelous work and a wonder..."
A Marvelous Work and a Wonder by LeGrand Richards
D&C 95:4; 101:95 "My strange act..."
Malachi 3:17

3 Nephi 20:16-22
Isaiah 11:11-14
3 Nephi 21:15-23
3 Nephi 16:13 "...they shall be numbered among my people, O house of Israel."
2 Nephi 4:34

Chapter Thirty-Six
Podcast 036 Glory

Well, tonight, brothers and sisters, I pray that the Holy Ghost will help so that this topic can be presented in plainness and that it's readily understandable. That is my prayer tonight because it's a topic that I've pondered on for a number of years, and this week I had some personal experiences as I studied this area. At 4 o'clock this morning, the Spirit of the Lord woke me up and said, "You need to teach that concept tonight." So, I pray for that direction. It's not an easy concept. It has to do with one of the ways in which the Gods, the Mothers and Fathers, progress. We've already had a lesson called Progression in Eternity, and we talked about some of these things. I'd like to take it a little step further.

It is true that the Fathers and Mothers progress as their children come up and inherit all that they have. Those inheritances include kingdoms, thrones, principalities, powers, dominions, and exaltations. Notice that all those words are plural, and that is the correct doctrine. As we've talked about before, there are many different levels of progression before and after the resurrection of the dead. One of these that I want to talk to you about tonight has to do with something called *glory*. The principle is called *glorification*. That's really an interesting subject because if you search on lds.org under the scriptures, and just type in the word *glory*, you'll see that it comes up many,

many times throughout all of the standard works. And its counterpart word, *glorification*, which describes a process, is also found under the word *glorify*. So, if you look up *glory* and *glorify*, and do a little study on those, compared with some of the things we'll talk about tonight, I feel that it will do for you what it has done for me and give you some added information. Remember, whatever principle of intelligence we attain unto in this life, will rise with us in the resurrection. And if a man gains more knowledge and intelligence in this life than another, through his diligence and obedience, he'll have so much the advantage in the world to come. I think it behooves us to look into and see all that we can about how the Gods, the Fathers and Mothers, progress and continue to move up. There is no place in eternity where intelligent beings have reached a certain level of Godhood or Godliness, where they are not progressing. This was solid doctrine taught by Joseph Smith and by the early brethren in the Church.

This principle of *glory* is an interesting one, so I'd like to just look at some scriptures. The first one is Moses 1, verse 39 and it's probably the one scripture mastery scripture that most members of the Church can quote.

> For behold, this is my work and my **glory**—to bring to pass the immortality and eternal life of man.

There's that word. That word comes up in all kinds of different places. What I'd like to do is plug in some feelings and some thoughts with that. So, God's work and His *glory* are, *"to bring to pass the immortality and eternal life of man." Immortality* is accomplished through the resurrection of the dead. *Eternal life* is reserved for those who obtain the celestial world as a husband and wife, and are authorized by the Council of the Gods to move forward and do what those Mothers and Fathers do. That's *eternal life*. It is the God's life. It is the Mother and Father's life and everything that entails. Anything short of that places you in the position of a servant. So, in eternity, we have two groups of people. We have those who have obtained kingdoms and rule and reign over kingdoms, as kings and priests, queens and priestesses. And then all others are servants; separate and single in their saved condition; saved either in a telestial world, in a terrestrial world, or in a celestial world without an exaltation. Here's a Brigham Young quote about that:

All of God's children will be saved in a kingdom of light, except the sons of perdition. They are the only ones upon whom the second death has any power.

Brigham Young taught that the second death means that after the resurrection and after judgment, these individuals go backward and retrogress into darkness to a point where they lose their very identities and go back into native element. And if they are ever able to come out of that again, it will be through reorganization, and it may take millions and millions of years to do that. That was taught by Brigham and Heber and the Pratt brothers and all the early Brethren in general conferences; it is the dissolution of the identity of a son of perdition.

Now, *glory* is something that pertains to all intelligent beings who are saved in a kingdom of light. So, you would have *glory* at a telestial level, you would have *glory* at a terrestrial level, and you would have *glory* in varying degrees and levels in the celestial world. That still doesn't answer for us what it is, but it kind of gives us an idea that you'll find *glory* everywhere in eternity but in outer darkness. In outer darkness, there is no *glory*, and there is no light. Light has to be present in order for there to be *glory*. That's the first rule I want to talk about.

Now, let's go over to Abraham chapter 3, verse 22 for just a minute, and let's look at another scripture that will kind of build a platform and build a little bit of a case for what we want to do here. Abraham, in vision, looks into the premortal, pre-earth life:

[22] Now the Lord had shown unto me, Abraham, the intelligences [notice that it is plural] *that were organized before the world was;*

Now, we can call these exactly what the scripture says: these are organized intelligences. This refers to the spirit offspring sons and daughters of the Mothers and Fathers in Heaven. This is that person who is inside your body. According to what we have been taught by the Brethren, this is an organized spirit that has gender and is male or female and comes into existence through birth. There has been controversy on this among the Brethren throughout the history of the Church. The prevailing consensus is that these come into existence through a spirit birth and that the Parents of these organized intelligences are resurrected Men and Women who have attained an exaltation in the celestial world. Back to verse 22:

*and among all these there were many of the noble
and great ones;*

So, now you've got two groups of people here. He has divided them into two groups. You have the organized intelligences, male and female offspring, and then within that group, you have another group (I assume smaller in number), that He refers to as *"the noble and great ones."* Verse 23:

*[23] And God saw these **souls** that they were
good,*

If you'll stop for just a minute and go over to section 88 in the *Doctrine and Covenants*, I'll show you an interesting little thing here. We read this so often and so fast that we don't stop to take a closer look at it. In verse 15, the Lord reveals to the Prophet Joseph Smith, the definition of *soul*. Now, in the *Book of Mormon*, Alma and Amulek referred to *the soul*, but they did not have complete information. The way they use *soul* in the *Book of Mormon* is referring to the spirit, in other words, these organized intelligences. Most Christians when they refer to *the soul of man* are talking about his spirit. But the *Doctrine and Covenants*, in verse 15, gives us a very interesting truth:

*And **the spirit and the body** are the soul of man.*

So, embodied spirits are souls. Now, when you go back to Abraham 3, and among these organized intelligences, which are spirit beings, there is another group called *the noble and great ones. "And God saw these **souls**..."* Interesting! Are we to take that literally, that in the premortal world there were not only spirit offspring, but that there were also embodied persons that the Lord refers to as *the noble and great ones*? Can we look at it that way? Just something to look at:

and he stood in the midst of them, [the noble and great ones] *and he said: These* [souls, the noble and great ones] *I will make my rulers; for he stood among those that were spirits,*

There's your big general group again:

> *and he saw that they were good; and he said unto*
> *me: Abraham, thou art one of them; thou wast*
> *chosen before thou wast born.*

Just something to think about.

Now, let's skip on down and look at verse 24, and I'll show you where I'm going with this.

Student 6: Okay, so Mike, you said that's, "something to think about." Are you going to address that?

Mike: No, I'm going to leave that open because I can't pull anything from the scriptures that would back up or give us added information on it. It's something for you to contemplate and ponder. I'm just saying, is it just a mistake in the Abraham manuscript, or are we talking about a group of people that were embodied that God calls *the noble and great ones*? He refers to one of them, interestingly, as *"Abraham, thou art one of them; thou wast chosen before thou wast born."* Now, obviously, that doesn't fit in with our theology and what's been revealed to us in the Restoration doctrine. So, what I'm trying to do here is to show how if you slow down and look at things, and if you can compare one scripture to the other, it gives insight that you otherwise wouldn't get if you were in a rush reading. I'm not making any kind of conclusions here. But, it's interesting anyway.

Student 6: Okay.

Mike: Verse 24:

> *And there stood one among them* [these noble and
> great ones] *that was like unto God, and he said*
> *unto those who were with him: We will go down,*
> *for there is space there, and we will take of these*
> *materials,*

We're going to find out in a minute that those materials are referred to as element.

> *and we will make an earth whereon these may dwell.*

These, meaning *these* spirit offspring, *these* organized intelligences:

> *[25] And we will prove them* [these intelligences]
> *herewith* [meaning on this new world], *to see if*
> *they will do all things whatsoever the Lord their*
> *God shall command them;*

270

So, verse 25 gives you the core reason for earth life and our existence in the telestial world. This part in verse 26 is where I want to go tonight:

> *[26] And they* [meaning those who were spirits]
> *who keep their first estate shall be added upon;*

Now, the first estate refers to the life before the telestial world. Whether you want to call that the premortal life, or whether you want to go into the temple allegory and say that it represents a terrestrial world, the Garden of Eden before the Fall—whatever you want to do there—it's before they come into this world. So, if they keep that first estate, they shall be *added upon.* All of us kept that first estate, meaning; you did not come out in open rebellion and join in the warfare against the Father and the Son. In James Talmage's book *Jesus the Christ,* the second chapter under the premortal world (you can look this up), he said that those who did not join in open warfare and rebellion against the Father and the Son obtained a body. They were able to merit a birth. And that's the *"added upon."* The physical body then becomes the item that's *added upon* your spirit. Now, watch the next one in verse 26:

> *and they who keep not their first estate shall not*
> *have **glory** in the same kingdom with those who*
> *kept their first estate;*

What this tells us is that whatever *glory* is, brothers and sisters, you who kept your first estate have been *added upon.* You can tell that you did because you're here in the telestial world, clothed upon with a physical body. What this verse is telling you is that before you came here, you obtained something called *glory.* You had it before you came here. Now, that's an interesting concept. And you'll see how we add on that as we go. Watch the rest of this:

> *they who keep their second estate* [which is the
> telestial world they're in] *shall have **glory** and*
> *added upon their heads for ever and ever.*

So, if you're faithful in the second estate and pass the second estate judgment, you'll obtain **additional** *glory* that will be added to the *glory* you already had before you were born into this world.

271

What we're talking about here is that at the end of each estate (first, second, third) there is an estate judgment. If you pass that judgment, you go into the next estate with more *glory* than you had before you came into the previous one. So, in this progression from one place to another, one of the benefits of being faithful and true and being qualified to enter into the next estate is that you're going to take two estates worth of accumulated *glory* with you into that third estate. The next estate for us will be the millennial, third estate, the terrestrial world. We still haven't defined what *glory* is, but you've already got some! That spirit inside of you, that man or that woman, is a being of *glory*. Now, when you're clothed upon with a body, it hides the *glory*. We'll see how that happens in just a moment.

Let's look at a couple of other things. I just find it so fascinating that the terms *glory* and *glorified* are used so much, and as you go into your lds.org scripture search, you'll see just how much this is used. I'm just so fascinated with it, and we know so little about it. And yet, we are in possession of it, and we are adding to it. Don't you think that if that's the case, then we ought to understand what's happening to us since we're in the process of it here? Let's go to section 93 and get a definition of it. First of all, section 93, verse 36 is a very, very famous and oft-used scriptural reference. In fact, it is written on the entrance walls to BYU. On one wall, it says, *"Enter to learn-Go forth to serve."* And on the other wall, it says, *"The glory of God is intelligence."* So, let's look at that verse.

The **glory** of God is **intelligence**, or, in other words,

"In other words" what? *"In other words"* other than *glory* and *intelligence* we've got synonymous words that mean the same thing:

or, in other words, **light** and **truth**.

So, now what have we got here? In that one little verse, we've got four words, and the Lord uses the phrase *"or, in other words,"* to tell us that the four words are all synonymous with each other. So, for example, if you want to define *glory*, according to verse 36, it would be easy by just looking at the other three words. *Glory* equals *intelligence*, *light*, and *truth*. If you want to define *intelligence*, you would say *intelligence* equals *glory*, *light*, and *truth*. If you want to define *light*, *light* equals *glory, intelligence,* and *truth*; and so on. So, there's your definition.

Now, that just gives us four terms to work with that are not really easy to understand. Let's take the *intelligence* part first of all. Let's go back to verse 29 in the same section. Now, section 93 is, in my mind, the deepest, most poignant, doctrinally profound section in the *Doctrine and Covenants.* I know 76 is great, and I know 88 is great, but boy, when it comes to deep truths, section 93 really is at the top. Hyrum Andrus used to call it the "Holy of Holies" of the *Doctrine and Covenants.* So, look at verse 29:

Man was also in the beginning with God.

Period. Just an interesting statement. You might ask, "Who is man?" Well, that's us. What's the beginning? Well, you have to discern these things. You have to say, "Is the beginning the first estate where we were organized as intelligent sons and daughters, male and female in gender, organized intelligences?" But, then He goes on. Look at this:

Intelligence [now look closely], *or the light of truth, was not created or made, neither indeed can be.*

Now, this becomes very confusing for Latter-day Saints. I know it was for me. And I'm not professing that I understand everything about it right now, but I'll share with you what I've learned. Look carefully at the wording:

[29] Intelligence [here's your definition], *the light of truth.*

Now, look at verse 36 again:

[36] ...intelligence, or, in other words, light and truth.

So, you have two terms here now. One is *light AND truth,* and the other is *light OF truth.*

[29] was not created or made, neither indeed can be.

The *intelligence* referred to in verse 29, and is also having reference to it in verse 36, is what some people call the CIA of the human being (CIA means Central Intelligence Agency). It is that part of you that is truly intelligent. Joseph Smith said it is co-eternal with God, is without beginning of days and end of years and without mother or father and has always existed and was not created, nor made, neither indeed can be. That's *intelligence*. Now, Lecture 5 in *The Lectures on Faith* is on the Godhead. This *intelligence* is referred to as *the mind of man*. That's an interesting concept. I think that it is the part of us that allows us to reason, and that can be capacitated for further instruction. Listen to the statement by the Prophet Joseph Smith. He said this in *The Teachings of the Prophet Joseph Smith*, page 51:

> *We consider that God has created man with a mind...*

Think *intelligence* now, not the organized spirits that Abraham was talking about, but something inside of us that's not created, or made, or organized. It's always been there. It has no beginning and no end.

> *We consider that God has created man with a mind capable of instruction, and a faculty which may be enlarged in proportion to the heed and diligence* [listen to this] *given to the **light** communicated from heaven to the intellect.*

This is what separates us, brothers and sisters: this mind, this *intelligence* of man, the mind of man, and it's also referred to as the *mind of God*. We'll talk about that in a second. But the name of *the mind of God* is called the *Holy Spirit*.

Student 6: Say that again.

Mike: I'll say that again. In Lecture 5, *the mind of God*, or God's mind, is referred to as the *Holy Spirit*. It's interesting that Paul says that when the saints in the *New Testament* obtained a certain level of excellency in their spiritual progression, of those who obtained this level of progression, "We have *the mind of Christ*." Isn't that interesting?

Student 6: And you said that the scriptures teach that this mind, or *intelligence*, has no mother or father.

Mike: Right. That fits in with the *Holy Spirit*, which is not a personage but is a channel through which the Gods perform their work, a medium, etc. And Lecture 5 says that the mind of the Father and the Son is the *Holy Spirit*. Okay, let me come back to this quote by Joseph Smith:

> *God has created man with a mind capable of instruction, and a faculty which may be enlarged*

> in proportion to the heed and diligence given to
> the light communicated from heaven to the
> intellect;

So, here's what he just said there. Now, remember the definition of *glory* is *light*. So, whenever we have *light* that comes from heaven into our mind, it enlarges it, increases its capacity for enlargement on gospel principles. Then the quote goes on like this:

> and that the nearer man approaches perfection,
> the clearer are his views and the greater his
> enjoyments, till he has overcome the evils of this
> life and lost every desire for sin;

So now, brothers and sisters, when you get to a point where, as King Mosiah says, *"[You] have no more disposition to [sin], but to do good continually,"* the reason you have that is because you have obtained **light** and **truth** and **intelligence** and **glory**, even though it may not show while you're embodied. The reason you lose all disposition for evil is that there has been an increase of **glory** in your being. Even though you may not notice it while you are embodied in the telestial world, you ARE being *added upon.* And if you were this person who has obtained *glory* after *glory*, *intelligence*, *light*, and *truth* to the end of their life, you lay your body down and go into the spirit world; you're going to see a person who is on fire! That's why when these persons go into the spirit world, it's an area of *light.* If you have the spirit of *a just man made perfect,* he appears to you in *glory.* That's the only way he can appear because he doesn't have a body to enclose that *glory* and that spirit. I'll go into that a little bit further, but let me finish the quote:

> and like the ancients, arrives at that point of faith
> where he is wrapped in the power and glory of his
> Maker,

That's while you're still here on this earth. This isn't talking about after this earth. So, it says:

> ...the nearer a man approaches perfection, the
> clearer are his views, and the greater his
> enjoyments, till he has overcome the evils of his
> life and lost every desire for sin; and like the
> ancients, arrives at that point of faith [while still

alive] *where he is wrapped in the power and glory of his Maker, and is caught up to dwell with Him. But, we consider that this is a station to which no man ever arrived in a moment:*

Do you want to know how to get there?

*he must have been instructed in the government and the laws of that kingdom by proper degrees, until his **mind** [think about what we're talking about in verse 89] is capable in some measure of comprehending the propriety, justice, equality, and consistency of the same.*

Now, what have we learned here? You come here with *glory*. What is *glory*? It's *intelligence, light,* and *truth.*

Skip over to section 88 for just a minute and let me show you an interesting little statement. You start to put all these things together, and you start to get a magnificent picture. We want to go to verses 5, 6, and 7. This is talking about:

[The] glory...of the church of the Firstborn, even of God, the holiest of all, through Jesus Christ his Son—

So, here we are talking about this *glory*. What's *glory* again? *Intelligence, light, truth,* and *glory*. That's talking about Jesus. It says, *"through Jesus Christ his Son—"* Verse 6, Christ is:

He that ascended up on high, as also he descended below all things, in that he might comprehend all things, that he might be in all and through all things, the light of truth;

Now watch, verse 7:

[7] Which truth shineth.

Isn't that an interesting little statement? A definition of *truth* is, *"Truth is knowledge of things as they are, and as they were, and as they are to come."* It's knowledge! It's a principle of *intelligence*. If you were to see a physical manifestation of *truth*, it would manifest itself in *light*, and it shines. Verse 7:

*Which truth shineth. **This** is the light of Christ.*

Let's go over and look at another thing here. Let's go to John in the *Bible*, and start to see some things here about this *glory*. Now, the first principle that I want to teach you is that the

276

obtaining of this *glory, intelligence, light,* and *truth* is the way the Gods increase and progress in the eternal worlds. One God, who is related to Another, can add *glory* to One by what He does. One person can be *glorified* in the works of another. So, the Father obtains this *glory,* and He is *glorified* through the works of His Son. In John chapter 17, we have something called *the great intercessory prayer.* This is the prayer that's spoken at the last supper, just prior to them leaving the upper room and going into Gethsemane that evening. Let's just go to verse 1, and look at this. It's interesting! I read this for years, and it just fascinated me, but I didn't understand it:

> *These words spake Jesus, and lifted up his eyes to heaven, and said, Father, the hour is come; glorify thy Son, that thy Son may also glorify thee:*

Now, we're starting to hit on something here. Whatever the Son does, in the name of the Father, it adds *glory* to the Father. What is *glory*? *Intelligence, light,* and *truth.* How is it manifested in physical form? In *light.* Have you ever heard the story that God dwells in everlasting burnings? It doesn't sound too compatible right now because of what we think of as fire. But, if you look into where God dwells, you're going to look into a fiery realm. The celestial world and the terrestrial world are estates of fire. They are fire-based worlds. The telestial world is a water-based world. The mean temperature of a water-based, telestial world is 70°. The mean temperature of a fire-based terrestrial world, where the Son of God reigns is 700°. The mean temperature of the celestial world, where the Father dwells in everlasting burnings is 7000°. Just to kind a give you an idea of the differences in these three places. What makes the difference? Why is one more *light*? Why is one more fire-based? Why is one hotter than another? We've got it all backward. When we say, "hot as hell," we've got it backward. Hell is cold. Heaven is hot. Isaiah said it, and it's also in the *Doctrine and Covenants;* God dwells in everlasting burnings. Verse 2 of John 17:

> *As thou hast given him* [the Son] *power over all flesh, that he should give eternal life to as many as thou hast given him.*

[3] And this is life eternal, that they might know thee the only true God, and Jesus Christ, whom thou hast sent.

[4] I have glorified thee [Christ speaking] *on the earth*:

How did he do it? How did the Father receive *glory* because of the Son? It tells you in the last part of the verse:

I have finished the work thou gavest me to do.

There's your key! So, the Father commands the Son to fulfill a mission. As the Son successfully fulfills that mission, not only is the Son *glorified* in the process and receives additional *light, truth,* and *intelligence,* but the Father also is increased. So, upon completion of the mission of the Son, the Father is *glorified* to a greater degree than He was before. Verse 5:

And now, O Father, glorify thou me with thine own self with the glory which I had with thee before the world was.

That's the same for you and me, brothers and sisters. Back in section 93, (and also Abraham 3) we learn that you came here with *glory*. And you're not only going to get that back but whatever you accomplish in this life, in your righteous endeavors, is going to add to that. Go down to verse 9:

[9] I pray for them [meaning the Twelve]*: I pray not for the world, but for them which thou hast given me; for they are thine.*

[10] And all mine are thine, and thine are mine; and I am glorified in them.

That's the Twelve. And then He goes on and talks about all those who believe in the words of the Twelve, how it *glorifies*. You see that each stewardship, each assignment that's given to us (if we successfully complete it), cannot be completed without adding *glory, intelligence, light,* and *truth* to who you are.

There's so much written on this that I was pondering about this thought today: every estate that we are in, whether it's the first estate, premortal life, or the second estate, mortal, telestial world, the Lord gives us opportunities to learn laws and commandments and enter into covenants and have ordinances performed. Now, in connection with all of this, I want to read to you this interesting statement from Joseph Smith in the King

Follett discourse. He's talking about creation and the difference between the terms, *create* and *organize*. And if you've read the King Follett discourse you know what I mean. He says:

> *It means to organize; the same as a man would organize materials to build a ship. Hence we infer that God himself had materials to organize the world out of chaos—chaotic matter, which is element, and in which dwells **all the glory**.*

That is a statement that just blows my mind! I've pondered and prayed on that. What he is saying is that element is defined as *chaotic matter*.

Now, go back to section 93 for a minute, and let's pull a couple of things together just to show you how we can use the scriptures as a guidebook to become detectives and see what the Lord is giving us here. There appears to be at least two main building blocks in eternity that the Fathers and Mothers use to organize all things. Look at verse 33:

> *For man is spirit.*

There's your first element. There's your first building block; spirit:

> *The elements are eternal* [there's your second one], *and spirit and element, inseparably connected, receive a fulness of joy.*

According to the scriptures and the *Book of Mormon*, the way that you inseparably connect spirit and element together is through the resurrection of the dead. We've already talked about our spirit inside of us. The physical body is made up of element. Now, go back to what Joseph Smith said. He said that chaotic matter (chaos) is element. And, *"...in chaotic matter...dwells all the glory."* It's not in organized matter but chaos; not ordered. The next statement in the King Follett discourse:

> *Element* [which is chaotic matter] *had an existence from the time He* [God] *had.*

It's always been there. When you become a Creator, you will use this element. The temple refers to it as *"matter unorganized."* It's chaotic. But, according to Joseph Smith, within that matter dwells *glory*. Which is what? *Intelligence, light,* and *truth*. The rest of the quote goes on like this:

> *The pure principles of element* [meaning chaotic matter] *are principles that can never be destroyed; they may be organized and re-organized, but not destroyed.*
>
> [Nothing can be destroyed] *They had no beginning and can have no end.*

They exist eternally. That's element. Well, your body is made up of element. It's made up of the things that the earth is made up of. It's organized now in a physical body, and upon death, it will become disorganized and go into a chaotic state. But it's still element. And that element is assigned to you, through birth, no matter how it's reorganized through the processes of death. Whether fire burns you, whether you fall overboard and are eaten by a shark and your remains are scattered all over the ocean floor, it doesn't matter. That pure principle of element that made up your physical body has your identity to it and will not ever belong to another person. That is yours. It belongs to you. And in the resurrection, it will be reordered and come back into its full and perfect stature.

So, I pondered this whole thing about this element residing in *glory*, in chaotic matter, and here are some things that I've come up with. I've given you doctrine here, and now I'm just going to give you Mike Stroud chapter 26, verse 32. My thought is that this *glory* dwells within chaotic matter in a somewhat dormant state. It's not in a position to be *added upon*, or diminished from, which are the two opposites. It appears that these elements have at least, from what Joseph Smith and others have said, a rudimentary ability to exercise some agency, but really limited in its unorganized, chaotic state. It's alive! This *intelligence*, this *light* and *truth*, this *glory* is alive! But, in order for it to come to a state where it can be *added upon* in intelligent beings, agency has to come into play and has to be acted upon. In other words, God said, "Let there be plants, let there be animals, let there be the various things that comprise the earth," and as He speaks, this chaotic matter obeys. It goes from a rudimentary, fundamental state into something more sophisticated where it now can progress because it's been *added upon*; in our case with a physical body, a spiritual body first. So, we are what the Brethren have called "triune people." Each one of us is a triune being, meaning that we're made up of three parts. One part never can have a beginning or an end and is without mother or father. It's without beginning of days or end of years. It's co-eternal with God. That is your primal life. That's the *intelligence* that's inside you. Another definition of that is *glory, light,* and *truth.* When it's *added upon* with the spirit body, and you become an organized male or female in spirit form, it's now capacitated, by being *added upon,* to now progress much further and gain additional *light* and knowledge and *truth* and *glory* that it otherwise couldn't in that rudimentary position. To be *added upon* again and have that spirit *added upon* with a physical body is the third part of you, the central primal life. Some people have referred to it as the "I am" that's in you. The "I am." It's your identity. It's your core. It's the mind of man added on first of all with the spirit, and then added again with the physical body; and with those three put together the door really opens wide, depending on how you use your agency. Whether you love *light* and *truth,* or whether you love darkness, depending on how you use your agency, you can really now be *added upon* with *glory.* That concept seems to fit with the other things that the scriptures have said.

Here's something else, too, that I found out. Anciently, element could be broken down into four general parts. This goes back to the ancient writings and different things like that. The four parts are earth, air, fire, and water. Those are your ancient definitions of element. Element is matter in its most basic form, simple and rudimentary. But, as Joseph said when capacitated through agency it can come up and have the ability to dwell among the Elohim and be one of Them. They are who They are, brothers and sisters. These People are who They are because They have something called "a fullness of *truth*; a fullness of *glory*; a fullness of *light*." How did They get that? We are learning the process here. I thought about covenants that are made in each estate. If you come into this world, how do you keep from losing *glory* earned from the previous world; how do you keep it? Because it is possible to lose it; it's possible to go backward. We don't want to go backward. We want to be *added upon.* We want to go forward. We don't want to look back. And it's my feeling that that's the purpose of covenants and ordinances. The word ordinance is interesting because it means "to put in order." Ordinances take chaos and confusion and bring them into order. Notice what the Lord says in section 132:

> *[8] Behold, mine house is a house of order, saith the Lord God, and not a house of confusion.*

Well, it's the ordinances and covenants and the corresponding doctrines and principles of the gospel that keep the order there. So, it seems to me that one way that we can maintain and **retain** and have *added upon glory* is through proper observance and faithfulness to the covenants and ordinances that we enter into. The word ordinance comes from order. Ordinances are designed to take things in the state of confusion and bring them into a state of order. Think of all the ordinances that we go through. What's the purpose of it? Is the purpose of these ordinances to help us retain what we've earned in the previous places so that we go forward and are added upon and not go backward and are diminished or dwindle? Is that what this is all about? You look at all the statements of the Prophet Joseph Smith, and you can see that that probably fits pretty well.

So, here are some thoughts: Our joy increases as we obtain *glory*. The more *light* and *truth* and *intelligence* and *glory* we obtain, the greater our joy. Something else that increases as *glory* increases is wisdom. The acquisition of Christ-like attributes that are bestowed upon us through the atonement adds *glory*. All of this adds *glory*, or in other words, *intelligence, light,* and *truth.* I looked it up, and the Hebrew word for *glory* is brightness, splendor, magnificence, and majesty of outward appearance.

I wrote this little note as I was pondering this and I'll end with it. Again, these are my thoughts as I studied this. Agency is limited in an elementary, rudimentary state. Agency causes element to become ordered. Covenants and ordinances order element. *Glory* is activated as a result when the creature is *added upon.* Back to our first statement:

> *For behold, this is my work and my* **glory**—*to bring to pass the immortality and eternal life of man.*

God our Father and all of the Elohim are *glorified* in the salvation and exaltation of their children. As we come up and obtain what They have, it adds to who They are.

I love the gospel! As I pondered these things this week, I just bowed my head at my desk, and said, "Father I don't understand these things. What does this mean?" Take a moment and order your questions. Give a little thought and put some time and consideration into what question you're going to present to the Father in the name of His Son. I want to testify to you, brothers and sisters, that if you ask specific questions, the time that you spend preparing that question will put you in a position to receive greater *light* and *truth* and knowledge and *intelligence* and *glory*. And God will more readily answer your question because you took the time to present Him with a well thought out, ordered, pondered thought. Remember what Joseph said, and I'll end on this, *"The things of God are of a deep import."* You may ask yourself, "So what? Why is this important?" Well, I think that anything that God speaks of in His word is important for me to understand. And since **glory** is the term that is used so ubiquitously throughout the scriptures, how many times do we stop and ask, "What the heck is this talking about?" And if you stop and start to ask questions like that, I testify to you that the Father and the Son are anxious to share with you these things. And they do make a difference. If for no other reason, I can approach them in prayer using different language, based on my new understanding, that puts me in a position to more readily receive information from Them.

Well, God bless you all, and I hope that you find this interesting. We'll call this podcast, guess what? *Glory*! How's that for original?! Any questions or comments or thoughts? This is at least one of those ways that the Mothers and Fathers progress in eternity. Thank you.

Student 6: I wanted to ask if you would please give me the reference on the quote that talks about your *intelligence* always existing, no beginning no end, no mothers, no fathers...

Mike: Yeah that's Joseph Smith. It's in verse 29 of section 93:

> *Intelligence, or the light of truth, was not created*
> *or made, neither indeed can be.*

But, there's another place where it says that it's without father and mother, beginning of days or end of years. Let me see if I can find it here real quick.

Student 6: Thank you!

Mike: Maybe I've got it right here. Here's a statement here by Spencer W. Kimball and it kind of ties in with it, and he says:

> *Our spirit matter was eternal and co-existent with God, but it was organized into spirit bodies by our Heavenly Father.*

Marion G. Romney of the first presidency, speaking of people's divine origin as children of God, stated:

> *Through that birth process, self-existing intelligence...*

Now, that's not your organized spirit persons. That's that part of you that cannot be created or made:

> *self-existing intelligence was organized into individual spirit beings.*

Brother McConkie said this:

> *Abraham used the name 'intelligences' to apply to the spirit children of the Eternal Father. The intelligence or spirit element became **intelligences** after the spirits were born as individual entities.*

So, that kind of fits in with what we're talking about. It's not the exact quote that you wanted, but I'll dig that up for you, and we'll put it on the Dropbox.

Here's one more that I want to give you. This all ties in with what we've talked about. Joseph Smith, *Teachings of the Prophet,* page 354:

> *God Himself, finding He was in the midst of spirits and **glory** [there it is again] because He was more intelligent, saw it proper to institute laws whereby the rest could have a privilege to advance like Himself. That advancement is called being added upon. The relationship we have with God places us in the situation to advance in knowledge.*

It's what we're talking about. So, if you ask what this is all about, why is this important? It's knowledge!

> *He has power to institute laws to instruct the weaker intelligences that they may be exalted with Himself so that they might have one glory upon another. And all that knowledge, power, glory, and intelligence, which is requisite, in order to save them in the world of spirits.*

What a marvelous quote! And I'll see if I can get that one for you, and we'll put it up. Any other questions?

Student 6: I have another question.

Mike: Ok, going ahead...

Student 6: You made reference to the fact that the telestial world has an assigned medium temperature and the terrestrial... and the celestial being 7000°, where can we reference that work?

Mike: That is Mike Stroud chapter 3, verse 16.

Student 6: Oh, ok.

Mike: Hahaha!

Student 6: Alright, thank you!

Mike: What I'm doing is just illustrating that *glorious light/truth* shines, and as you move up the *light* is going to get hotter, and it's going to get brighter. So, I just put some Fahrenheit degrees to it to illustrate a point.

Student 6: I see. Thank you.

Mike: Hahaha! I was wondering if anyone was going to pick up on that! I'll probably hear from a lot of people on that, from the podcast, saying, "Where in the heck did you get that?" It's just to illustrate a point. Alright, Thanks, brothers and sisters! Love you all, and we'll see you next week.

References:
Moses 1:39
Brigham Young, "Union, etc.," (7 October 1859) *Journal of Discourses* 7:281
D&C 76:37
Abraham 3: 22-26
D&C 88:15
James Talmage, *Jesus the Christ*
D&C 93:36
D&C 93:29
The Teachings of the Prophet Joseph Smith page 51
The Lectures on Faith Lecture 5, Joseph Smith
Mosiah 5:2 "...we have no more disposition to do evil, but to do good continually."
D&C 93:23 "And truth is knowledge of things as they are, and as they were, and as they are to come."
D&C 88:5-7
John 17:1-4
Isaiah 33:14; D&C 133:41: everlasting burnings

Joseph Smith taught, "All men who are immortal (i.e., resurrected beings in any of the degrees of glory) dwell in everlasting burnings" (*TPJS*, pp. 347, 361, 367)
King Follett Sermon
D&C 93:9
D&C 93:33
D&C 132:8
Spencer W. Kimball, *The Miracle of Forgiveness,* 5.
Marion G. Romney, November 1978 *Ensign*
Bruce R. McConkie, *Mormon Doctrine*, 2 Ed. [1966], p. 387
Joseph Smith, *Teachings of the Prophet,* page 354

ABOUT THE AUTHOR

Mike Stroud was born March 1944 to Walt and Eileen Stroud in Salt Lake City, Utah. He attended BYU and received a BA and MA degree.

He is trained in Outdoor Survival and Primitive Living; he has spent a lifetime in the outdoors as a hunter, tracker, and outdoorsman.

Mike enjoys training horses and has spent many years exploring wild places on horseback. He is a western history lover and re-enacts the mountain man era, and the old west.

He served a mission to Bavaria, Germany, and he and Margie have served missions together in Mongolia, Central Philippines, and in New Jersey.

Mike has spent his lifetime as a teacher, working 27 years in The Church of Jesus Christ of Latter-day Saints Church Education System. He retired from CES in 2006.

Mike and Margie reside in Eagar, Arizona. He is the father of 12 children, 29 grandchildren, and 7 great-grandchildren.

Made in the USA
San Bernardino, CA
07 April 2018